Commonhold

Related titles by Law Society Publishing:

Conveyancing Handbook, 12th Edition
General Editor: Frances Silverman
1 85328 928 0

Environmental Law Handbook, 6th Edition (November 2005)
Trevor Hellawell
1 85328 978 7

Licensing for Conveyancers: A Practical Guide
Tim Hayden and Jane Hanney
1 85328 966 3

Planning and Compulsory Purchase Act 2004: A Guide to the New Law
Stephen Tromans, Martin Edwards, Richard Harwood, Justine Thornton
1 85328 925 6

Profitable Conveyancing: A Practical Guide for Residential Conveyancers
Stephanie F. Dale
1 85328 862 4

Titles from Law Society Publishing can be ordered from all good legal bookshops or direct from our distributors, Marston Book Services (tel. 01235 465656 or e-mail **law.society@marston.co.uk**). For further information or a catalogue, e-mail our editorial and marketing office at **publishing@lawsociety.org.uk**.

COMMONHOLD

Law and Practice

Gary Cowen,
James Driscoll
and
Laurence Target

The Law Society

Appendix E reproduced by permission of the Council of
Mortgage Lenders.

Crown copyright material is reproduced with the permission of
the Controller of Her Majesty's Stationery Office

ISBN 10: 1-85328-867-5
ISBN 13: 978-1-85328-867-8

Published in 2005 by the Law Society
113 Chancery Lane, London WC2A 1PL

Typeset by J&L Composition Ltd, Filey, North Yorks
Printed by Antony Rowe Ltd, Chippenham, Wiltshire

Contents

Preface

There is now an alternative to the leasehold system for interdependent buildings such as blocks of flats or office blocks. This system is called commonhold. It is available for new developments and for the conversion of existing leasehold or freehold developments into a commonhold. In this short work we have written a general account of commonhold and how it works. We examine how a development can be set up as a commonhold and how it is managed under the rules of a commonhold. It will not be too long before solicitors, legal executives and other legal advisors will be advising on how a commonhold is created or advising a prospective purchaser who is buying a commonhold flat, house or a commercial commonhold unit. One of the great attractions of commonhold is the standardised documentation for the creation of the commonhold association and the commonhold community statement, which defines the properties within the commonhold, the rules of the commonhold and how they can be applied and enforced. This work also explains how these documents are drafted and considers the ways in which the commonhold form of ownership and management has advantages over the traditional freehold/leasehold forms.

We are grateful to various colleagues with whom we have discussed commonhold as we have been writing this book. Gary would like to express this thanks to colleagues in Falcon Chambers and James and Laurence would like to record their thanks to their colleagues at Trowers & Hamlins. Thank you also to our Publishers.

Gary Cowen, James Driscoll and Laurence Target
July 2005

Table of cases

Table of statutes

Page numbers in **bold** indicate where the legislation has been set out in part or in full.

Table of statutory instruments

Page numbers in **bold** indicate where the legislation has been set out in part or in full.

CHAPTER 1

Background to the commonhold legislation

James Driscoll

1.1 INTRODUCTION

The enactment of the Commonhold and Leasehold Reform Act 2002 (the Act) heralds one of the most important innovations in English property law for many decades. This work has been written for practitioners who advise developers and also for practitioners who are either advising the purchaser of a commonhold unit, or who need to become familiar with the new commonhold legislation and the opportunities it brings to the property industry. Unless it is otherwise stated then references in the text are to the Commonhold and Leasehold Reform Act 2002.

In this introductory chapter 'commonhold' is defined and the background to the Act is examined. The leasehold reform provisions in Part 2 of the Act are also briefly considered. Although the two parts to the Act may appear unrelated, Part 2, which makes enormous improvements to the legal position of leaseholders of flats and houses, is designed to make the residential leasehold system fairer and more workable for leaseholders. Part 1, in contrast, introduces a new way of delivering freehold ownership of units such as flats or offices within a statutory framework which allows for the management of the development as a whole. Commonhold is available for new developments and also for leasehold and freehold developments where all parties agree to the conversion of the property to commonhold. It can be used for commercial, residential and mixed-use developments. Commonhold came into force in England and Wales on 27 September 2004. The leasehold provisions have been brought into force in stages since 2002 and are expected to be fully in force by the end of 2005.

1.2 WHAT IS A COMMONHOLD?

Commonhold is the new way in which interdependent properties can be owned and managed. Equally accurately, it might be defined as a new land ownership scheme, the purpose of which is to regulate relations between owners of separate properties which lie in close proximity to each other and are interdependent. Commonhold is suitable for developments such as blocks of flats, but it is not limited to residential property, though many of the concerns that have led to commonhold being developed are based on the often unhappy experience of many flat owners (see, for example, the consultation paper *Residential Leasehold Reform in England and Wales* (DETR, November 1998) which contained proposals for reform leading to Part 2 of the Act, and Cole and Robinson, 'Owners yet tenants: the position of leaseholders in flats in England and Wales', *Housing Studies*, 15: 4 (2000), pp. 595–612).

In introducing the legislation which has created commonhold the then Lord Chancellor, Lord Irvine described it as:

> ... a scheme which will combine the security of freehold ownership with the management potential of positive covenants which could be made to apply to successive owners of interpendent property ... I believe that the commonhold concept is worthy of, and will receive, wide acceptance.

> Although commonhold has been widely described as a new way to own flats, and of course that is the most likely use for it, it is also available for any development where the occupants owe duties to one another related to their proximity to one another and to the need to manage and maintain common parts of a development ...

> The standardisation of documentation is one of the most important features of commonhold ...
> Lord Irvine, Lords, *Hansard*, January 29 2001, cols 455, 466

In a commonhold, each owner of a unit such as a flat, office or other commercial unit, owns a freehold estate in the unit coupled with the right to a concurrent membership of a commonhold association (CA) which owns and manages the common parts of the building. Following the development of a new commonhold, only unit-holders can be members of the CA and the developer of the commonhold no longer has any proprietary interest in the commonhold. Unlike a leasehold development there are no superior interests (such as a landlord).

Commonhold ownership, in contrast to leasehold ownership, is not time-limited. The other striking feature of commonholds is the use of standardised documentation which is prescribed by statutory instrument. Although the practical features of particular commonholds will vary widely (and could include large Marina developments containing flats, houses, recreational facilities, shops, restaurants, etc., new developments of offices, a block of flats, a mixed-use block with flats over a shop or some other commercial development) the essential features of the documentation is similar.

As will be seen in this book, each commonhold will have a 'commonhold association', a company limited by guarantee, whose memorandum and articles of association are prescribed by statutory instrument, and a 'commonhold community statement' whose form is also prescribed and which defines the number of units and sets out the rules of the commonhold.

The other essential feature of a commonhold is that it can only be created in relation to registered land. Each commonhold must, therefore, be registered at the Land Registry.

1.3 WHY COMMONHOLD?

There are several problems with the existing leasehold system which explain the pressure for reform. These are the problem of enforcing positive freehold covenants, difficulties with redevelopment and the growing complexity of the leasehold legislation.

1.3.1 Freehold covenants

A fundamental problem arises when the owner of a freehold property enters into a positive obligation connected with that ownership, as there is no direct way to enforce that obligation against successive owners of property. This difficulty is best illustrated by a block of residential flats where the very stability of the building requires proper repairs and maintenance of the individual flats as well as the building itself. If the developer/landlord were to sell the flats freehold, the obligations would only bind the original parties. Exactly the same concerns apply to other developments such as a block of offices or a mixed-use building.

This principle, that positive covenants do not run with the land, has been firmly established in English land law. Most recently it was reaffirmed by the House of Lords in *Rhone* v. *Stephen* [1994] AC 310. Various attempts have been made to mitigate the inconvenience of the rule: for example, through a chain of covenants where the seller takes a covenant from the purchaser to comply with these obligations and the purchaser takes like promises when selling the land. The obvious disadvantage of this device is that the chain may break down if, for example, an intermediate purchaser disappears or dies. (It is possible, though, under the Contracts (Rights of Third Parties) Act 1999 for the original covenantee to sue on the promise made by the current owner of the land). Other devices include requiring the consent of the covenantor before a subsequent sale takes place; using the doctrine in *Halsall* v. *Brizell* [1957] Ch 169 whereby the purchaser cannot enjoy the benefit of a right without accepting the correlative obligation (in this case a purchaser could not use a private road without complying with the positive obligation to contribute towards the costs of its upkeep).

Using leases

The most common way to avoid the difficulty with enforcing positive covenants has been to grant leases of the interdependent units (such as granting leases of flats). This provides a solution to the problem of enforcing positive covenants such as repairing obligations and service charge contributions. Each successive owner of the lease can be forced to comply with such obligations if they are set out in the lease, and the obligations also bind successive owners of the freehold. This in turn has led to other difficulties: a lease is by definition a time-limited estate in land and its value can diminish rapidly as the term of the lease draws to an end. Another practical problem is that there is no uniformity in the drafting of leases which can increase the costs of conveyancing or make enforcement of leasehold obligations difficult or impossible if the lease is badly drawn (see again the consultation paper *Residential Leasehold Reform* referred to at **para.1.2**).

Leasehold management (at least in the residential context) has been notoriously unsatisfactory with wide-spread complaints regarding poor management and overcharging for services. For decades, successive governments have introduced legislation to ameliorate the position by the enactment of such reforms as the regulation of service charges and allowing certain leaseholders or tenants to appoint a new manager. This has found further expression in Part 2 of the Act which has made some fundamental changes to the framework governing residential leases but at the expense, no doubt, of a very complicated system of legal rights and obligations which may prove costly to administer.

1.3.2 Leasehold redevelopment

Existing leasehold developments do not usually make provision for a case where the property needs to be redeveloped. The need for this could arise in several ways: the property may have become dilapidated, seriously damaged or a commercial opportunity may have arisen which makes redeveloping the building an attractive proposition to the current owners. As long as the leasehold units in the building continue, such redevelopment cannot be achieved without the agreement of all the leaseholders (many of whom may also have statutory rights to extend their leases as residential long leaseholders). Commonhold has a number of flexible features which allow for the termination of the arrangements and many of the essential features of this can be settled in advance in the original commonhold documentation.

1.4 AN ALTERNATIVE TO THE LEASEHOLD SYSTEM

In 1965 the Wilberforce Committee on Positive Covenants Affecting Land recommended that positive covenants should bind successive owners of land (Cmnd 2719, 1965). It also recommended the introduction of so-called 'strata title', based on a scheme operating in New South Wales, under which mutual rights and obligations of owners of flats in blocks of flats and other multiple developments could be regulated. These recommendations have not been adopted. In a later report the Law Commission recommended the introduction into property law of a new interest in land, the 'land obligation', which would impose a burden on one owner for the benefit of another owner or as part of scheme of development regulating the interests of the owners of separate properties within a defined area. Such land obligations would run with the land which benefited and that which is burdened, and would be enforceable by and against the current owners of each such property (*Transfer of Land – The Law of Positive and Restrictive Covenants*, Law Com. No. 127, 1984).

Several commentators (including many who commented on the Wilberforce Report, see Law Commission report, Cm 179, 1987) suggested the introduction of condominium legislation which allows for freehold ownership of flats or other units; a management body composed of all the unit-holders; shared ownership of the common parts of the buildings and mutual rights and obligations imposed by statute. Condominium legislation has operated successfully in Canada and the United States, and under the name 'strata title' in Australia and New Zealand as well as in Europe since the 1930s.

By request of the Lord Chancellor, the Law Commission set up a Working Party to propose details of such legislation. The Working Party's report recommended legislation to introduce 'commonhold' as a new term '. . . for a system of land ownership where the emphasis is on co-operation between owners living within a defined area . . .' (*Commonhold: Freehold flats and freehold ownership of other interpedendent buildings,* Cm 179, July 1987). It should be noted then that commonhold is not simply an academic idea, it is based on the experience of conceptually similar systems which have worked successfully in both commercial and residential property contexts for several decades (for a review, see Ian Cole and Yvonne Smith, *Liberating the Leaseholder* (Joseph Rowntree Foundation, 1993), Chapters 3 and 4).

1.5 COMMONHOLD AND LEASEHOLD REFORM ACT 2002

Draft Bills were published for consultation in 1990, 1996 (Cm 1345) and in 2000 (Cm 4843). A Bill was introduced in 2000 but was lost with the 2001 Election so several decades passed until the Law Commission's 1987 report proposals were finally enacted by Part I of the Act (which received Royal Assent on 1 May 2002). The Act sets out the basic principles of commonhold in just 70 sections; much of the practical detail was left to secondary legislation. After protracted consultations, the Department for Constitutional Affairs (the successor to the Lord Chancellor's Department) produced the final drafts of secondary legislation which were laid before Parliament in July

2004 and which came into force on 27 September 2004 (Commonhold Regulations 2004, SI 2004/1829 (CR) and Commonhold (Land Registration) Rules 2004, SI 2004/1830 (CLRR)). It was the consultation and drafting of these rules and regulations which largely accounts for the delay in the commencement of Part I of the Act until 27 September 2004.

Further regulations are likely to be laid by the end of 2005 or in 2006. These will deal with shared ownership leases, Islamic mortgages, the Commonhold Ombudsman Service, compulsory purchase and insolvency (for a review of the legislation see *Commonhold: The Dawning of New Age?* 26th Blundell Lecture, 2001 and an analysis of the Act by D.N. Clarke *The Enactment of Commonhold – Problems, Principles and Perspectives* [2002] 66 Conv 349.)

1.5.1 The Rules and Regulations

Land can only be registered as commonhold land if it is registered land with absolute title. If the title is unregistered, application must be made for a first registration at the Land Registry. Land which has, for example, contingent title cannot be registered as commonhold land. Matters relating to registration of commonhold at the Land Registry are regulated by the CLRR. The Land Registry has issued a Practice Guide (No. 60) on the procedures leading up to a commonhold registration (see **www. landregistry.gov.uk**). Particular emphasis has been laid on the importance of ensuring that the plans which must accompany the commonhold community statement (CCS) conform to the Rules. The Land Registry will consider whether the plans proposed for a new commonhold application are in the required form in advance of an application for registration of land as commonhold land.

The Department for Constitutional Affairs has produced 'Non-Statutory Guidance' to the CLRR (see **www.dca.gov.uk**). Specimen clauses which can be used in drafting the local rules for a commonhold have also been published with guidance and a worked example of a CCS (DCA, December 2004).

1.5.2 Getting advice on commonhold

Advice on commonhold is available from the Leasehold Advisory Service (**www.lease-advice.org**). Once the Commonhold Ombudsman Service has been established under the Act, it is also expected that they too will publish advice on dispute settlement. It is an important characteristic of commonhold that all commonholds must use conciliation and other types of dispute settlement whenever possible, as opposed to litigation, to resolve disputes and enforce where necessary the rules of the commonhold. (It should, however, be borne in mind that in recovering money from a unit-holder or in an emergency, the CA may use legal action and using conciliation is not required in such cases.)

1.5.3 Components of a commonhold

No land can be registered as commonhold land unless the applicant has first set up a company called a 'commonhold association' (CA), a private company limited by guarantee with a constitution (that is the memorandum and articles of association) which has been prescribed by the CR (Scheds. 1 and 2). This CA must be first registered at the Companies Registry. Clearly such an association must be incorporated before an application can be made for land to be registered as commonhold land. Only limited changes can be made to the prescribed constitution of the CA. A certified copy of the certificate of incorporation must be lodged with the application to the Land Registry. The role of the CA is to manage the common parts and to apply the rules of the commonhold and to manage it under the rules applicable to that commonhold.

An application cannot be made for registration of land as commonhold land unless the applicant has prepared a CCS. This statement must also be in the prescribed form (s.31; CR, reg.15 and Sched.3). The purpose of this statement is two-fold: it defines and describes the properties which are within the commonhold and defines the rules of that commonhold. The regulations require each CCS to be in a common form with four parts, each part being divided into sections with four annexes which correspond to each part. The document must be completed with the insertion of the details of the commonhold concerned in each of the annexes. Any additional clauses can also be added to each of the parts. An additional annex or annexes can be added, for example where a developer for a new commonhold wishes to reserve rights to complete the commonhold development. The principles and other statements included in these annexes are known as the 'local rules' of the commonhold concerned. A copy of the CCS must also be lodged at the Land Registry. If the CCS is later amended, the amended version only takes effect when it is registered at the Land Registry.

The existence of these two key documents (the constitution of the CA and the CCS) in a standard form, contributes to the goal of having standardised documentation for all commonholds, whatever their size or location. In other words, every commonhold will have a CA and a CCS in a common form.

In order to further this standardisation of documentation, 'voluntary clauses' have been produced as part of the Non-Statutory Guidance issued by the Department of Constitutional Affairs.

Commonhold is available for new developments. It is not compulsory, nor retrospective, but the availability of freehold ownership of flats and other units, combined with membership of a company which owns and manages the common parts, using standardised documentation should prove attractive for new developments. It is also possible for existing leasehold developments to convert to a commonhold. Similarly existing freehold flats (which are usually difficult to sell or mortgage) could convert into a commonhold.

Under Part 2 of the Act massive changes are made to the laws governing residential leases of flats and houses. Although the connection between the first and second part of the Act may not seem immediately obvious, there clearly is a relationship as the Government has previously stated that it does not consider the leasehold system to be a suitable tenure for owner occupation (*Leasehold Reform – a consultation paper,* DTLR, November 2002). This led to the detailed legislative proposals which are to be found in Part 2. Long-term, the Government hopes that commonhold will establish itself as the preferred choice for new interdependent buildings: pending this, it has taken steps to improve the legal position governing long residential leasehold properties.

1.5.4 The Commonhold Ombudsman Service

As noted at **para.1.5.2**, it is an important characteristic of every commonhold that disputes between the CA and a unit-holder or a tenant of a unit, or between unit-holders or tenants of units, should be resolved, wherever possible, by using conciliation and mediation; using legal proceedings only as a last resort. Indeed the directors of the CA, who are under a duty to manage (s.35), 'need not take action if they reasonably think that inaction is in the best interests of establishing or maintaining harmonious relationships between all the unit-holders' (s.35(3)(a)). Under the standard rules of each commonhold (CR, Sched.3) conciliation and mediation are to be used wherever possible, except (as noted at **para.1.5.2**) in an emergency, or to recover monies. For example, the directors need not use conciliation where a unit-holder fails to pay his dues under a commonhold assessment.

This policy of using conciliation or mediation wherever possible and appropriate is buttressed by the power given to the government to appoint an approved ombudsman under s.42 of the Act. Regulations to be made under s.42 may provide that a CA shall be a member of an approved ombudsman scheme. Once such a scheme is established (and this is unlikely to occur before 2006 at the earliest) each unit-holder will have power to refer to the ombudsman, a dispute between the unit-holder and a CA which is a member of the scheme (s.42(2)(c)). Similarly the CA could refer such a dispute (s.42(2)(d)). Such a reference will trigger the ombudsman's powers to investigate and determine the dispute, to require the CA to co-operate in the investigation of the determination of the dispute and to comply with the ombudsman's decision (s.42(2)(e)–(g)). Any unit-holder could apply to the High Court for an order requiring the CA to comply with the regulations (s.42(4)). For example, unit-holders can in this way, insist on their CA becoming a member of such an approved ombudsman scheme. As the reference to a unit-holder is defined as including a tenant of a unit, tenants can also refer disputes to the scheme (s.42(5)).

1.6 LEASEHOLD REFORM

1.6.1 Overview

Part 2 of the Act makes enormous changes to residential leasehold law by increasing the rights of leaseholders of flats and houses. These changes, which are designed to make the residential leasehold system work more fairly, are summarised in **para.1.6.2** below. They include reforms to enfranchisement and lease extension rights for both flat and house leaseholders, changes to valuation and procedures, a new statutory right for leaseholders of flats to take over the management of their block under a radical new right to manage (RTM) as well as major reforms to the laws governing leasehold management, such as new service charge consultation requirements. The main changes are listed below.

1. It makes enfranchisement and lease extension of flats and houses easier (mostly commenced on 26 July 2002 for dwellings in England – the only outstanding changes yet to be commenced are those relating to Right to Enfranchise Companies).
2. It gives greater protection to leaseholder's monies (many provisions commenced in September and October 2003 – the remainder in 2005).
3. It makes other changes to the management of leasehold properties (some of these – the requirement that a landlord must serve a notice in a prescribed form before ground rent is due – came into force on 28 February 2005 and the remainder, such as new notices accompanying service charge demands and statements of account are likely to commence by the end of 2005).
4. It makes further restrictions on the forfeiture of leases (commenced on 28 February 2005).
5. It introduces a new right to manage (commenced on 30 September 2003).

1.6.2 Summary of the changes

The new provisions are summarised below.

1. Leaseholders have a new no-fault-based RTM which allows them to take over the management of their block of flats without having to show any default on the part of the current landlord and without having to pay the landlord any compensation. As the qualifying conditions for the RTM are the same as they are for enfranchisement the RTM may well prove to be popular with a group of leaseholders who have a long term

commitment to living in their block of flats and who would prefer to take over the management of the flats (probably coupled with the appointment of their own managing agents for the day to day management of the block) rather than acquiring the freehold through the enfranchisement process. Unlike enfranchisement no premium is payable and the responsibility for the landlord's costs is far more limited under the RTM than it is under enfranchisement.

2. Reforms have been made to the qualifications for leasehold enfranchisement and lease extension, with certain changes to valuation and with a new procedure which will apply (if brought into force) to groups of flat leaseholders who wish to enfranchise.

3. New rules governing the recovery of service charges and related matters are made. In particular, the landlord's obligations to consult the leaseholders before entering into works contracts (and before entering into certain long term agreements) are more onerous than was previously the case. Leaseholders are also entitled to regular statements relating to the service charge and its expenditure, coupled with notices advising them of their new rights along with the right to withhold payments in certain circumstances. 'Administration charges' as well as charges for improvements are also brought within the new framework. (Landlords will not be able to recover ground rents until they have first served a notice on a leaseholder in a prescribed form.)

4. New restrictions apply to forfeiture of residential leases which are likely to make forfeiture a weapon of last resort (the government has indicated that further reforms to forfeiture and the determination of leases are likely to take place in future).

5. Leasehold Valuation Tribunal's (LVT) jurisdiction over leasehold matters has been further extended: the LVT service has a broader jurisdiction in relation to service charge disputes and will also be dealing for the first time with matters such as applications for variation of leases.

Most of these changes are made by amendments to existing legislation. As is well known, the Leasehold Reform Act 1967 is the legislation that gives qualifying leaseholders of houses the right to enfranchise and (in the case of lower value houses) a separate right to extend their lease.

Under the Landlord and Tenant Acts of 1985 and 1987 leaseholders have several statutory rights relating to the management of leasehold property from the right to challenge unreasonable service charge expenditure, to applying to the LVT for a manager to be appointed, applications for the terms of the lease to be varied and related matters.

Under Part 1 of the Leasehold Reform, Housing and Urban Development Act 1993, groups of qualifying leaseholders of flats have the right collectively to enfranchise and thereby acquire the freehold to their block of flats along with a separate individual right to extend their leases.

This body of legislation was last amended by provisions in the Housing Act 1996 although the amendments made by Part 2 of the Act are more far reaching.

Whilst most of the reforms are effected by amendment to this body of legislation, some of these changes are contained in Part 2 of the Act itself including the new right to manage and the new restrictions on forfeiture of leases.

1.7 SUMMARY

Taken together the two parts of the Act make major changes to property law in England and Wales. For the first time it is now possible to create new developments of commercial, mixed-use and purely residential units, where freehold ownership of units such as an office, retail premises, flats and houses, can be provided in a development with an enforceable system of duties and obligations with a communal system of management. This is called commonhold. It came into force on 27 September 2004 and can be used for new property developments as well as for leasehold or freehold developments where the parties concerned have unanimously agreed to convert. Part 2 of the Act applies only to residential leases and it has introduced major reforms making it easier for qualifying leaseholders of flats or houses to enfranchise as well as introducing a radical overhaul of residential leasehold management in various ways.

Chapter 2 summarises the main features of commonhold in more detail.

CHAPTER 2

What is a commonhold?

James Driscoll

2.1 OUTLINE

This chapter summarises the main features of a commonhold. In general terms a commonhold may be described as a property development which has shared facilities, benefits and obligations, and which provides for freehold ownership of units, where the common parts are also held freehold and are owned by the commonhold association (CA). The CA is a private company limited by guarantee with a prescribed constitution (ss.34–36; Commonhold Regulations 2004 (CR), Scheds.1 and 2). In the case of both completed development or conversion, only the current unit-holders or owners can be members. Commonhold associations are described in more detail in **Chapter 7**.

Other features of a commonhold are 'self management' by unit-holders through the CA (rather than a landlord or other third party) with standardised documentation. Each CA must have a memorandum and articles of association in the form prescribed by statutory instrument.

Each commonhold must also have a commonhold community statement (CCS) whose form complies with the CR and the Act (ss.31–33; CR, reg.15 and Sched.3). The function of the CCS is to define the properties in the particular commonhold, to specify the rules of the commonhold and explain how these rules are to be applied and enforced. The CCS is examined in more detail in **Chapter 6**.

The individual properties in the commonhold development are called commonhold units. They may consist of two or more separate areas of land such as a flat and a garage, or a shop with a separate storage area. Commonhold units can be divided vertically or horizontally, or they might be free-standing (such as an office block, flats over commercial premises, or a row of houses). However, no part of a commonhold unit can be over or under any part of a building which is not part of the same commonhold. A commonhold development must, in that sense, be self-contained. No commonhold can be created unless there are at least two unit-holders (it would not make sense to have a commonhold for a single unit).

To summarise, the owner of a commonhold unit has two proprietary interests in the commonhold development: freehold ownership of the unit and membership of the CA which owns the freehold of the common parts.

2.2   WHAT IS COMMONHOLD LAND?

Almost any land which has a registered title can be registered as commonhold land provided that the applicant owns an absolute freehold estate in that land. In the case of unregistered freehold land there must first be an application for registration with absolute title. This is provided for in section 1 of the Act. Land may be registered as commonhold land where there is a freehold estate registered with absolute title and where the land concerned is specified in the memorandum of association of the CA as land in relation to which the association is to exercise functions. Land cannot be registered as commonhold land unless a CCS, which makes provision for the rights and duties of the CA and unit-holders, has been prepared in the prescribed form and registered with the other documents at the Land Registry. To reiterate, both the CA constitution and the CCS must be in the form prescribed by regulations made under the Act and the CA must be a company which has been registered at Companies House under the Companies Act 1985.

2.2.1   Land which cannot be registered as commonhold land

Only in very limited cases is land incapable of being registered as commonhold land. This is provided for in section 4 of and Schedule 2 to the Act and encompasses the following categories: developments in which it is intended to create a commonhold in land above ground level where the grounded part of the structure is not part of the same commonhold application; agricultural land; a case where the freehold title is contingent upon some specified future circumstance; leasehold land and land which is already commonhold.

2.2.2   Applications for land to be registered as commonhold land

Land must be registered as commonhold land by registration at the Land Registry. This is governed by section 2 of, and Schedule 1 to the Act and the Commonhold (Land Registration) Rules 2004 (CLRR).

Under section 2 of and Schedule 1 to the Act, the Land Registry must register freehold land which is the subject of a commonhold application as a 'freehold estate in commonhold land' on an application by the registered freeholder, provided that no part of the land is already commonhold land. In making an application for land to be registered as commonhold land the following documents must be lodged: the CA's certificate of incorporation (and any altered certificate); the memorandum and articles of association of the CA; the CCS; and certificates by the CA's directors that the documents are compliant with the Act and CLRR and certain consents.

Consents required

The consent of those who have an estate or interest in the land must be obtained and lodged with an application for land to be registered as commonhold land. Consents are required from the registered proprietor (the developer in the case of a new commonhold development) and any mortgagee which has a charge over the land. For new developments, these are likely to be the only persons who have to consent to the land becoming registered as commonhold land. In some cases there may be others who have a legal interest in the land such as a lease. Certainly a leasehold conversion is only possible if all of the leaseholders will consent to the conversion. So too with any mortgagee where any of the leases have been mortgaged. The cases where additional consents may be required can be set out in regulations made under the Act.

The reason for leaseholders having to give consent is that after the land has been registered as commonhold then land leases are automatically extinguished (ss.7 and 9). As expanded in **para.2.4**, the Act and the regulations both require the applicant for registration of the land as commonhold land to obtain consent from the owners of a freehold or leasehold granted originally for more than 21 years and any mortgagees of such estates or interests. The regulations then go further and require the consent of (it appears) any leaseholder or tenant of any term unless they have been granted a replacement lease or tenancy.

Under section 2 of the Act consent is required from the registered proprietor of the freehold estate (whole or part) (usually the developer in the case of a new development) and the registered proprietor of any leasehold estate (whole or part) where the lease was granted for more than 21 years (presumably usually only an issue in the case of a leasehold conversion) and the registered proprietor of any charge over the whole or part of the land. Under section 3 of the Act and regulation 3 of the CR the following additional categories of consent must be obtained: the owner of an unregistered freehold estate (whole or part); the owner of an unregistered leasehold estate (whole or part) where the lease was granted for more than 21 years; the owners of any mortgage, charge (or other lien for money or money's worth) over the whole or part of any unregistered land included in the application; and the holder of a lease granted for a term of not more than 21 years which will be extinguished under ss.7 or 9. This consent is not required if the lessee is entitled to a replacement lease (see **para.2.5**). Regulation 3(2) makes provision for a replacement lease and contains detailed requirements for its terms and protection of entitlement to it at the Land Registry.

The combined effect of the Act and the CR is that any such consent is binding on the person giving it and lasts for 12 months from the date on which it was given (CR, reg.4). Moreover, a certificate must be given by the CA's directors to confirm that the memorandum and articles of association and the CCS comply with the provisions of the Act, that the application is not in relation to land which may not be commonhold land, and that the CA has not traded and has not incurred any liability which has not been discharged.

2.2.3 Documents registered at the Land Registry

The Land Registry will have records of the CCS and the memorandum and articles of association and other documents submitted (such as any consents and certificates) and these will be referred to in the property register of the common parts title. If either the CCS or memorandum or articles of association is amended at a later date, then the amended document must be lodged for registration. The CLRR, rules 13 and 19 require the Land Registry to enter a note of the amended version 'in a manner that distinguishes it from previous versions'. An amended CCS of a CA is only effective once it has been registered at the Land Registry.

2.3 NEW DEVELOPMENTS

In the case of a new development the application is for the land to be registered as commonhold land without unit-holders (s.7). Once registered in this way the developer builds and sells the units. Once a successful application is made by the developer, the whole title (that is for all the units and the common parts) is registered in the name of the developer who becomes the registered proprietor of commonhold land. Each of the units and the common parts titles is allocated its own title number.

There follows a 'transitional period' (s.8) which starts with the date of this registration and ends with the date of the registration of the first unit title in the name of the buyer following the sale of the first unit. During this transitional period the developer can change the development by making appropriate amendments to the CCS or the CA and having the amended version registered at the Land Registry. Throughout the transitional period the rules in the CCS do not have effect and the CA has no role in managing the commonhold. This picture changes once the first unit is sold.

When the registration application for that first title is completed, the provisions of the CCS come into effect, the common parts automatically vest in the CA under a separate title and the developer's charge is extinguished over the common parts (s.28(3)). The charge will then transfer to the unsold unit titles. The remaining unit titles remain vested in the developer pending sale.

Obviously those lending on a commonhold development (who will have to consent to the registration of the land as commonhold land) will do so recognising that they will lose their security on the 'common parts' element of the land but will retain it on the remainder of the land. In the usual way, they will agree to a discharge of their mortgage over an individual unit when it is sold on part repayment of the loan. On registration of the land as commonhold land, the Land Registry allocates a title number for the common parts and title numbers for each of the units: so, when a unit is sold it is treated as a transfer of the whole of the title in that unit.

The other consequence of the transitional period coming to an end is that any lease, of the whole or a part of the commonhold land, granted before the CA becomes entitled to be registered as the proprietor of the common parts title, is automatically extinguished. This may not in practice be an issue for a new development as the developer will probably own a title to the land to be developed which is unencumbered by leases or other estates or interests. In contrast, if leaseholders or freeholders wish to convert to a commonhold, each leaseholder or freeholder (and any mortgagee if their flats are mortgaged) must consent. The decision to consent must be unanimous.

Clearly during the transitional period, the developer has sufficient flexibility to respond to commercial circumstances, an issue which is examined in detail in **Chapter 9**. For example, the developer can apply for the land to cease to be registered as commonhold land under section 8 provided consent is obtained from all necessary parties. Alternatively, the developer might decide to change some aspect or aspects of the development plans, for example, by changing the number of units, or by adding or removing land. This would require the redrafting of the CCS to change the number of the units and possibly other changes, such as changes to the proportions each unit-holder has to contribute to the expenditure, or redrafting of the CA's constitution if land is added. That flexibility is lost to a certain extent once the transitional period ends. From then until the sale of the last unit and the completion of the development the developer needs to have at least the same degree of flexibility as they do with a modern leasehold development. This can be achieved by the developer reserving 'development rights' in the CCS (s.58). By doing this the developer can reserve the right to add or remove land, to change the CCS without the consent of the CA and to appoint and remove directors.

2.4   EXTINGUISHMENT OF LEASES

Any lease of the whole or part of the commonhold is automatically extinguished at the end of the transitional period as discussed at **para.2.4** (s.7(3)(d)). Where an existing leasehold scheme is converted into a commonhold any lease of whole or part is also extinguished (and the former leaseholders become registered as the owner of a unit) (s.9(3)(f)). This explains why leaseholders have to give their consent before the land can be registered as commonhold land. Thus a leaseholder whose lease was granted for a term of more than 21 years must consent and the consent of lessees of leases of 21 years or less is also required unless they are entitled to a replacement lease under CR, reg.3(2). This is described as a 'compensatory lease' in the DCA's Non-Statutory Guidance; it will be for the unexpired residue of the extinguished lease and of the same premises, terms, rent (including rent review) and will take effect immediately after extinguishment of the prior lease. Such an entitlement to the replacement lease should be protected by registration against the freehold title before the application for the registration of the commonhold is made. It appears that periodic tenancies (for example, assured and statutory tenancies) are also extinguished, so presumably the entitlement to a replacement lease extends to those tenants too. Under section 10 of the Act, lessees whose leases are extinguished and whose consent is not required are entitled to compensation from either the freeholder or the immediate landlord.

2.5 COMMONHOLD ASSOCIATION

A CA has to be set up before application for registration can be made. The Act makes provision for the constitution and role of the CA in sections 34, 35 and 36 and Schedule 3. A CA is a private company which is limited by guarantee where its memorandum and articles of association are as prescribed in regulations made under Schedule 3. These regulations were formalised as the Commonhold Regulations 2004 (CR). Under these regulations the memorandum (reg.13) and the articles of association (reg.14) must be in the form in Schedule 1 (Memorandum) and Schedule 2 (Articles) to the CR though a form 'to the same effect' may be acceptable.

So far as the memorandum is concerned each provision in the Schedule 1 form has effect whether or not it is adopted (CR, reg.13(2)). Regulation 13(3) requires the name of the CA to be included on the front page and in paragraph 1 and the name of the commonhold to be included in paragraph 3. Regulation 13(4) permits additional provisions to be added as paragraph 6 but only if these appear under the heading 'additional provisions specific to this commonhold association' and are sequentially numbered.

As to the articles each provision in the Schedule 2 form has effect whether or not it is adopted (CR, reg.14(2)). Regulation 14(3) requires the name of the CA to be included on the front page. Regulation 14(4) allows for limited changes to be made (such as the periods for calling meetings). The balance of regulation 14 allows additional provisions and controls any right conferred by the CCS on the developer to appoint and remove directors with provisions which are deemed to be included.

Any alteration to the constitution of the CA has no effect until the altered version has been registered at the Land Registry, and any application to register an altered version must be accompanied by a certificate given by the directors of the CA that the altered version complies with the regulations. In other words the version registered retains effect until such time, if ever, that an altered version is registered at the Land Registry

A fundamental requirement is that the memorandum of association must state that one of its objects is to exercise functions of a CA in relation to land and specify £1.00 as the amount to be contributed by members in the event of the company's liquidation (Companies Act 1985, s.2(4)). It should be noted that under regulation 12 the CA's name must end with 'commonhold association limited' (or the Welsh equivalent).

Other factors are that the CA cannot be a member of itself although it can own units. Post-development, once the developer has sold the last unit no other members are permitted except for unit-holders. A director need not be a member of the CA (thus allowing for the appointment of professional directors). Membership takes effect only with registration in the company's register.

Under Schedule 3 to the Act, there is provision for membership over three separate phases. First, pre-commonhold – starting with the incorporation of the CA and ending when the land specified in the memorandum of association becomes commonhold land. During this period the members of the CA comprise the subscribers to the memorandum who will ordinarily be appointed by the developer. This is followed by the transitional period – the subscribers and anyone who is for the time being a developer of all or part of the commonhold is entitled to be a member. Third, after the first unit is sold – the first and subsequent unit-holders are entitled to be members on becoming registered as proprietors of the unit titles. Once all the units are sold only unit-holders can be members of the CA.

Where there are joint unit-holders only one of them can be a member. Nomination can be made (see prescribed art.2(d)). If no nomination is received within 7 days beginning with the date the unit-holder is entitled to be registered at the Land Registry, the member will, by default, be the first named on the proprietorship register.

Further factors relating to membership are provided for in Schedule 3(12) to the Act. This makes provision for membership to be terminated when the unit-holder ceases to be a unit-holder. It should be noted that unit-holders cannot resign from membership whilst they remain unit-holders, the only members who can resign are subscribers and developer members. Membership consists exclusively of all unit-holders in the development once all the units have been sold and the developer ceases automatically to have an interest in the development.

As noted at **para.2.5**, whilst the development is underway, the developer will wish to exercise control over the CA so far as possible. It is possible to make provision in the CCS giving the developer the right to appoint and remove directors of the CA (note that this is not included in the prescribed form of CCS and will need to be added expressly).

Under regulation 14(8) the following provisions relating to these developers rights are to have effect whether or not they are adopted: during the transitional period the developer can appoint up to two directors in addition to any appointed by subscribers and may appoint or remove any director so appointed. At the end of the transitional period and for so long as the developer retains title to at least one quarter of the total number of units, he can appoint up to a maximum of one quarter of the maximum number of directors and may appoint or remove any director so appointed. Such an appointment or removal must be by written notice signed by or on behalf of the developer and takes effect when received by the CA or as from the dates specified in the notice. Once the developer ceases to be a unit-holder of more than a quarter of the total number of units he may no longer appoint, replace or remove a director and any director previously appointed by him will cease to hold office immediately.

Further coverage of the CA is contained in **Chapter 7**.

2.6   COMMONHOLD COMMUNITY STATEMENT

Regulation 15 of the CR states that the CCS must be in the form provided in Schedule 3 to those regulations (or in a form to the same effect) and will be treated as including provisions in that Schedule. The CCS performs a dual function of defining the physical attributes of the development and specifying the rules and regulations by which it will be conducted.

Although this commonhold documentation is standardised and prescribed by regulations, a large degree of flexibility is permitted to allow for the development of different types of residential, mixed-use and commercial developments by the use of additional provisions.

Under section 31 of the Act, every CCS must contain provisions relating to the rights and duties of the CA and its unit-holders.

The duties are defined as, to:

- pay money (including interest for late payment);
- undertake works;
- grant access;
- give notice;
- refrain from entering into specified transactions;
- refrain from using the whole or any part of the unit for certain purposes;
- refrain from undertaking works, causing nuisance, etc.;
- indemnify the CA or other unit-holders in respect of costs arising from the breach of a statutory requirement.

2.6.1 The prescribed form of the CCS

Under regulation 15 of the CR, there is provision for what must be included, what may be omitted and what provisions are deemed included in the absence of alternative provisions made in their place. Any statement included in a CCS which is contrary to the regulations governing the prescribed form or inconsistent with the Act or the memorandum and articles of association has no effect (s.31(9)). Further requirements are that the CCS must include the name of the CA on the front page and the relevant information in Annexes 1–4 of the general form prescribed in Schedule 3 to the CR. However, it need not include either the allocation of the reserve fund levy in Annex 3, para.2 if the directors have not established such a fund or the insured risks in Annex 4, para.5 if there are no other risks insured other than fire.

Regulation 15(6) treats the CCS as including 0 per cent as the prescribed rate of interest unless different provision is made in Annex 4, para.1.

Additional provisions can be added, whether by way of definitions or substantive clauses. Any additional definitions have to be inserted into para. 1.4.5 of the form provided and additional substantive provisions can be inserted at the end of a Part or Section or in an Annex provided regulations 15(9) to (11) are satisfied. These requirements are that the numbering must be continued; each additional provision must be preceded by a heading 'additional provisions specific to this commonhold'; that the table of contents must reflect additional provisions and if development rights are added these must appear as the last Annex (reg.15(10)).

Duties conferred by the CCS are binding on the CA or unit-holder without further formality (s.31(7)).

2.7 APPLICATIONS TO ADD LAND

An application to add land to the commonhold can only be made by a CA if approved by unanimous resolution of the members (but note that the developer can reserve the right to add land without such consent).

2.8 RESTRICTIONS ON TRANSACTIONS

Under sections 15(2) and 20 of the Act, the CCS may not prevent or restrict the transfer or charge of the whole of a commonhold unit. In other words, an owner of a unit is free to deal with it by charging it or selling, though there are leasing restrictions which apply to residential units. Points to note are that: section 22 prevents the creation of a charge of part only of a unit; and that sections 17–19 impose restrictions on leasing residential commonhold units; whilst section 21 restricts the sale of part only of a unit on a freehold basis without the consent of the CA (requires a 75 per cent majority voting in favour).

2.9 LEASING RESTRICTIONS

2.9.1 Background

It may seem odd that the owner of a freehold residential commonhold unit should be prevented from leasing it. The explanation is that the government decided that unit-holders should not be allowed to sell units on a long lease at a premium as this would perpetuate the very long leasehold system that commonhold is designed to replace. The restrictions on leasing residential units do not prevent the owner from letting short-term, so that commonholds are entirely suitable for buy to let and other investors. It should be noted though that these restrictions, in their present form, rule out the grant of shared ownership leases by registered social landlords (RSLs), though, not of course renting them on standard tenancies.

Under sections 17–19 of the Act, any resultant regulations must make restrictions on leasing of residential commonhold units and more generally must require tenants to make payments to the CA or a unit-holder which are due to the CA under the CCS and leave commercial leases free from restriction unless the CCS makes provision for them.

2.9.2 Restrictions on leasing a residential commonhold unit

In line with sections 17 to 19 of the Act, restrictions on leasing a residential commonhold unit are provided for in regulation 11 of the CR. In summary, a residential unit can be leased provided the tenancy or lease is not granted for a premium and that it is for no more than 7 years, nor pursuant to an option or agreement capable of taking the term beyond 7 years, nor renewable or capable of extension beyond 7 years. Nor can a residential unit tenancy or lease require a tenant to make payments to the CA in discharge of payment which the CCS requires the unit-holder to pay. More generally, before granting a tenancy of a commonhold unit the prospective landlord must give the prospective tenant a copy of the CCS, relevant plans and a Form 13 Notice to a Prospective Tenant (see CR, Sched.4). The landlord must reimburse loss suffered by the tenant if obligations 'not reproduced in the tenancy agreement' are enforced against him.

Other provisions require a notice of grant of tenancy in prescribed Form 14 Notice of Grant of Tenancy of a Commonhold Unit within 14 days of grant. In addition, before assigning the tenancy the outgoing tenant must give the prospective assignee a copy of Form 15 Notice to a Prospective

Assignee of a Tenancy. Failure by the outgoing tenant renders him liable to the assignee to reimburse loss sustained. A Form 16 Notice of Assignment of Tenancy of a Commonhold Unit must also be given within 14 days of the assignment and any inconsistent provision is void (s.17(1)).

If the tenant fails to comply with any of these obligations, causing the CA to suffer a loss as a result, and the obligation is one which must be complied with by the unit-holder and tenant, then the CA may give notice requiring the unit-holder to reimburse it for the loss.

Note also that regulation 11(2) permits a lease for a term of up to 21 years if it is a lease in compensation for an extinguished lease under s.7(3)(d) or s.9(3)(f).

2.9.3 Social housing

As the leasing restrictions would prevent social landlords such as RSLs from granting shared ownership leases, there will be a separate set of regulations to cater for RSLs. These are expected at a later date as the details were not settled by the first set of commonhold regulations

The problem arises because of the practice of RSLs of using shared ownership leases as a way of promoting home ownership. These leases can be used for houses or flats. In either case the leaseholder is in the position of being part-owner part-tenant and is usually granted a 99 year lease at a premium with the option of acquiring further tranches of the equity. The leaseholders pay a rent in respect of that part of the equity which they do not own.

Clearly, shared ownership leases cannot be granted in their present form under the current leasehold regulations which govern residential commonholds. Nonetheless it is possible for a social landlord to enter into a form of joint ownership where the 'tenant' has a right to occupy and own a share of the equity.

2.9.4 Commercial units

Note that these leasing restrictions do not apply to a commercial unit. The only restrictions which apply to commercial units are those (if any) which are contained in the CCS (s.18).

2.10 CONVERTING EXISTING LEASEHOLD OR FREEHOLD BUILDINGS

This may prove popular with very small leasehold buildings, such as a block of flats or those cases where flats have been sold freehold.

2.10.1 Generally, under section 9

The general principle was noted at **para.2.2.2**: unanimity amongst all who have an estate and certain other interests in the land is required before the land can be registered as commonhold land. The Act makes provision for application to the Land Registry for such a conversion. This application must be accompanied by a statement by the applicant asking for section 9 to apply. This statement must include a list of the commonhold units, the proposed initial unit-holders and, under regulation 6 of the CR, addresses for service, the unit number and postal address if available. This application must be accompanied by the following documents: the certificate of incorporation of the CA; the memorandum and articles of association of the CA; the CCS; director's certificates that the documents are compliant with the Act and the Regulations; and the consents (in this case, in particular the consents of all of the leaseholders and freeholders and any mortgagees).

2.10.2 Converting existing leasehold schemes

Whether the reversion is held by a freeholder who is independent of the leaseholders, or a company which comprises the leaseholders (either as shareholders or members) or by some other combination of leaseholders, the freeholder has to agree and is the person/entity which applies for the registration.

A new company will be required satisfying the requirements of the Act generally and any charge over the freehold reversion will have to be discharged.

As noted earlier at **para.2.2.2**, the creation of the commonhold will bring the leases to an end, which is why any mortgagees of those leases will be required to consent and in return will expect a substituted security in the form of the commonhold unit. After the commonhold is created, new mortgages will have to be executed and registered and any sub-tenancies must end and any substitute lease will have to comply with the restrictions on leasing.

2.10.3 Converting existing freehold schemes

The freehold flat owners will be joint applicants and their lenders will have to consent. Replacement charges over the commonhold units will be required in place of the mortgages over the freehold flats. If there are no common parts in the freehold flat scheme these will have to be created. This may require some redefinition of the extent of the units in the CCS to make provision for common parts which will have to be vested in the CA.

2.11 SUMMARY

This chapter has summarised the essential features of commonhold land. Land can be registered at the Land Registry as commonhold land if the applicant owns the registered freehold estate, the land is referred to in the constitution of a CA and where the land is described in a CCS which also contains the rules of the commonhold. In making this application the applicant must have the consent of the owner of the freehold (the applicant in this example) and the owner of any leaseholds and mortgages. A commonhold can also be established in relation to a leasehold or a freehold development if all concerned agree to the land being registered as commonhold land. For example, in the case of a block of flats held by leaseholders, they must acquire the freehold and then may convert to commonhold if they are unanimous and have the consent of any mortgagee. Conversion is also possible in a freehold development consisting of freehold flats provided all of the flat owners (and any mortgagees) agree they may convert to commonhold.

CHAPTER 3

Setting up a commonhold

Gary Cowen

3.1 INTRODUCTION

In this chapter, we will deal in general terms with the steps which must be taken to establish a commonhold. Specific elements of the procedure will be dealt with in more detail in other chapters. Registration procedures are dealt with in detail in **Chapter 4**. The commonhold community statement (CCS) is discussed in **Chapter 6**. The commonhold association (CA) is dealt with in detail in **Chapter 7**.

It is important to understand that a great deal of preparation will have to be carried out by the person proposing to establish the commonhold before the commonhold can come into existence. The CA will have to be established and registered, a CCS drafted, requisite consents obtained and applications for registration made. Each of these steps will require careful planning and the input of expertise to ensure that the documents drafted to govern the management of the commonhold land for the foreseeable future are completed in a form which is acceptable to all of those concerned with the future of the development. It is important therefore that the planning and preparation of the necessary documentation commences sufficiently early to allow ample time for it to be completed before it is envisaged the commonhold will commence.

3.1.1 Five requirements for setting up a commonhold

In order to establish a commonhold, those proposing the commonhold must ensure that the following five requirements are satisfied:

- establishing the freehold land which is to form the commonhold;
- obtaining all requisite consents from those persons with interests in the land which is to form the commonhold;
- establishing a CA and registering it as a company;
- preparing a CCS;
- registering the land as a commonhold at the Land Registry.

Each of these elements will be considered in turn in this chapter.

3.2 FREEHOLD LAND

Land is defined as commonhold land by section 1(1) of the Act, if:

(a) the freehold estate in the land is registered as a freehold estate in commonhold land,

(b) the land is specified in the memorandum of association of a commonhold association as the land in relation to which the association is to exercise functions, and

(c) a commonhold community statement makes provision for rights and duties of the commonhold association and unit-holders . . .

Section 1 of the Act therefore requires that the land which will be commonhold land will be freehold land. Additionally, section 2 provides that only the registered freehold owner of the land is entitled to apply for the land to be registered as commonhold land. Leasehold land may not be registered as commonhold. For example, the owners of long leasehold interests in a block of flats or an estate must acquire the freehold interest in the block or the estate if they wish to convert their development into a commonhold and accordingly, must act unanimously.

The Act also provides that certain categories of land cannot be commonhold land (s.4). These are set out in Schedule 2 to the Act and are:

- flying freeholds;
- agricultural land; and
- contingent estates.

Whilst it is a pre-requisite of registration of land as a freehold estate in commonhold that the person making the application to register is the registered freeholder of the land, that definition is extended in section 2 of the Act to include any person who has applied and who, the Registrar is satisfied, is entitled to be registered as the freeholder of the land. There is no provision in the Commonhold (Land Registration) Rules 2004 (CLRR) for a single application for registration to be made where the land is formerly unregistered land. It would appear necessary, therefore, for two separate applications to be made; first for registration as freehold owner of the land and then for registration of the proposed commonhold. There is no reason why those applications should not be made simultaneously (see paragraph 4.1. of the Land Registry Practice Guide No. 60).

No application for registration as a commonhold can be made in respect of land of which any part is already an existing commonhold (s.2). This is to prevent subdivision of existing commonholds.

3.2.1 Flying freeholds

It is not possible to register even freehold land as commonhold if it is a 'flying freehold'. A flying freehold is defined in Schedule 2 as 'land above ground level ("raised land")'. Schedule 2 provides that an application to register land which comprises or includes 'raised land' may not be made unless all the land between the ground and the raised land is the subject of the same application.

The practical consequences of this provision are that it is not possible to have a commonhold of an upper floor of a building unless every floor beneath the upper floor in question down to ground level also forms part of the same commonhold. This may be of particular significance in buildings of mixed use where there may be commercial units at ground level with residential flats on the floors above. The residential flats in such a situation would not be able to be a commonhold without the commercial units also becoming part of the same commonhold. It should be noted that the same does not necessarily hold good in reverse. A commonhold may include ground floor premises without necessarily including the upper floors of the same development.

It seems that the reference to 'ground level' means that a basement or underground car park could be excluded from a commonhold even if the property immediately above it is part of the commonhold.

An application to add land which is wholly or partly raised to an existing commonhold may be made, pursuant to s.41, provided that all the land between the ground and the raised land forms part of the commonhold to which the raised land is to be added (Sched.2, para.(2)). Thus, an additional floor constructed at the top of an existing building can be added to the existing commonhold provided that each floor below the additional land forms part of the existing commonhold to which the new raised land is to be added.

3.2.2 Agricultural land

Land or a part of land which is agricultural land may not be registered as a commonhold (Sched.2).

Agricultural land is defined in Schedule 2 as:

- Land which is agricultural land as defined in the Agricultural Holdings Act 1947:

  - The 1947 Act defines agricultural land as 'Land used for agriculture which is so used for the purpose of a trade or business, or which is designated by the Minister for the purposes of this subsection, and includes any land so designated as land which in the opinion of the Minister ought to be brought into use for agriculture'.

- Land which is comprised in a tenancy of an agricultural holding within the meaning of the Agricultural Holdings Act 1986.
- Land which is comprised within a farm business tenancy within the meaning of the Agricultural Tenancies Act 1995.

3.2.3 Contingent estates

Land or a part of land which is a contingent estate may not be registered as a commonhold (Sched.2, para.(1)).

A contingent estate is defined in Schedule 2 as an estate which is liable to revert to or vest in a person other than the present registered proprietor on the occurrence or non-occurrence of a particular event where that reversion or vesting occurs pursuant to one of a number of specified enactments.

The relevant enactments are:

- the School Sites Act 1841;
- the Lands Clauses Acts;
- the Literary and Scientific Institutions Act 1854;
- the Places of Worship Sites Act 1873.

It is not clear why, in three of these cases, the land should not be able to be converted into commonhold land. The School Sites Act 1841, Literary and Scientific Institutions Act 1854 and Places of Worship Sites Act 1873 must each now be read in the context of the Reverter of Sites Act 1987 (1987 Act). The 1987 Act which effected a significant change in the law relating to each of the situations covered by those statutes in order to cure the problem which flowed from the potential inability to trace the successors to the original estate owners.

In each of the statutes, land which formed part of an estate could be conveyed for use for particular purposes but would revert back to the estate in the event that use of the land for those purposes ceased. 'Particular purposes' would be educational purposes in the case of the School Sites Act 1841, use as literary and scientific institutions in the case of the Literary and Scientific Institutions Act 1854 and use as a place of religious worship or burial or as accommodation for a minister in the case of the Places of Worship Sites Act 1873. In the case of the Literary and Scientific Institutions Act 1854, 'the estate' would be settled land, land held on trust or land held by various duchies, ecclesiastical or lay corporations.

Sections 1 and 7 of the 1987 Act provide in each case that the land may now be conveyed free of the obligation to revert to the original estate but that the proceeds of sale of any such conveyance would be held on trust for the successor in title of the original estate owner.

There would not seem to be any good remaining reason, therefore, why such land could not be sold to become commonhold land, with the proceeds of sale being held on trust for the successor in title of the original estate owner. Indeed, it seems that the bar on commonhold ownership of such land will be relatively easy to circumnavigate by conveying the land in accordance with the 1987 Act before any application for registration as commonhold is made.

The other category of contingent estate referred to in the Act is contingent estates under the 'Land Clauses Acts'. This appears to be a reference to the Land Clauses Consolidation Act 1845 which contains a procedure for compulsory purchase of land pursuant to which the acquiring party executes a deed poll and pays the purchase monies into court, the effect of which is to vest the land in the acquiring party. The Land Clauses Consolidation Acts Amendment Act 1860 contains no vesting or reverter provisions. Other Land Clauses Acts were repealed by the Compulsory Purchase Act 1965.

The 2002 Act provides for regulations to add or remove enactments from the list. The Commonhold Regulations 2004 (CR) make no such provision.

3.3 OBTAINING CONSENTS

In order to register land as commonhold land, the consent of a number of persons is required. Those persons are:

- the registered freehold owner of the land;
- the registered owner of any leasehold interest in the land granted for a term in excess of 21 years;
- the registered owner of any charge over the land;
- other persons whose consent is required by regulations.

3.3.1 The registered freehold owner

Only the registered freehold owner of the land is entitled to apply for the land to be registered as commonhold land (s.2(1)(a)). Therefore, the consent of the registered freehold owner must implicitly be forthcoming. However, consent is also explicitly required (s.3(1)(a)).

There is nothing in the Act about obtaining the consent of a beneficial owner of the freehold interest in the land and it would appear that the consent of such a beneficial owner is not required. Some doubt remains about whether a commonhold will be registered by the Land Registrar where a beneficial owner of the freehold interest in the land has placed a notice on the Register of his beneficial ownership. However, as there is nothing in the Act which requires the consent of such a beneficial owner, it is thought unlikely that the Registrar will interfere with the process. It may be that a beneficial ownership in the freehold interest will attach itself to the proceeds of sale of the commonhold units upon conversion to commonhold.

In addition the CR require consent to be obtained from the owner of an unregistered freehold estate in the whole or part of the land.

3.3.2 Registered leasehold owner

The consent of the registered owner of a leasehold estate in the whole or any part of the land intended to be converted to commonhold is required provided that the lease in question was granted for a term in excess of 21 years (s.3(1)(b)).

It should be noted that it is not sufficient that the leasehold owner should have occupied the land for a period in excess of 21 years if, in fact, his occupation was pursuant to two or more consecutive leasehold interests adding up to more than 21 years. In addition, a leasehold interest is not prevented from being a leasehold interest for a term in excess of 21 years merely because it contains an option to determine the lease prior to the end of the contractual termination date or a right of re-entry on the part of the landlord.

It follows that consent is not required from:

- the beneficial owner of a leasehold interest of any length;
- the owner of a so-called equitable lease of any length (where the lessee occupies the premises pursuant to a binding and enforceable agreement for lease which, in equity, is treated as if the lease had been granted).

The CR have added significantly to the provisions of the Act relating to the consent required from persons holding leasehold interests in the land or part of the land. These regulations are dealt with throughout this chapter.

One important effect of this provision is that, in order to convert an existing leasehold development to commonhold, the consent of every registered long leasehold owner will be required and a failure to consent on the part of one such leaseholder will have the effect of blocking the conversion to commonhold. Given the experience that many legal advisors will have of the types of disputes which tend to surface in leasehold blocks of flats, it may very well be the case that the fear that very few existing leasehold developments will convert to commonhold will be justified.

3.3.3 Owner of a registered charge over the land

The consent of a registered owner of a charge over the land or a part of the land to be converted to commonhold is required (s.3(1)(c)).

It is not clear whether the reference in the Act to the 'registered proprietor of a charge' extends to the owner of an equitable mortgage or equitable charge over the property which has been protected by notice on the register. It is submitted that it very arguably would not. It would be stretching the language of the Act to suggest that an equitable mortgagee whose interest is protected by notice on the register is a 'registered proprietor' of a charge. He may be the equitable chargee and may have registered his equitable charge by notice but it is suggested that that would not be sufficient to constitute him as a 'registered proprietor' of a charge. Additionally, the use of those words suggests very strongly that it was intended that it should apply only to the proprietor of a registered charge, something which would be consistent with the position relating to leasehold interests.

In addition the CR require consent to be obtained from the owner of a mortgage, charge or lien for securing money or money's worth over unregistered land. This is dealt with **para.3.3.4** below.

3.3.4 Other persons whose consent is required by regulations

Paragraph 3 of the CR provides that, in addition to the persons listed in section 3(1) of the Act, the consent of the following persons is required before an application may be made to register land as commonhold land:

- the owner of any unregistered freehold estate in the whole or part of the land;
- the owner of any unregistered leasehold interest in the whole or part of the land granted for a term of more than 21 years;
- the owner of any mortgage, charge or lien for securing money or money's worth over the whole or part of any unregistered land included in the application; or
- subject to the CR, reg.3(2), the holder of a lease granted for a term of not more than 21 years, which will be extinguished by s.7(3)(d) or s.9(3)(f) of the Act (CR, reg.3(1)(d)).

Unregistered freehold owner

Consent is required from the owner of any unregistered freehold estate in the whole or part of the land (CR, reg.3(1)(a)). This is a curious provision. As has been stated, the only person who is entitled to apply to register a commonhold is the registered proprietor of the freehold estate in the land (s.2(1)(a) and s.2(3)). It may be that the addition of this provision at a late stage in the process was designed to encompass the extended definition of the registered proprietor to include a freehold owner of unregistered land who would be entitled to make an application to register land as commonhold provided the Registrar is satisfied that he would be entitled to be registered as the proprietor of the freehold land (s.3(b)). However, the CR, reg.4(5)(a) provides that consent will be deemed to have been given by the applicant for registration.

Unregistered leasehold owner

Consent is required from the owner of any unregistered leasehold estate in the whole or part of the land granted for a term of more than 21 years (CR 2004, reg.3(1)(b)). The wording mirrors that relating to registered leasehold interests and the same considerations concerning the length of term will apply. The obvious problem with such a provision is that it may, occasionally, be difficult to identify an unregistered leasehold owner.

Mortgagee of unregistered land

Consent is required from the owner of any mortgage, charge or lien for securing money or money's worth over the whole or part of any unregistered land included in the application (CR, reg.3(1)(c)). Again, this would appear to be aimed at a situation where the land proposed to be registered as a commonhold has not yet been registered at the Land Registry but where the owner of the land would be entitled to be so registered (this situation is dealt with by s.2(3)(b)). The chief difficulty once again may be in identifying the persons from whom consent must be obtained.

Leases of not more than 21 years

The CR, reg.3(1)(d) also provides that subject to certain provisions dealt with below, consent is required from the holder of a lease granted for a term of not more than 21 years which will be extinguished by s.7(3)(d) or s.9(3)(f) of the Act.

Section 7(3)(d) of the Act provides for the extinguishment of leases upon registration of a commonhold where there are no proposed existing commonhold units (i.e. where s.9(1) does not apply) and s.9(3)(f) provides for the extinguishment of leases where existing commonhold units are proposed. A detailed discussion of the extinguishment of leases upon the registration of the commonhold appears in **Chapter 4**.

However, no consent is required from the holder of a lease granted for a term of not more than 21 years if two conditions apply (CR, reg.3(2)).

The first condition is that the person who holds the lease in question is 'entitled' to the grant of a term of years absolute:

- of the same premises as are comprised in the extinguished lease;
- on the same terms as the extinguished lease except to the extent necessary to comply with the Act and the CR and excluding any terms that are spent;
- at the same rent as payable under, and including the same provisions for rent review as were included in, the extinguished lease as at the date on which it will be extinguished;

- for a term equivalent to the unexpired term of the lease which will be extinguished;
- to take effect immediately after the lease is extinguished by virtue of s.7(3)(d) or s.9(3)(f).

It is suggested that the reference to the tenant's 'entitlement' to the grant of such a term of years is a reference to a binding legal entitlement. It will be necessary, therefore, for the developer who proposes to convert to commonhold and who will require the consent of such a tenant, to enter into a fully binding and specifically enforceable agreement for lease which meets all of the requirements referred to in the preceding paragraph in order to avoid the necessity for obtaining that tenant's consent to the registration of the commonhold. Clearly, the intention behind such a requirement is that the holder of such a lease should not be prejudiced by the change to commonhold and should be in a position to legally enforce his right to a new tenancy, putting him in the same position as he was in prior to the application to register as commonhold.

The second condition is that prior to the application for registration as a commonhold being made, the tenant's legal entitlement to the grant of a further term of years absolute has been protected by a notice in the Land Register of the freehold title for the land comprised in the proposed application or, in the case of land which is at that stage unregistered, by an entry in the Land Charges Register in the name of the estate owner of the freehold title (CR, reg.3(2)(b)).

It is not clear that this second condition will provide any greater protection for the tenant than is provided by the first condition. If it is a condition of dispensing with his consent that he must be legally entitled to a new tenancy to take effect immediately after his existing lease is extinguished, then such a condition would be sufficient, it would seem, to protect the tenant's position.

3.3.5 Form of consent

Section 3(2) of the Act also provides for regulations to be made concerning consents and in particular, for regulations to:

- prescribe the form of consent;
- make provision about the effect and duration of consent (including provision for consent to bind successors);
- make provision about withdrawing consent (including provision preventing withdrawal in specified circumstances);
- make provision for a consent given for the purposes of one application to register as a commonhold to have effect for the purposes of another such application;

- make provision for consent to be deemed to have been given in certain circumstances;
- enable the court to dispense with the requirement for consent in specified circumstances.

An order made by the court under such regulations to dispense with the requirements for consent may be made absolutely or conditionally and may include any other provision which the court thinks appropriate (s.3(3)).

In a case where consent is required to an application to register land as a commonhold (s.2) the CR, reg.4(1)(a) provides that the consent must be in Form CON1. In a case where consent is required to an application to cancel the registration of a commonhold during the transitional period (s.8(4)) the CR, reg.4(1)(b) provides that the consent must be in Form CON2.

Once given, the consent is binding upon the person who gives the consent or who is deemed to have given the consent (CR, reg.4(2)). A person is deemed to have given consent if, in fact, they are the person making the application (either under s.2 or s.8(4)) and where their consent would otherwise have been required but has not expressly been given (CR, reg.4(5)(a)). So, the owner of the freehold interest in the land who also owns a long leasehold interest in the land would not have to give a separate consent in respect of his long leasehold interest. In addition, the successor in title to a person who has given consent or who is deemed to have given their consent is likewise deemed to have given their consent (CR, reg.4(5)(b)).

Consent may be given subject to conditions (CR, reg.4(3)). There is no reference in the CR to what such conditions might encompass and this has the potential to give rise to difficult questions. It would seem that a person who is required to give consent has a free hand as to the conditions which he can impose, including presumably, the requirement of payment of a monetary sum in return for consent being given or, in the case of a lender, the grant of a new charge over the commonhold unit. Given that consent is required prior to an application for registration being made, it is not clear what would be the effect of a consent subject to a condition which could only be fulfilled following registration as a commonhold and where that condition was not subsequently fulfilled. It is thought that notwithstanding that the condition was not subsequently fulfilled (so that the consent itself was colourable) at the time of registration, a valid consent would be in place so that registration would be valid. If a person required to give consent wishes to impose a condition upon the grant of his consent, such a condition should therefore ideally require fulfilment by the time of the application for registration.

Subject to any condition which is attached to a consent and which imposes a shorter period, any consent given or deemed to have been given will lapse if no application has been made within a period of 12 months from the date of the consent (CR, reg.4(4)).

If consent is given in respect of a proposed application, that consent will only have effect for the purposes of a different application where the new application is submitted in place of the application which has been withdrawn by the applicant or rejected or cancelled by the Registrar. The new application must be made within 12 months of the date of the consent (CR, reg.4(5)).

A consent which has been given may be withdrawn at any time before the date upon which the relevant application is submitted to the Registrar (CR, reg.4(7)).

3.3.6   Dispensing with consent

The requirement for consent to be obtained from each of the persons described above has the serious potential consequence that a refusal by any person from whom such consent is required, no matter how arbitrary, could prevent a commonhold from coming into existence. In addition, a commonhold might be frustrated by an inability to locate an individual from whom consent is required.

The Government decided at an early stage of the legislative process that it would not make regulations which would enable the court to dispense with consent where it was said to have been unreasonably withheld. The Government considered that defining an unreasonable withholding of consent would be difficult and time consuming and that in any event, conversion to commonhold is not something which should be the subject of compulsion, no matter how unreasonable the withholding of consent.

As a result the Act provides for regulation to make provision for the court to dispense with the requirement for consent only in respect of a person who cannot be located. It should be noted that these provisions apply only to a consent required in respect of an application to register a commonhold under s.2 and not an application under s.8(4).

The CR, reg.5 provides that the court may dispense with a consent which would otherwise be required:

- where the person whose consent is required cannot be identified after all reasonable efforts have been made to ascertain his identity;
- where such a person can be identified but cannot be traced after all reasonable efforts have been made to trace him;
- where such a person has been sent a request for consent and all reasonable efforts have been made to obtain a response but he has not responded.

Thus, if a person from whom consent is required takes a positive decision not to reply to a request for consent in order to frustrate the registration of a commonhold, the court may, if satisfied that all reasonable steps have been taken, dispense with such consent. Yet, a person with the same objective might reply positively refusing consent. In the latter case, there would be nothing which the freehold owner could do to overturn that position.

3.4 ESTABLISHMENT OF A COMMONHOLD ASSOCIATION

The detailed provisions concerning the establishment of a CA are dealt with in **Chapter 7**. This chapter will give a relatively brief overview.

3.4.1 Nature of a commonhold association

A CA is a private company limited by guarantee set up to oversee the management of the commonhold (s.34(1) and s.35). The members of the company are the unit-holders within the commonhold and no other person is entitled to become a member of the company after registration of the commonhold (CR, Sched.3, paras.7 and 10). Because the CA is a company, it is governed by the general law relating to companies although the Act and the CR make some specific provisions where the Companies Act 1985 does not apply to a CA or applies in a modified form.

The CA is bound by the CCS which governs the rights and obligations of the members of the commonhold. The obligations owed by individual unit-holders of units within the commonhold will be owed to the CA. Conversely, the rights which individual unit-holders hold are enforceable against the CA.

3.4.2 Registration of a commonhold association

A CA is formed in the same manner as any other company, by sending the appropriate documents to the Registrar of Companies. The documents which must be sent are:

- The memorandum and articles of association as prescribed in the CR (Companies Act 1985, s.10(1)).
- A statement in the prescribed form containing the name and particulars of the first directors and the first secretary of the company signed by the subscribers (Companies Act 1985, s.10(2)). The statement must include a consent from each of the persons named as a director or secretary and must specify the address of the intended registered office of the company.
  - The particulars which are required in respect of a director are the name and any former names of the director, his usual residential address, his nationality, his business occupation, his date of birth and details of any other directorships held by him or which have been held by him.
  - If the proposed secretary is an individual, only the name, any former names and the usual residential address of that person are required.

36

– In the case of a corporate secretary, only the corporate name and its registered office need be provided.

The application to register the company must also be accompanied by the appropriate fee. If the Registrar is satisfied that the documentation is in order and that the relevant fee has been paid, he will issue a certificate of incorporation and the company will exist from that date (Companies Act 1985, s.13). The subscribers will automatically become the first members of the company upon its registration (Companies Act 1985, s.22(1)).

3.4.3   Membership of the commonhold association

The Act makes provision for limiting the persons who may be members of the CA. The membership of the CA will be limited in accordance with the various stages of registration of the commonhold.

Following incorporation of the CA but prior to registration of the land as a freehold estate in commonhold, the only persons entitled to be members of the company are the subscribers (Sched.3, para.5) who have applied for registration of the company in the manner described above. There must be at least two such subscribers (Companies Act 1985, s.1(1)) and they will automatically become members of the company upon a certificate of incorporation being issued (Companies Act 1985, s.22(1)). Some ambiguity is created by paragraph 5 of Schedule 3 to the Act, which makes express reference to 'the subscribers (or subscriber) to the memorandum' being 'the sole members (or member) of the association' suggesting that a single subscriber is sufficient to create a CA. However, this is at odds with the Companies Act 1985 and it is thought that it perhaps reflects only the fact that a member is entitled to resign as a member at any time after incorporation of the company.

During the transitional period between the registration of the land as a freehold estate in commonhold and the date upon which the first unit-holder becomes entitled to be registered as a proprietor of an individual unit, the subscribers may remain as members of the CA or may resign as members (Sched.3, para.6(2)).

However, during the transitional period, the developer for the time being of all or part of the commonhold may also become a member of the CA (Sched.3, para.6(3)). The developer is either:

• the person who made the application for the land to be registered as commonhold land (s.58(1)); or
• a person to whom the freehold estate in the whole of the commonhold has been transferred during the transitional period (s.59).

Strangely, upon such a transfer, the Act does not prevent the original developer from remaining a member of the CA. However, it is thought likely that the new developer would be likely to wish to make it a condition of any sale that the original developer resign as a member of the CA.

At the end of the transitional period, when a person other than the developer becomes entitled to be registered as proprietor of one or more individual commonhold units (but not all of the units), then any person who becomes the unit-holder of an individual unit in relation to which the CA exercises functions is entitled to be registered as a member of the CA (Sched.3, para.7). It should be noted that a person becomes the unit-holder as soon as he is entitled to be registered as the proprietor of the unit (this may therefore be prior to his actual registration as proprietor of the individual unit, s.12). Once the transitional period has come to an end (usually upon the sale of the last unit), the developer will no longer be entitled to be a member of the CA and ought to resign as a member if he has not already done so.

A person who is not a unit-holder of a commonhold unit may not become a member of the CA (Sched.3, para.7). Indeed, when an individual unit-holder or joint unit-holder ceases to own a unit, he will automatically cease to be a member of the CA though this will not affect any accrued rights or liabilities during the period of his membership (Sched.12, paras.12(a) and (b)). A unit-holder may not resign his membership of the CA during the period of his ownership or joint ownership of the commonhold unit (Sched.12, para.13). Only a subscriber or a developer may resign as a member of the CA but neither is required to do so, even if they do not own any commonhold units. A CA cannot be a member of itself (Sched.12, para.9).

A person who is entitled to become a member of the CA does not do so automatically. An application must be made to register him in the register of members for the company. Once registration has taken place, he becomes a member of the CA and becomes entitled to exercise his voting rights (Sched.12, para.11). However, it should be noted that the company has a duty to register the member promptly pursuant to section 352 of the Companies Act 1985. The Act provides for regulations to be made which provide specifically for the manner in which the duty to register new members is to be performed (Sched.3, para.14(1)) and the period within which the new member must be registered (Sched.3, paras.14(2) and (3)) but no such regulations have yet been made.

A person who is entitled to be registered as a member of the CA need not be so registered if he chooses not to be. However, he will not be entitled to vote in matters concerning the management of the commonhold if he is not a member of the CA.

3.4.4   Joint unit-holders

If a unit is owned jointly, the unit must still only have a single member of the CA in order to avoid having a disproportionate benefit in voting rights.

The rules for determining which joint unit-holder is entitled to be a member of the CA are given in Sched.3, para.8. In the first instance, the joint unit-holders may nominate one of their number to be the member of the CA. Nomination is made in writing and must be addressed to the CA. The nomination must be made before the end of a prescribed period but neither the Act or the CR prescribes what this period is to be.

In the event that no nomination is received by the CA within the prescribed period, the person whose name appears first in the proprietorship register will be deemed to be the only person entitled to become a member of the CA although another joint unit-holder may apply to the court to be substituted as the member of the CA in the event that such a deeming takes effect (Sched.3, paras.8(4)–(5)).

After the end of the prescribed period, the joint unit-holders can nominate one of their number to be entitled to become a member in place of another of their number who became a member as a result of a nomination within the prescribed period or an order of the court in the circumstances described in the previous paragraph (Sched.3, para.8(6)).

It should be noted that the court may only intervene to replace as the member of the CA one of a number of joint unit-holders in the very limited circumstances where, in default of a nomination within the prescribed period, the first-named registered proprietor is the only person entitled to be registered as the member of the CA. In the absence of such circumstances, any change of the identity of the member must be consensual. There is no procedure in the Act whereby a joint owner who is dissatisfied with the way in which his joint owner is exercising his voting rights can apply to have that joint owner replaced.

Of course, in the absence of a prescribed period defined either in the Act or the CR, it remains to be seen precisely how the courts will seek to enforce these provisions.

3.5   COMMONHOLD COMMUNITY STATEMENT

In order to register land as a freehold estate in commonhold, it will be necessary to have prepared a CCS in advance of the application for registration as commonhold land. This document, which must be in a prescribed form, defines the rights and obligations of the CA and the individual unit-holders and may also make provision about the taking of decisions in connection with the management of the commonhold or any other matter concerning it (s.31(1)–(3)).

The detailed provisions concerning CCSs are dealt with in **Chapter 6**.

3.6 REGISTRATION OF THE COMMONHOLD

Once the CA has been established, the final task in setting up the commonhold is to apply to have the freehold land registered as commonhold land at the Land Registry.

In brief, the application to the Land Registry must be made on Form CM1 (Commonhold (Land Registration) Rules 2004, Sched.1). The application must be accompanied by the following documentation:

- the CA's certificate of incorporation under section 13 of the Companies Act 1985 and the memorandum and articles of association of the CA (Sched.1, paras.2 and 4);
- the CCS;
- any relevant consent forms as well as any order of the court dispensing with the requirement for consent pursuant to s.3(2)(f) (Sched.1, paras.2 and 4);
- a certificate given by the directors of the CA that the commonhold complies with the various requirements of the Act and the CR; and
- unless the Registrar otherwise directs, a statutory declaration made by the applicant.

The detailed provisions concerning application for registration of the land as commonhold land are dealt with in **Chapter 4**.

3.7 SUMMARY

This chapter has summarised in general terms the manner in which a commonhold must be established. In order to establish land as commonhold land, an applicant must first identify the freehold land which is to comprise the commonhold. He must then obtain consents from any person with an interest in the land whose consent is required under the Act. He must additionally form a CA and register it as a company. The rules governing the commonhold will be contained in the CCS and the applicant must have formulated those rules and established the CCS before an application to register land as commonhold can be made. It is only once those steps have been taken that the applicant can perform the last task, applying to the Land Registry to register the land as commonhold land.

CHAPTER 4

Registration procedures

Gary Cowen

4.1 INTRODUCTION

This chapter deals with the procedures for registration of the commonhold land and the consequences of that registration. The chapter will additionally deal with the specific procedures laid down for conversion of an existing lease-hold scheme to commonhold and the position in the event of a registration of a commonhold in error.

4.2 UNREGISTERED LAND

It is a prerequisite of registration of land as a freehold estate in commonhold that the person making the application to register is the registered freeholder of the land (s.2(1)(a)). However, that definition is extended to include any person who has applied and who, the Registrar is satisfied, is entitled to be registered as the freeholder of the land (s.2(3)(b)). There is no provision in the Commonhold (Land Registration) Rules 2004 (CLRR) for a single application for registration to be made where the land is formerly unregistered land. It would appear necessary, therefore, for two separate applications to be made for registration as freehold owner of the land and for registration of the proposed commonhold. There is no reason why those applications should not be made simultaneously (see paragraph 4.1 of the Land Registry Practice Guide No. 60).

4.3 APPLICATION FOR REGISTRATION

A proposed commonhold cannot take effect as such until it is registered at the Land Registry as commonhold. It is the responsibility of the person proposing the commonhold to make an application to the Land Registry for registration of the freehold estate as a freehold estate in common-hold pursuant to section 2. The application must be made to the Land Registrar.

The application for registration must be made on Form CM1 (CLRR, Sched.1). Additionally, where the commonhold is to be registered with existing unit-holders (that is to say, where an existing leasehold development or development of freehold flats is to be converted to a freehold estate in commonhold), the application must be accompanied by the statement required by section 9(1)(b) to the effect that section 9 of the Act is to apply. Form CM1 includes a tick-box at paragraph 13 to that effect, but Form CM1 must also be accompanied by a further Form COV complying with s.9(2) (CLRR, r.5(2)). If the commonhold is to be registered prior to the sale of any of the units section 9 will not apply and the statement need not be provided on registration.

The Form CM1 also:

- permits up to three addresses to be provided for service of notices and correspondence upon the applicant, one of which must be a postal address though not necessarily in the United Kingdom. The other addresses may be a postal address, a box number at a UK document exchange or an electronic address. Care should be taken to comply with this provision as the Land Registry has indicated that it will reject applications where this formality is not complied with (Land Registry Consultation Paper, paragraph 49 and the Land Registry Practice Guide, paragraph 5.2);
- enables the applicant to provide the name and address of a third party (such as the applicant's solicitor) to whom the Land Registry should:

  - send confirmation of registration; and/or
  - raise any requisition or queries; and/or
  - issue a copy of the commonhold community statement (CCS) and/or the memorandum and articles of association;

- requires up to three addresses to be provided for service of notices and correspondence upon the proprietor of any proposed charge, one of which must be a postal address though not necessarily in the United Kingdom. The other addresses may be a postal address, a box number at a UK document exchange or an electronic address.

4.4 SUPPORTING DOCUMENTATION

The Form CM1 must be accompanied by the following further documentation.

- *Documentation relating to the commonhold association.* This documentation comprises the CA's certificate of incorporation under Companies Act 1985, s.13, any altered certificate of incorporation issued under section 28 of the Companies Act 1985 and the memorandum and articles of association of the CA (Sched.1, paras.2–4).

- The CCS (Sched.1, para.5). Particular care should be taken to provide a clear and accurate plan of the land intended to form the commonhold land with the CCS. The Land Registrar has a specific power to reject an application on delivery or to cancel an application at any time thereafter if the plans submitted with the application are insufficiently clear or accurate (CLRR, r.8). Reference should be made to the Land Registry Practice Guide No. 60 which contains detailed guidance on the preparation of plans at paragraph 4.3.

- *Documentation evidencing consents.* Such documentation would comprise any relevant consent forms as well as any order of the court dispensing with the requirement for consent pursuant to s.3(2)(f) (Sched.1, para.6(1)(a) and (b)). A consent form must be in the prescribed Form CON1 (CLRR, r.7). In addition, if any consent is deemed to have been given by virtue of s.3(2)(e) of the Act or if any order of the court makes consent conditional pursuant to s.3(3)(a) of the Act, such evidence as may be required to demonstrate the deemed consent or the compliance with conditions should also be provided by way of statutory declaration (Sched.1, para.6(1)(c) and 6(2)).

- *Director's certificate.* A certificate given by the directors of the CA (Sched.1, para.7) that:

  - the memorandum and articles of association submitted with the application comply with the regulations under Sched.3, para.2(1) concerning the form and content of the memorandum and articles of association;
  - the CCS submitted with the application satisfies the requirements of the Act;
  - the application satisfies Schedule 2 to the Act. In other words, that the application does not comprise land which may not be commonhold land;
  - the CA has not traded; and
  - the CA has not incurred any liability which has not been discharged.

- *Statutory declaration.* Unless the Registrar otherwise directs, a statutory declaration made by the applicant (CLRR, rr.5 and 6) that:

  - lists the consents, or orders of court dispensing with consent, that have been obtained under or by virtue of section 3 of the Act;
  - in a case where there is a restriction entered in any individual Register affected by the application, confirms that either the restriction does not protect an interest in respect of which the consent of the holder is required or, if it does, that the appropriate consent has been obtained;
  - confirms that no other consents are required under or by virtue of section 3 of the Act, that no consent has lapsed or been withdrawn, and that if a consent is subject to conditions, all conditions have been fully satisfied;

– in a case where the application involves the extinguishment under section 22 of the Act of a charge that is the subject of an entry in the Register, identifies the charge to be extinguished, identifies the title of the owner of the charge, gives the name and address of the owner of the charge, and confirms that the consent of the owner of the charge has been obtained.

4.4.1 Nature of the documents to be submitted

In the case of the CA's certificate of incorporation, any altered certificate of incorporation, the memorandum and articles of association of the CA, any altered memorandum or articles of association of the CA, a CCS, any amended CCS, an order of the court under the Act and a termination statement, the applicant may submit the original documents or may submit a certified copy of the original documents instead. If an original document is submitted, a certified copy of the original must also be submitted (CLRR, r.4).

4.4.2 Consents relating to unregistered land

In addition, where a consent required under or by virtue of section 3 of the Act has been submitted which relates to an interest which is unregistered or is the subject of only a notice, caution or restriction in the Register, the applicant must also submit sufficient evidence to satisfy the Registrar that the person whose consent has been submitted is the person who was entitled to that interest at the time the consent was given (CLRR, r.9(1)). The Registrar may accept, as sufficient evidence of entitlement, a conveyancer's certificate that he is satisfied that the person whose consent has been lodged in relation to that interest is the person who was entitled to it at the time the consent was given and that he holds evidence of this (CLRR, r.9).

4.4.3 Effect of the statutory declaration

The Registrar must accept the statutory declaration referred to above as conclusive evidence that no additional consents are required under or by virtue of section 3 of the Act and must cancel any entry in the Register relating to an interest that has been identified in the statutory declaration to be extinguished (CLRR, r.6(6)).

4.5 COMPLETION OF REGISTRATION

If the Registrar is satisfied that the application has been made in accordance with section 2 of the Act, he must complete the application. The manner in which the registration takes place will depend upon whether it is proposed that the registration will proceed with individual unit-holders. In a case where there are no individual unit-holders, so that section 9 of the Act does not apply, the Registrar will complete the registration (CLRR, rr.27 and 28) by:

- registering the applicant as proprietor of the registered title of each of the individual units;
- registering the applicant as proprietor of the registered title of the common parts;
- entering a note in the individual registers of the affected registered titles that the freehold estate is registered as a freehold estate in commonhold;
- entering a note in the individual registers of the affected registered titles of the memorandum and articles of association of the CA and the CCS;
- entering a note in the individual registers of the affected registered titles that the rights and duties conferred and imposed by the CCS will not come into force until the end of the transitional period;
- entering a restriction in Form CA in Schedule 2 in the individual register of the common parts title;
- entering a restriction in Form CB in Schedule 2 in the individual register of each unit title.

In a case where there are pre-existing individual unit-holders, for instance, in respect of the conversion of an existing leasehold development into common-hold, if the Registrar is satisfied that the application has been made in accordance with section 2 of the Act, the Registrar must:

- register the CA as proprietor of the freehold estate in the common parts (s.9(3));
- register the person or persons who have been listed as the proposed initial unit-holder or joint unit-holders pursuant to section 9(2) of the Act as proprietor or joint proprietors of the freehold estate in the unit;
- cancel notice of any lease extinguished by section 9(3)(f) of the Act (CLRR, r.28(2));
- close the title to any extinguished lease if the leasehold interest was registered (CLRR, r.28(2)).

In such a case, no further application need be made to register the proposed initial unit-holders or joint unit-holders as proprietors of the individual units nor to register the CA as proprietor of the common parts (s.9(3)(d)).

4.6 MULTIPLE SITES

Where it is proposed that a commonhold should comprise more than one existing site owned by two different persons, registration as a commonhold is permissible even where the two sites are not contiguous. However, under section 57(2) of the Act, provision for all of the land comprising the proposed commonhold must be made in a single CCS. The only regulations made pursuant to section 57 of the Act provide that, in addition to complying with the requirements of section 11(3) of the Act in defining the extent of a commonhold unit, the CCS must also provide for the extent of each commonhold unit to be situated wholly upon one part-site and not situated partly on one part-site and partly on one or more other part-sites.

4.7 CONVERSION OF EXISTING LEASEHOLD AND FREEHOLD DEVELOPMENTS

The only person entitled to apply to register land as commonhold is the registered freehold owner of the land (s.2(1)(a)). It should therefore be clear from the outset that in order to convert any existing leasehold development into a commonhold, the leaseholders will be required to acquire the freehold of the development. Such an acquisition would presumably take place either by negotiation and agreement with the existing freehold owners or pursuant to the collective enfranchisement provisions of the Leasehold Reform Housing and Urban Development Act 1993, the details of which are outside the scope of this book.

Pursuant to the 1993 Act, a successful collective enfranchisement will result in ownership of the freehold of the development, usually by a company formed and owned by the participating leaseholders. It seems likely, thereafter, that any application to convert the development into a commonhold will be made by such a company although there is no requirement that that should be the case.

Once the freehold has been acquired, the application for registration will proceed in the manner described above. As well as the Form CM1 and the documents listed above, the application must be accompanied by Form COV (CLRR, r.5(2)) which lists:

- the full name of the proposed initial unit-holder or if there are proposed joint unit-holders the full name of each of them;
- the address for service of the proposed initial unit-holder or, as the case may be, the address for service of each proposed joint unit-holder;
- the relevant unit number of the commonhold unit for each proposed unit-holder or joint unit-holders;
- the postal address of the relevant commonhold unit if it has one (Commonhold Regulations 2004 (CR), reg.6).

Rule 3(3)(f) of the CLRR amends the Land Registration Rules 2003 to enable any person interested in the conversion process to obtain an official search with priority.

It is not clear at this stage to what extent existing leasehold developments will convert to commonhold. One potential difficulty is that the Act requires the consent of all registered proprietors of leasehold estates for periods in excess of 21 years (s.3(1)(b)). Therefore, one leasehold owner could, in theory, prevent the conversion from leasehold development to commonhold by refusing to provide consent to the conversion. The power of the court to dispense with the requirement for consent (CR, reg.5) does not extend to cases where a leaseholder has been identified and asked for his consent but simply refuses to give it, however unreasonably. Practitioners with experience of leasehold developments will know how often it is the case that, for whatever reason, one or more leaseholders sets their face against the majority will. Whereas in respect of a claim for collective enfranchisement, such recalcitrant elements can simply be left aside, a single dissenter in the ranks of a leasehold development will, it seems, cause insurmountable problems for a conversion to commonhold. It remains to be seen, therefore, the extent to which existing leasehold developments will, having already acquired the freehold of their developments, seek to additionally take advantage of the benefits of commonhold.

4.8   EFFECT OF REGISTRATION

4.8.1   Transitional period

In a case where there are no proposed unit-holders in respect of individual units, so that section 9 of the Act does not apply, the registration by the Registrar of the applicant as proprietor of each of the individual commonhold units as well as the common parts marks the commencement of what is known in section 8 of the Act as the transitional period.

The transitional period is the period between registration of the freehold estate in land as a freehold estate in commonhold and the time at which a person other than the applicant becomes entitled to be registered as proprietor of the freehold estate in one or more, but less than all, of the commonhold units (i.e. upon the sale of the first unit) (ss.8(1) and 7(3)). It should be noted that the transitional period does not come to an end if the applicant disposes of its interest in all of the commonhold units. This will enable a developer to dispose of its interest in its new development without bringing about the end of the transitional period. Furthermore, the transitional period ends when a person other than the applicant is 'entitled to be' registered as proprietor of a commonhold unit. It is suggested, therefore, that the transitional period will continue until the transfer of the first commonhold unit is completed, at which stage the purchaser will be 'entitled to be' registered as proprietor of the unit.

During the transitional period

During the transitional period:

- the freehold estate has become a freehold estate in commonhold;
- the applicant remains the proprietor of every part of the commonhold land including each individual commonhold unit and the common parts (s.7(2));
- the rights and duties conferred and imposed by the CCS shall not come into force (s.7(2));
- leases of any part of the land continue to exist and are not yet extinguished (s.7(3));
- the registered proprietor may make an application to the Registrar to cancel the registration of the land as commonhold (s.8);
- the owner may exercise any rights as he may be permitted to exercise during the transitional period by the articles of association of the CA.

The Act provides for regulations to be made which would permit certain provisions contained within the Act, the CCS or the memorandum or articles of association of the CA to apply during the transitional period with specified modifications (s.8). No such regulations were made in the CR or the CLRR.

After the transitional period

The question of *when* the transitional period comes to an end is dealt with above. Upon the termination of the transitional period (i.e. upon the sale of the first unit) (s.7(3)):

- the CA becomes entitled to be registered as proprietor of the freehold estate in the common parts;
- the Registrar will register the CA as proprietor of the freehold estate in the common parts without any further application having to be made;
- the rights and duties conferred and imposed by the CCS shall come into force;
- any lease of the whole or any part of the commonhold land is extinguished. This includes any lease granted for any term before the CA becomes entitled to be registered as the freehold proprietor of the common parts. This would apply to any lease granted at any time before the end of the transitional period;
- the owner loses the right to make an application to cancel the registration of the land as a freehold estate in commonhold.

4.8.2 Where section 9 applies

Where it is proposed that the commonhold will commence with existing individual unit-holders so that section 9 of the Act applies (in the case of a conversion of an existing leasehold development for instance), there is no transitional period. Immediately upon registration of the land as a freehold estate in commonhold (s.9(3)):

- the CA becomes entitled to be registered as proprietor of the freehold estate in the common parts,
- the Registrar will register the CA as proprietor of the freehold estate in the common parts without any further application having to be made;
- the person specified in the application as the initial unit-holder of a commonhold unit shall be entitled to be registered as proprietor of the freehold estate in the unit;
- any person specified in the application as an initial joint unit-holder of a commonhold unit shall be entitled to be registered as a joint proprietor of the freehold estate in the unit;
- in each case, the Registrar will register the unit-holder as proprietor of the freehold estate in the unit without any further application having to be made;
- the rights and duties conferred and imposed by the CCS shall come into force;
- any lease of the whole or any part of the commonhold land is extinguished. This includes any lease granted for any term before the CA becomes entitled to be registered as the freehold proprietor of the common parts. This would apply to any lease granted at any time before registration.

4.9 MORTGAGES

In the case of a development to be converted from an existing freehold or leasehold development to a commonhold, the position of mortgagees must be considered as, in the usual case of a block of residential flats or estate of residential houses, many of the freehold or leasehold interests will be subject to mortgages.

As has already been noted, the effect of registration of the land as a freehold estate in commonhold will be that any leasehold interests in the land will be extinguished. Such extinguishment will also extinguish the mortgage as the security for the mortgage will cease to exist. In its place, the leaseholder will become the freehold owner of the individual unit and this will normally provide the mortgagee with better security than previously existed.

However, the Act does not automatically transfer any mortgage from a former leasehold interest to the freehold interest in the relevant commonhold unit. Instead, because the consent of any proprietor of a registered charge is required to convert an existing leasehold interest into a freehold interest in a commonhold unit (s.3(1)(c)), it is thought likely that in practice, mortgagees will simply grant consent conditional upon the grant of a new charge over the freehold interest in the commonhold unit in place of the existing charge which will be extinguished.

4.10 EXTINGUISHMENT OF LEASES

One of the important effects of the creation of a commonhold is that any lease of the land which formerly existed will be extinguished upon the creation of the commonhold. In the case of the conversion of an existing development, this will occur upon the date upon which registration is completed (s.9(3)). For a new development, it will take place at the end of the transitional period.

The extinguishment of leases applies to every existing leasehold interest of whatever length whether the consent of the leaseholder was required or not. The conversion of an existing development throws up the potential for the extinguishment of a leasehold interest against the wishes of the leaseholder and without his consent having to be obtained.

However, leases which are granted after the CA becomes entitled to be registered as proprietor of the freehold estate in the common parts are not extinguished (s.7(4)(b) and s.9(4)(b)). This would apply, therefore, to a lease granted after the CA is entitled to be registered but before registration is actually completed.

The extinguishment also applies to any derivative interest. So, any underlease created out of an existing lease will also be extinguished.

Some interesting questions arise concerning the extinguishment of leases which might otherwise qualify for security of tenure. A number of possibilities need to be considered.

4.10.1 Rent Act 1977

The Rent Act 1977 (RA 1977) distinguishes between a protected tenancy, where the contractual term continues, and a statutory tenancy, which arises upon the termination of a protected tenancy. It is trite law that, despite the name often applied to it, a statutory tenancy is not in fact a tenancy. The statutory tenant has no interest in the premises in respect of which he occupies and his status, whilst he remains in occupation of the premises, is that he has a personal right to remain in occupation and no more.

The 2002 Act has the effect of extinguishing any lease of the premises of whatever length. It is thought, therefore, that because a statutory tenant has no 'lease', his status of irremovability will remain unaffected by the conversion to commonhold.

A protected tenant under the RA 1977 does have a lease however, and it would appear, therefore, that the conversion to commonhold would have the effect of extinguishing that lease. The interesting question is whether, assuming the formerly protected tenant remained in occupation of the premises, the tenant would become a statutory tenant under the RA 1977. It is suggested that there is nothing in the 2002 Act which detracts from the effect of s.2(1) of the RA 1977 so that a formerly protected tenant would become and would remain a statutory tenant for as long as he continues to occupy the premises as his residence.

4.10.2 Housing Act 1988

There are a number of critical distinctions between the RA 1977 and the assured tenancy regime created by the Housing Act 1988 (HA 1988). One of these distinctions is that upon the determination of the contractual tenancy, whereas the RA 1977 protected tenant retains only a personal right to remain with no interest in the land, an assured tenant with the protection of the HA 1988 is entitled to remain in occupation as a result of a statutorily-created periodic tenancy arising by virtue of section 5(2) of the HA 1988.

Thus, whereas there is a good argument for suggesting that a statutory tenant under the RA 1977 retains his right to occupy as a result of the fact that he has no 'lease' which would be extinguished by the Act, the statutory periodic tenant under the HA 1988 can not make the same claim in the light of the fact that his right to occupy derives from a 'lease' which will also be extinguished upon conversion to commonhold.

It would seem, therefore, that any tenant who relies upon the HA 1988 for protection will lose his tenancy upon conversion to commonhold whether his original contractual term has been brought to an end or not.

One question which remains is whether it can be argued that a contractual assured tenant whose tenancy is brought to an end upon the conversion to commonhold can then claim a statutory periodic tenancy pursuant to section 5(2) of the HA 1988 or whether that further statutory periodic tenancy would also be extinguished simultaneously. That would leave an anomalous position whereby a statutory periodic tenant whose tenancy arose prior to the conversion to commonhold would have that tenancy extinguished whereas a statutory periodic tenancy which arose as a result of the conversion to commonhold would survive. It is questionable whether that analysis can have been what Parliament intended and it is thought likely that all tenancies with the protection of the HA 1988 will be extinguished upon conversion to commonhold.

4.10.3　Landlord and Tenant Act 1954

It is thought that a tenancy with the protection of the Landlord and Tenant Act 1954 (LTA 1954) will nonetheless be extinguished upon the conversion to commonhold as it is a 'lease'. There may be an argument that protection continues as a result of section 24 of the LTA 1954 but it is again difficult to see how that could be what Parliament intended. The better view would appear to be that the provisions of the Act which provide for extinguishment of all leases impliedly repeal section 24 of the LTA 1954 so far as it is necessary to do so in relation to land converted into commonhold land.

4.10.4　Compensation

Upon conversion to commonhold, any lease is automatically extinguished and the freehold owner of any commonhold unit will automatically be entitled to possession of that unit with no further notice required unless the lessee has secured an agreement which entitles him to a replacement lease. If there is no such agreement, possession proceedings may be commenced immediately. Clearly, the extinguishment of all leases has the potential to cause significant hardship to tenants who may not have been required to consent to the conversion to commonhold and who may find their interests in their leasehold premises at an end through no fault of their own.

The Act therefore provides for compensation to be paid to lessees whose leases have been extinguished after a conversion to commonhold. However, such compensation is payable only to those lessees whose consent was not required for the conversion to commonhold. If the consent of a lessee was required and was given, the lessee is not entitled to compensation under the Act although compensation may have been agreed as a condition of giving such a consent.

Compensation is paid by the freehold owner or by the lessee whose interest was superior to that which was extinguished and from whom consent was required. So, for example, in the case of premises which were subject to a 30 year lease out of which was carved a periodic tenancy, both the 30 year lease and periodic tenancy will come to an end on the conversion to commonhold but only the owner of the 30 year lease would have been required to give his consent to the conversion to commonhold. If he gives his consent with the result that the property is converted to commonhold and both his lease and the periodic tenancy are extinguished, the owner of the periodic tenancy will be entitled to look to the owner of the former 30 year term for compensation under the Act.

Each underlessee must look to the first superior interest above him in the chain in respect of which consent was required and given. So, to take a different example, where premises are subject to a 125 year lease out of which has been carved an underlease of 10 years and a sub-underlease of 3 years, both the owner of the underlease and the sub-underlease would look to the owner of the 125 year lease for compensation. There is no limit to the number of derivative interests which can look to the same person for compensation.

Where there is no head leasehold interest, the compensation is liable to be paid by the freehold owner (s.10(4)).

The compensation payable is for 'loss suffered' (s.10(2)–(4)). No explanation is forthcoming in the Act as to how that loss is to be calculated. Clearly, one aspect of the lessee's loss will be the value of the leasehold interest which has been lost. That will be a matter for valuation evidence. In addition, the lessee will be entitled to costs directly associated with the loss of his tenancy such as removal costs. However, what is not clear is whether the lessee will be entitled to any indirect losses. A tenant who would otherwise have had the protection of the LTA 1954 may lose a tenancy which (if it is at a rack rent) may have little or no value as such but the tenant will also lose the right to carry on his business from those premises. That may cause losses to the value of the tenant's business both in terms of a reduction in goodwill and possibly, losses incurred as a result of trading from alternative, less attractive premises. It remains to be seen whether the courts will be prepared to saddle freehold owners and long lessees with the payment of compensation of that nature.

4.11 SUMMARY

The essence of commonhold lies in the registration of the land as commonhold land. Accordingly, it is of vital importance that the initial application for registration of the land as commonhold complies with the Act, the CR and the Rules. An application which does not comply fully is liable to be rejected by the Land Registry, potentially delaying the implementation of the development as commonhold land. Once an application has been duly made and the land has been registered as commonhold land, existing leasehold interests in the land will be extinguished. Unit-holders will own a freehold interest in their units and the freehold interest in the common parts will be owned by the CA.

CHAPTER 5

Commonhold units

Laurence Target

5.1 INTRODUCTION

This chapter deals with units in commonhold. They are the parts that will be occupied, let, bought and sold regularly.

The commonhold unit is likely to be the key economic part of a commonhold. The unit will be the main vehicle for investment and economic return, whether through owner-occupation or letting. The unit will be transferable as a whole quite readily, unlike the common parts, which can only be owned by the commonhold association (CA) while they form part of the commonhold. Units have the meaning given to them by section 2 of the Act. It is helpful because it avoids the difficulties sometimes found in leasehold schemes where the definitions of demised premises and common parts can be confusing.

Each commonhold must contain at least two units, and they are to be defined in the commonhold community statement (CCS). The CCS must define the extent of the units, and must refer to a plan, whose standards are prescribed in rule 16 of the Land Registration Rules 2003; but rule 8 of the Commonhold (Land Registration) Rules 2004 (CLRR) provides an additional and wide discretion for the Land Registry to reject an application if plans submitted (whether as part of the CCS or otherwise) are insufficiently clear or accurate. Conveyancing plans have often been of a poor quality, and often criticised by the courts. In relation to commonholds that should be a thing of the past, for it will not be possible for land to be registered as commonhold at all unless the prescribed standards are met.

Almost all dealings with the land will be with units as a whole, but if dealings with parts of units are in fact permitted by the CA then the CCS itself will have to be amended, including its plans, to the prescribed standards. Commonhold associations should ensure that those who want to carry out such dealings are fully responsible for all the costs of carrying them through.

5.2   DEFINITION AND PLANS

Commonhold has been widely thought of as a replacement for long residential leases. The prescribed standards will make plans reliable and helpful when dealing with a block of flats or a conversion.

The same standards will apply to all plans for all kinds of commonhold land. Practitioners should not resent any over-specification. It will lead to a general improvement in standards.

The definition of a unit may 'refer to an area subject to the exclusion of specified structures, fittings, apparatus or appurtenances within the area' and 'may exclude the structures which delineate the area referred to' (s.(3)(b) and (c)).

There is no obvious difference between where an area may be referred to 'subject to exclusions', and where structures that 'delineate' the area may be excluded. It means that it will be possible, for example, to define a commonhold unit as 'all that land edged red on the plan but excluding the communal heating system' or 'excluding the walls forming part of the structure of the building'.

It is also initially surprising to see only one half of the familiar pairing 'fixtures and fittings', but it is surely correct. Fixtures are those things that do form part of the land in consequence of having been fixed to it, whereas fittings retain their character as chattels.

It is difficult to interpret the provision that allows reference to an area subject to the exclusion of appurtenances within the area. Appurtenances are those incorporeal rights that belong to land, such as easements or profits. It is, therefore, odd to talk about excluding appurtenances within an area since appurtenances are necessarily burdens on land elsewhere. Probably the intention is to allow the CCS to ensure that units do not necessarily get all of the appurtenances that benefit the entirety of the land before it is converted to commonhold, although new legislation was not required to achieve that goal. This could also be helpful when dealing with commonhold developments, when units will be sold out of common ownership and section 62 of the Law of Property Act 1925 would otherwise apply, thus creating easements appurtenant to units on each sale, some over other units (depending on the order of sale) and others over the common parts. This provision is not excluded in the standard CCS (Commonhold Regulations 2004 (CR), Sched.3).

It may be thought desirable that a commonhold should operate entirely as set out in the commonhold documentation, and thus that the creation of such rights should be excluded. A carefully drafted CCS can ensure that all rights and responsibilities affecting units as against the other units and the common parts are actually commonhold rights with their manifold advantages over easements, profits, covenants, and restrictions. The form of CCS annexed to the CR leaves this option open, but is itself in addition to any rights and duties that may exist as part of the general law.

An important feature is the fact that a unit need not be a single parcel of land, and that the parcels that comprise a unit need not be contiguous. The obvious example is that of a flat with its associated parking space, but there might be a grouping of commercial facilities, or even separate floors of a building.

Commonhold is not restricted to buildings – car-parking spaces, coupled with an obligation to pay for maintenance, would not contain any part of a building. There could also be a 'Building unit', so called by analogy with a 'Building Lease'. Used in this way, the sale of units could be the mechanism for funding and carrying out a development, allowing investors and developers to take part on a larger scale than they might otherwise be able to do; and opening the investment market in such developments to a wider range of people than is possible now.

5.2.1 Units and common parts

Every part of a commonhold that is not a unit is defined by section 25 of the Act as being common parts, which are discussed in **Chapter 6**.

5.3 INVESTMENT CONSIDERATIONS

People promoting and considering investments must always be careful about collective investment schemes under section 235 of the Financial Services and Markets Act 2000. Collective investment schemes are:

> any arrangements with respect to property of any description, including money, the purpose or effect of which is to enable persons taking part in the arrangements (whether by becoming owners of the property or any part of it or otherwise) to participate in or receive profits or income arising from the acquisition, holding, management or disposal of the property or sums paid out of such profits or income.

It must be the case that the persons who are to participate do not have day-to-day control over the management of the property, whether or not they have the right to be consulted or to give directions. The arrangements must also have either or both of the following characteristics:

(a) the contributions of the participants and the profits or income out of which payments are to be made to them are pooled;
(b) the property is managed as a whole by or on behalf of the operator of the scheme.

It could be suggested that the common parts in a commonhold represent pooling. Profits may well arise from the common parts. Normally, CAs and commonholds will fall within paragraph 16 of the Schedule to the Financial Services and Markets Act 2000 (Collective Investment Schemes) Order 2001 (SI 2001/1062). They will be schemes where the predominant purpose of the arrangements is to enable the participants to share in the use or enjoyment of property, or to make its use or enjoyment available gratuitously to others. Practioners should be cautious if the predominant purpose of any commonhold seems to be different, or where there seems to be significant income from the common parts.

5.4   ALLOCATION OF RESPONSIBILITIES

The same kind of principles that apply to decisions about landlords' and tenants' responsibilities and the extent of the demise will govern the choices about whether unit-holders or the CA should take responsibility for specific functions (such as repair and insurance), and about what should be included within a unit.

If units are, for example, houses on an estate with common services, it will usually make sense for the entire structure of the house to form part of the unit. This is the norm under regulation 9(1)(a) of the CR, and it will rarely be sensible to depart from it. The structure will rarely be the whole of the unit, for there will be gardens, garages, and so on. The unit-holder should be responsible for insurance and repair of the entire unit. Common services, however, would be excluded, as would all conduits or other service media that do not exclusively serve the unit – they would be common parts. In the case of a block of flats, however, it would be sensible for there to be a very different division. The main structure should form part of the common parts and the CA should be responsible for its insurance and repair. This is required by regulation 9(1)(b) of the CR.

5.5   LEGAL AND BENEFICIAL OWNERSHIP

Units may be held legally and beneficially by a sole owner, like any other land. They may, however, also be held on a trust of land. In the case of a private or non-charitable trust that means that the legal estate may be vested in no more than four persons as trustees. As with other freehold land, the land may be held for the beneficial owners as tenants in common or as joint tenants, in which case it passes by survivorship, unless severed by notice to the trustees. A legal estate held by joint tenants always passes by survivorship. The beneficial owners may, or may not, be identical to, or overlap with, the trustees.

Solicitors should always advise clients about beneficial ownership when clients purchase property together, or even when they are just contributing to the purchase price. An express declaration of trust is always desirable, and is increasingly demanded by the courts. If a contribution to the purchase price or running costs is not intended to give one or more of the contributories a beneficial interest, or a security interest, in the property then the intended effect of the arrangements should be clearly documented. The evicted boyfriend or girlfriend who finds that ten years' contributions of half the mortgage payments were really rent will not be happy, and if solicitors were involved may look to sue them.

5.6 OWNERSHIP AND MEMBERSHIP OF THE COMMONHOLD ASSOCIATION

With co-ownership of a unit the need for an express declaration of trust dealing with the matter is more pressing. The necessary provisions will be more complicated. Ownership of a unit carries with it the entitlement to be a member of the CA, but membership is limited to one person for each unit, even though there may be more than one registered proprietor, and any number of beneficial owners.

It has often been assumed that unit-holders have to participate in the CA, i.e. to become members of it. This even seems to be assumed in some parts of the standard documentation, e.g. forms for notification on change of unit-holder, but it is not the case under the Act or CR that unit-holders are obliged to join the CA. Paragraph 7 of Schedule 3 to the Act clearly provides that a person is *entitled* to be entered on the register of members of a CA if he becomes a unit-holder. Paragraph 11 of Schedule 3 to the Act provides that a person who is entitled to become a member of the CA actually *becomes a member* on entry of his name on the member's register. There are forms of notice to be used on dealings in units, and they seem to assume that new unit-holders will provide one of themselves as a member of the CA, but there is nothing automatic or obligatory in the legislation.

It would be helpful for there to be an additional requirement (a local rule) in the CSS, to the effect that:

- a sole unit-holder is obliged to be a member of the CA;
- joint members are obliged to provide one of themselves as a member; and
- notification of a change of unit-holder is to be deemed to be an application for entry in the register of members.

A person who becomes entitled to be registered as proprietor of a unit must inform the CA within 14 days of the date of the disposition or the date of becoming aware of the fact that he is entitled to be registered. Strictly speaking, nobody is entitled to be registered at the Land Registry without having made an application in good form and paid the fees. There would, however, seem to be little point in imposing a period and then leaving the choice of date on which it starts to run entirely up to the new unit-holder, i.e. the date on which he chooses to make an application to the Land Registry.

The period of 14 days is short, especially perhaps in the case of dispositions by operation of law, e.g. when the entitlement has arisen on bereavement. During the first fortnight after death the bereaved have a great deal to think about and to do. The imposition of fines for non-notification to a CA would be heartless, and the CR have not made use of the power in section 15(4)(c) of the Act to make provision, including a requirement for the payment of money, about the effect of failure to give notice.

The practical conclusion for solicitors is that they must act promptly, and must advise prompt action.

Joint registered proprietors may decide which of them is to be the member of the CA, and may do so by notice to be served within a prescribed period. The period is within:

- 14 days of becoming entitled to be registered at the Land Registry as owner of the unit if the new unit-holder has become entitled by a registrable disposition, or
- 14 days of becoming aware of his entitlement to be registered as owner of the unit if the new unit-holder has become entitled by operation of law.

If no nomination is served within this period then it is the first named registered proprietor who is entitled to membership.

From Schedule 3, paragraph 8(4) of the Act it appears that after the prescribed period the co-owners cannot easily change their minds as to who should be the member of the CA. Schedule 3, paragraph 12 of the Act provides that a nomination only takes effect when a person ceases to be a unit-holder or joint unit-holder. The arrangements prescribed by the CR in Schedule 2 (articles of association) are more practical. Article 2(d)(iv) allows new nominations by the joint unit-holders. This sensible provision might go beyond what section 64 of Act itself allows to be done by regulations, but who could have any reason to object?

Power is given to the court by the Act to order that a different unit-holder may be substituted for the one who is a member of the CA (Sched.3, para.8(5)). The right to make an application is limited to joint unit-holders themselves: the CA itself is given no standing, and the beneficial owners of the unit are themselves given no standing as such.

Membership of a company limited by guarantee (such as a CA) is often analysed as a personal rather than a proprietary right and so there are some theoretical difficulties in thinking of it as part of the trust fund when a unit is held on a trust of land.

Entitlement to membership of a CA is, however, clearly an inseparable incident of the land, the unit. Thus, practically speaking, membership is part of the trust fund once it has been created. The principles of trust law will apply to membership of the CA just as to any other asset or power in the trust fund.

The unit-holder who serves as the member of the CA must act in the best interests of the beneficiaries, and in accordance with the express provisions of any trust instrument. It would normally be right to consult with the beneficiaries, and to exercise any commonhold rights in accordance with the wishes of the majority owners by value. A duty so to do will be implied by the Trusts of Land and Appointment of Trustees Act 1996 unless expressly excluded or limited. Membership of the CA can be thought of not merely as a personal right but also as a chose or thing in action, and thus it can be one of the assets of the trust fund.

5.7 LIABILITIES OF JOINT UNIT-HOLDERS

The Act is elaborate and not very straightforward in the way that it deals with the liability of joint unit-holders, i.e. those entitled to be registered as proprietors. It divides liabilities into those that are jointly owed by the unit-holders and those that are jointly and severally owed by the unit-holders (see **Tables 5.1** and **5.2**). The rationale behind the distinctions is explained in the Department for Constitutional Affairs' Non-Statutory Guidance. The prudent course for any CA that needs to take proceedings will be to issue all proceedings in joint names. It will not be able to rely on its membership register or on the title at the Land Registry, but will need to maintain separate records of who is entitled to be registered as a joint proprietor whether or not they are so registered. It is to be hoped that the courts will take a

Table 5.1 Joint liability

Liability	Section
Insurance repair and maintenance	s.14(2)
Notification of transfer	s.15(3)
Consent to redefinition of unit	s.23(1)
Payment of assessment	s.38(1)
Payment of assessment fund	s.39(2)

Table 5.2 Joint and several liability

Liability	Section
Duties in the CCS	s.1(1)(c)
Duties acquired on transfer	s.16(1)
Duties in the CCS	s.31(1)(b),(3)(b)
To indemnify the CA and other unit-holders in respect of costs arising from the breach of statutory requirements	s.31(5)(j)
Payment of compensation	s.37(2)
Co-operation with the developer if required by the CCS	s.58(3)(a)

flexible view, but that is difficult in the face of express statutory provisions imposing procedural complexity.

Section 13 of the Act lists most sections where a reference to a unit-holder is a reference to joint unit-holders together and where such references are to joint unit-holders individually and together.

Regulations may prescribe construction in the case of joint unit-holders in the commonhold documentation, and in 'another document' (s.13(6)(d)). The Lord Chancellor has power to amend section 13(2) and (3) by negative resolution regulations. This power has been exercised, and the CR have amended and simplified the complex provisions originally in the Act. The Act must, of course, be read in its updated form.

5.8   NEW UNIT-HOLDERS

New unit-holders must tell the CA about the transfer, and section 15 of the Act allows a financial penalty for failure. No financial penalty has been imposed so far by the prescribed parts of the CCS. The main sanction, however, is really the inability of a new unit-holder, who has not given notice, to join the CA, and thus take part in its deliberations. He will nonetheless be bound by its decisions since the provisions of the CCS have direct effect on unit-holders whether or not they become members of the CA (s.31(7)).

The prescribed forms have wording that envisages that non-notification within the 14-day time limit will end the unit-holder's entitlement to membership, either absolutely or at the discretion of the CA. There is no basis for this in the Act. A late applicant who is otherwise entitled to join the CA should always be entered in the register of members.

5.9   RIGHTS AND DUTIES

5.9.1   Use of unit

A CCS must make provision for rights and duties of unit-holders – it is one of the tests laid down in section 1 of the Act as to whether or not land is commonhold at all. It is also required that the CCS must make provision regulating the use of units.

Regulations may require detailed provision. The CCS must list any restrictions on user of units, common parts, and of any restricted use areas in Annex 4.

The question of the user must in any event be crucial for those setting up commonholds. The common law allows any user of freehold land, though imposing liability in damages for any user that causes a nuisance; and equity may restrict or prohibit such user by injunction; statute regulates user generally through the planning process. That should be the starting point when considering user of commonhold land.

Commonhold units are freehold – that is a great attraction of this system of land ownership. Owners should be allowed to do what other freehold owners can do, unless the law of planning and nuisance is plainly inadequate.

In commercial developments there may be legitimate restrictions on user to reflect the diversity of unit-holders' interests.

In residential developments it should usually be enough to prohibit non-incidental non-residential user.

In particular circumstances it may be desirable to restrict user further, say to people over 55 in sheltered accommodation. It is to be hoped therefore that practitioners will not nervously or unthinkingly adopt the kinds of restrictions common in leases.

Commonhold is meant to be a new start and a new form of ownership without the power struggles between landlord and tenant that user clauses frequently reflect. Without the possibility of forfeiture, a lease-style clause may be practically unenforceable, although injunctions could be considered in extreme cases. In most cases there will be no need to prohibit auctions and political meetings, or illegal or immoral use – at least not by the land law devices of conveyancing. These limitations are not found in other dealings with freehold land and should not be copied thoughtlessly into commonhold from leasehold conveyancing.

5.10   TRANSFER OF UNITS

A unit can be transferred without any limitation in the CCS (s.15(2)) but there is nothing to prevent some other instrument's doing so. A members' agreement, on the analogy of a shareholders' agreement (as to which see **Chapter 12**), appropriately protected by restrictions in the title at the Land Registry, could do so. This could be useful if controls over user are not, in any particular case, adequate protections for the other members of the community. There might be circumstances when, as in a true co-operative, the members needed to ensure that in-comers shared their values and approach, or where it was necessary to restrict ownership as well as occupation to a particular class of person, e.g. to people over 55 in sheltered developments. It is difficult though to think of realistic cases where controls of user would not afford adequate protection.

The question of what happens to the liabilities of a former unit-holder on transfer is completely central to the operation of commonhold. The English legal system has used long leases as a vehicle for owner occupation because it has not been possible to make positive covenants bind successors in title of freehold land. There is a great deal of complexity, even artificiality, in leases, and much case law and complicated statutory reform applies to them.

Commonhold duties owed by unit-holders remove the difficulty about positive covenants and ensure that each successive owner is bound. An additional advantage is complete freedom for unit-holders to transfer their units to whomsoever they want.

Section 16 of the Act achieves this goal and deals with arrears. It provides that a right or duty conferred or imposed by a CCS or by section 20 of the Act affects a new unit-holders in the same way as it affected the former unit-holder. Balancing that acquisition of rights and duties by a transferee is the provision that the transferor is not to acquire any new liabilities after the transfer because of anything in the CCS or done under section 20.

A prudent purchaser will satisfy himself about the extent of any liabilities that the vendor had, and will seek appropriate adjustments to the price or require prior discharge before completion. The purchaser can require a commonhold unit information certificate under paragraph 4.7.1 of the CCS, and will not be liable for more than it certifies.

There is nothing like original tenants' liability throughout the term, and no chain of indemnities to be followed. There is no need for a CA to be especially vigilant about securing debts to it, and no arguments about mortgagees' priority. In most cases the indebtedness of a unit-holder or any security that he has given will not imperil the functioning of the commonhold. Whoever owns the unit will have to meet the commonhold obligations of the unit.

Paragraph 4.7 of the CCS makes it abundantly clear that each new unit-holder may be required by the CA to discharge the obligations of the former unit-holder.

Paragraph 4.7.7 of the CCS provides that discharge of these obligations by the new unit-holder in accordance with paragraph 4.7.5 (i.e. within 14 days of the demand) is deemed to be an assignment to him by the CA of its rights to recover from the former unit-holder. It is not to be expected that the courts would interpret the time limit strictly. A new unit-holder who pays, even late, should have the right to be subrogated to the CA, or to whoever else may have had commonhold claims against the former unit-holder.

These matters should also be dealt with in any contract between buyers and sellers of units.

5.11 LEASING RESIDENTIAL UNITS

Section 17 of the Act reflects concern about the leasing of residential units. The Government is convinced that the long lease is a fundamentally unsatisfactory tenure for owner-occupation and is determined to ensure that it should not be possible to mingle leasehold and freehold ownership in residential commonhold. Indeed, to have long leaseholders who have paid a capital premium as tenants and occupants of units while landlords with merely nominal reversions were the unit-holders and members of the CA would be nonsense. It would reintroduce the institutionalised conflict of interests that is inherent within the landlord and tenant relationship into the management decisions of the commonhold.

Regulations may specify conditions that leases of units must satisfy, and may relate to:

- length;
- the circumstances in which the term is granted; and
- any other matter.

There has been extensive consultation and regulation 11 of the CR now prescribes that leases in relation to residential units:

- must not be granted at a premium;
- cannot be for a term of more than seven years (unless it is a compensatory tenancy granted to a leaseholder whose consent would otherwise be required for conversion to commonhold);
- cannot require the tenant to pay to the CA what the CCS requires the unit-holder to pay.

Section 17(3) of the Act provides that an instrument or agreement is to be 'of no effect' to the extent that it purports to create a term of years in contravention of subsection 17(1).

The extent or effect of the statutory avoidance is difficult to assess. The failure to create a term would, presumably, be a breach of a condition of the contract that would entitle the putative tenant to accept the instrument or agreement as repudiated. It would not necessarily allow the tenant to recover the money, or any premium or money paid under the instrument or agreement. Such moneys are prima facie repayable – but the landlord might not be able to repay them. It would not necessarily give the tenant the security of occupation, or even any occupation at all, that he had bargained for. Those consequences weigh heavily on the tenant, who will have paid and may not have investigated title. The ingenuity of the courts will be tested to ensure that this is not too unjust to tenants.

Property lawyers are familiar with the distinction between equitable interests that bind the parties and those with notice or against whom they have been protected on the one hand and legal interests powers and estates that bind the world on the other. It is enshrined in section 1 of the Law of Property Act 1925, and is fundamental to post-1925 property law. If that distinction had been used practitioners could have advised with reasonable certainty. Instead they must make more or less educated guesses as to what the court will do in exercise of its powers under subsection (4).

5.11.1 'Shared ownership' leases

One consequence of the prohibition of leases of more than seven year terms is that the so called 'shared ownership' lease will not be permissible. These are normally leases of 99 or 125 years where the tenant pays a premium of 25 per cent of the value, and pays rent for the rest. He can reduce the rent by a process known as 'staircasing' in which he pays a further premium in exhange for a reduction of rent, usually in steps of 25 per cent. At the end of the process the rent is merely a ground rent, as with other long leases of residential property.

Shared ownership leases have been widely used by registered social landlords (RSLs) to extend home ownership. There may be other ways for RSLs to achieve the benefits of home ownership, actually at a lower cost and with more transparency than with the shared ownership lease. The Housing Corporation and some RSLs are considering the viability of such arrangements. The shared ownership lease is ingenious, and the purpose is worthwhile, but it is complicated and costly, and shares all the well-documented drawbacks of the long lease as a vehicle for owner occupation.

There is continuing discussion as to whether shared ownership leases of commonhold units should be allowed, though further regulations would be required.

5.12   LEASING NON-RESIDENTIAL UNITS

There are no statutory restrictions on the leasing of non-residential units. The owner has the same freedom to let the land as the owner of any other freehold land. Although the heading (Other transactions) leads the reader to expect it to be limited to transactions that are not leases, section 20 actually provides that the CCS cannot prevent or restrict the creation, grant, or transfer of an interest in the whole or part of his unit. Section 17 merely provides that a lease will take effect subject to the provisions of the CCS. Those provisions will be in relation to the matters provided for in section 19, allowing some obligations to be enforced directly against tenants, and as set out in detail in paragraph 4.2 of the CCS. They principally allow for diversion of rent in specified circumstances.

A CCS may however make other provision, and regulations have left those decisions up to those setting up and running commonholds – leaving the decisions where they belong. Commercial purchasers of units will need to check the right version of the CCS (at the Land Registry, and as currently prescribed under the CR) and to consider the chances and risks of amendment to ensure that units are suitable for their purposes. There is further discussion of amendment to the CCS in **Chapter 6**.

It is clear that a CA needs to be able to ensure that tenants comply with the provisions of a CCS. Tenants may also need to be consulted about commonhold decisions – clearly, tenants of long leases with low rents should have a say. Section 19 acknowledges those concerns, and allows regulations to make provision such that a CA may be allowed a direct right of action against tenants, and that tenants may be able to discharge liabilities to their landlords by discharging corresponding liabilities to the CA.

There is also a power given by section 19 to the Lord Chancellor (who is now also the Secretary of State for Constitutional Affairs) that regulations may modify any rule of law derived from common law or from any enactment about leasehold estates in relation to a term of years in a commonhold unit. There does not appear to be any difference intended between 'leasehold estates' and 'term of years'.

The power is circumscribed in several ways: it permits modification only; it does not go so far as to permit the disapplication or abrogation of the rule. The rule must still apply, but in a different way. It may not, arguably, apply to any rules of law derived from equity. Two of the three sources of English law are clearly picked out, and the parliamentary draftsman must be presumed to have deliberately omitted the third. It expressly relates only to leasehold estates, i.e. the legal estates created by leases. Leases have a dual aspect: the estate and the contract. The courts have been much concerned in recent years by these two aspects and questions of how they should be balanced. The tendency of most cases recently has been to stress the contractual aspect, even in construction, as against the estate aspect. Regulations under the Act cannot modify any rules relating to contract, only those rules that relate to the aspect of the estate can be modified. This distinction may be unhelpful in practice and the courts may be able to ignore it. To date no regulations have been made under this power.

There are many other transactions that a freehold owner may wish to enter into in relation to this land, apart from leasing the whole or part at law or in equity. There is an obvious policy goal that other unit-holders and the CA should know with whom they have to deal; and another that the size of units should not change without the giving of careful thought to the making of consequential amendments.

5.13 VOTING RIGHTS

It has been recognised that the interests of each unit need to be protected and may not be equal. A large retail unit on the ground floor may deserve more than a studio flat, small office, or even a car parking space held as a separate unit. After considerable consultation, the CCS is permitted to make different provisions, allocating different votes to each unit-holder in respect of the unit – those voting rights will be set out in Annex 3 of the CCS.

Mortgagees in possession, trustees in bankruptcy and similar persons will have the right to vote in place of the unit-holder by virtue of the prescribed Articles 29–31 of the CA.

CHAPTER 6

The commonhold community statement

Laurence Target

6.1 INTRODUCTION

The commonhold community statement (CCS) is the central document for the functioning of a commonhold. The memorandum and articles of association will govern the powers and corporate action of the commonhold association (CA), but matters of day to day management, and the commonhold rights and duties as they relate to the property, will be set out in the CCS. It is here too that the individual features that are peculiar to any particular commonhold will be found. It is the CCS that will require the most attention from the property lawyer and clients when a commonhold is being set up; and from conveyancers when there are dealings, whether dealings with the common parts or with units.

The Act deals with the CCS in sections 31–33 and the Commonhold Regulations 2004 (CR) make provision in Part 4.

It is a new departure for property law that so central a document is prescribed and that the content prescribed is so extensive. Regulation 15 of the CR provides that the CCS 'must be in the form set out in Schedule 3, or a form to the same effect' (CR, reg.15(1)). The particular details of typography and layout may not matter, but the text and the structure clearly do. The wording in regulation 15 seems more liberal than the requirement in section 31(2) of the Act itself that a CCS 'must be in the prescribed form', but the CR are obviously more practical.

One of the most attractive features of commonhold is the standardisation that will be achieved, and that can only be done with the use of such documents. The prescribed CCS is not perfect, but nobody's drafting ever is, and it is much better drafted than most residential leases that the authors have seen. There are useful specimen clauses for local rules in the DCA's Non-Statutory Guidance, available on the DCA website (**www.dca.gov.uk**).

The widespread use of documents like this should do something to modernise and raise standards amongst conveyancers and other lawyers.

It remains to be seen how these documents will function in practice. Disputes cannot be ruled out completely, but at least the CSS should not play a very great role in generating disputes. It is to be hoped that lawyers and their clients will be able readily to interpret them and enforce them in ways that are not too widely felt to be unjust. As far as can be judged without having actually used the new documentation, it is well put together.

It is structured in a way that makes sense and is straightforward, and is written in plain English. The drafters have obviously thought long and hard about the task, and have attended carefully to representations made by those who have taken part in the consultation process leading up to the implementation of commonhold.

Advisers will be able to become familiar with the prescribed material and so the task of advising will become more simple than it ever can be with leasehold law and individual leases. Each lease is individually drafted and represents a separate bargain, and must be individually considered in the light of the circumstances; with commonhold there will be one form of documentation, with defined choices to be to be made within it, which will need to be applied to the circumstances. The writing is clear and normal, and most welcome to those who usually have to interpret the artificial convolutions and legalese so often found in leases.

6.2 RIGHTS AND DUTIES IMPOSED

The rights and duties of the CCS bind the CA as a legal person – it may be considered to have bound itself. They also bind unit-holders, and those who occupy units. They do this in a way quite different (in analysis at least) from contract, when there must be offer and acceptance, intention to create legal relations, as well as consideration passing. It goes beyond privity of estate, for there can be no privity of estate between CAs and unit-holders or their tenants, or between different unit-holders. The reason is that the estates in units are not derived from the estate held by the CA. Commonhold is not the creation of new form of tenure: it is freehold land.

Commonhold does not act like the restraining hand of equity, enforcing restrictive covenants against successive owners who take with notice of them, for it imposes positive obligations as well.

Conceptually the rights and duties are unique. That has been recognised by an amendment to the Limitation Act 1980 specifying the period of limitation for breaches of commonhold duties as six years. It is recognised as a unique kind of obligation and given its own period of limitations (Sched.5, para.4 of the Act).

Section 31 of the Act is drafted so as to allow a CCS to make provision about the rights and duties of CAs and unit-holders. Section 31(5) sets out expressly a whole range of particular duties included within the general language of section 31(3). The purist may feel that this is unnecessary, but it does put matters beyond doubt.

6.3 LEVELS OF AUTHORITY

The constitutional arrangements of a commonhold are ranked hierarchically. The Act itself has absolute authority, then the regulations made under the Act (CR), then the documents prescribed under those regulations.

The documents prescribed by the regulations take their authority from the fact that they have been used for the commonhold. In many cases no formal adoption is necessary (e.g. under CR, reg.13(2)).

First in priority come the memorandum and articles as between the members of the CA; and then the CCS as between unit-holders, tenants, sub-tenants, and others deriving title from unit-holders.

Nothing in the CCS is to have effect if it is not consistent with the Act, the CR or the memorandum and articles.

Nothing in a CCS is allowed to provide for the transfer or loss of an interest in land on the occurrence or non-occurrence of a particular event (s.31(8)). This is to prevent the introduction of forfeiture by the back door.

The CR do not, however, provide that no other agreement to which the CA is a party can make such provision. It will be possible for commonholds to be set up in which the unit-holders' levies (their contributions to service charges) are secured by rent charges with a power of forfeiture, or by a registered charge. There could even be options to similar effect, allowing the CA to buy units at a prearranged price in the event of default. It would inevitably be damaging to use these devices, because the market advantages of commonhold would be destroyed by the presence of features like these. Units in commonholds where they had been introduced would not be so attractive.

6.4 FORM AND CONTENT

Section 32 of the Act deals with what regulations can require in relation to a CCS. This allows the legislature to control what might be drafted in any particular circumstances. Under section 32(3) certain provisions may be deemed to be included or excluded no matter what has happened in practice. The CR have not used this device, but have merely specified matters to be included, using the method of control over the form of the CCS given by section 32(2).

When practitioners are dealing with any parts of a CCS that are not prescribed (mainly the local rules) they will need to check to see that they do not contravene those provisions.

The format of the CCS has been designed to ensure that it will be easy to distinguish between the parts that are derived from prescribed forms and those that are variable or particular. The latter will be set out in Annexes, and known as 'local rules'; or may be set out in each Part. If set out in a Part they must carry a heading, use numbering consecutive with the material that precedes them and be introduced with the words 'additional provisions specific to this commonhold'.

6.5 AMENDMENT

Section 33 of the Act deals with the important question of amendment. The rights of unit-holders and of the CA itself, are important property rights; they are legal rights that should be protected against the world. So too will be the rights of tenants, sub-tenants and mortgagees. The rights of others with an interest in the unit, e.g. judgment creditors, also need to be secure. It is particularly important, therefore, that they should not be subject to arbitrary change, even if it is made by a majority vote. The decision of the majority of the members of a CA should, of course, prevail in accordance with its constitution – but the majority must not be allowed to invade the core area of rights conferred by ownership of a unit. The owner of a unit must not have his rights of using and dealing with the property taken away, and must not unwillingly be made subject to disproportionate burdens.

The CR require each CCS to make standard provision about amendment.

A paragraph in Parts 1 to 4 of the CCS cannot be amended unless it is a local rule. Except where a CCS provides otherwise (and subject to the Companies Act 1985) local rules need an ordinary resolution in favour to be amended.

The CCS recognises the importance of user, and provides that the permitted use of a unit is capable of change only by special resolution with the written consent of the unit-holder.

It is also vital that prospective purchasers of units, whether freehold, leasehold, or mortgagees, should be able to know reliably what the CCS provides. This is achieved by section 33, which requires any CCS to set out provision for its amendment, and provides that amendments are to be 'of no effect' unless and until they have been registered at the Land Registry. Any application for registration must be accompanied by a certificate from the directors that the process of amendment satisfied the requirements of the Act.

The giving of such certificates will impress on the directors the need to get the amendment process and the amendments themselves right.

It is always difficult for practitioners to advise about the consequences of a statutory provision that something is to be 'of no effect'. Where justice requires, the courts are willing to use the flexibility of equity to ensure that statute is not used 'as an engine of fraud'. It could well be thought that justice required that amendments that were of no effect because of non-registration should bind the parties and those who have relied on them, just as an unregistered, but otherwise completed, transfer will be enforced and registered even after application should have been made. The responsibility has been left to the courts. They will probably apply the analogy of other unregistered agreements that do bind the parties, and can bind non-parties as well. Purchasers of units will probably not be bound, even if they have knowledge of the amendment, since section 16 provides only that obligations in the CCS affect new unit-holders in the same way as old unit-holders, and that wording is hardly apt to include matters that are 'of no effect'. Any such matters would need to be dealt with as between vendor and purchaser, and there might be delicate issues to resolve where late registration took place, when obligations that might not have bound a purchaser will do so as actually and legally being part of the CCS.

Only local rules will be capable of amendment by the CA. The local rules are the matters applicable to a particular commonhold. They will have been decided on by the relevant community, and so can be changed by that community. Matters that are dealt with in prescribed forms apply to commonholds as such and so cannot be changed locally.

6.6 INTERACTION WITH GENERAL LAW

It would have been possible for commonhold to have been created as a comprehensive system of law governing the rights and duties of unit-holders within each commonhold. The mechanisms of easements, profits and covenants, whether restrictive or positive could have been disapplied and replaced altogether with commonhold rights and duties. That radical choice is not the one that has been made. The prescribed CCS expressly provides that the commonhold rights and duties set out in it are in addition to the general law (paragraph 1.1.3). Occupants will, therefore, have a choice of remedies against their neighbours within a commonhold. This may mean that common law or other remedies that are not affected by the dispute resolution provisions of commonhold will be used instead of remedies through the commonhold structure. In many cases the use of mediation or other forms of dispute resolution will be preferable, as envisaged by the Act.

6.7 PRESCRIBED FORMS

In accordance with regulation 16 of the CR, the CCS has promulgated with it a series of forms to be used for many of the occasions which will mark the stages of the life of a commonhold. They will be readily available online, and in expandable field versions through the usual legal stationers.

CHAPTER 7

Commonhold associations

Laurence Target

7.1 INTRODUCTION

A commonhold association (CA) must be a private company limited by guarantee that complies with the requirements of section 34 of the Act. It will be a company incorporated under and subject to the requirements of the Companies Acts and company law generally, as well as subject to the special requirements of the Act.

Like any corporation, a CA will have a legal personality separate from that of its members. Corporate property will be held by the CA for itself beneficially, although in certain circumstances a CA may hold property on trust for others, perhaps after an express declaration of trust, or imposed in a constructive or resulting trust. In the normal course of its business, a CA should not hold property on trust for others, whether its members or third parties.

7.2 COMPANIES LIMITED BY GUARANTEE

Companies limited by guarantee have been available and used for various purposes since the Companies Act 1862. They are generally used for the incorporation of public benefit organisations (such as learned societies) and educational institutions (such as the new universities). Companies House does not have records readily indicating how many such companies there are, but it is thought to be only few (perhaps 40,000) of the approximately 1.8 million registered companies. There is little jurisprudence concerning such companies, and little space devoted to their treatment in the standard company law textbooks.

Companies limited by guarantee will, however, become much more familiar, at least to property lawyers, in the future. They are the prescribed vehicles for the right to enfranchise and the right to manage under Part 2 of the Act, as well as for CAs.

7.3   MEMORANDUM AND ARTICLES

Section 34 of the Act requires that the memorandum of a CA must state that an object of the company is to exercise the functions of a CA in relation to specified commonhold land. This does not mean that the land must be commonhold before the creation of the CA: that would be impossible, because land cannot be commonhold unless it is registered at the Land Registry as commonhold, specified in the memorandum of a CA, and subject to a CCS (s.1). The requirement is simply that the land that is to be commonhold must be specified in the memorandum, and that the company must have appropriate objects.

The requirement will be a continuing requirement. If any land is added to (enlargement under s.41) or removed from the commonhold (allowed under s.27, or following a legal mortgage under s.29) then the memorandum of the CA will need to be changed as well.

Part 1 of Schedule 3 to the Act makes provision for the memorandum and articles of association of CAs. While there are some matters laid down in the Act, most of the detail is in the Commonhold Regulations 2004 (CR), which make provision about the form and content as provided for under paragraph 2(1) of Schedule 3 to the Act.

Some parts may be adopted from the CR (Sched.3, para.2(2)), and other parts may have effect whether or not they have been adopted (Sched.3, para.2(3)). In fact, the CR have used this device, and it is stipulated that the memorandum must be in the form (or a form to the same effect) as that in Schedule 1 to the CR, and that each provision will have effect whether or not it is adopted.

The more certain procedure will still be for the subscribers to adopt the form.

If there are to be any additional provisions in the memorandum that are specific to any particular commonhold, they must be clearly headed as such, and must appear consecutively numbered.

Provisions in the memorandum and articles that are inconsistent with the CR are to have no effect to the extent that they are inconsistent (Sched.3, para.2(4)).

Paragraph 2(5) of Schedule 3 to the Act provides that regulations are to have effect irrespective of the date of the memorandum and articles, though subject to transitional provisions.

If a CA does not simply adopt provisions from the CR for its memorandum and articles then it will be necessary to work through these rather complicated provisions. People dealing with a CA, especially those looking to join one, will want to check:

- that the documents registered at Companies House correspond to those registered at the Land Registry; and

- that they do actually comply with what is laid down in the current regulations.

It must be remembered that the constitutional documentation prescribed by the CR will prevail.

A purchaser may wish to require that the constitution is in good order before buying a unit or joining a CA.

The most legally certain route would be for material in the CR simply to be adopted, but that must be at the cost of not having easily useable documentation containing all of the matters agreed. On the other hand, if there is documentation setting such matters out in full then anybody using it will need to check that the forms at Companies House and at the Land Registry correspond and comply with the current set of regulations. This is a cumbersome arrangement, and the most cautious advice is that CAs should adopt the prescribed content, and use their own wording only for matters peculiar to their own commonholds.

This is rather complicated, especially for what are expected frequently to be amateur-run organisations. The drafting technique of referring to statute or statutory instruments is considered unfair in standard form contracts offered to consumers (see Office of Fair Trading's *Guidance on unfair terms in tenancy agreements* (OFT356) paragraph 19, discussing the requirement that such contracts should be in 'plain, intelligible language') and it is certainly not user-friendly. It should be noted though, that commonhold documentation is not legally bound by the need for plain and intelligible language because purchasers of units are not, technically, consumers: they will probably use lawyers when purchasing their units, and the arrangements will have been prescribed by parliamentary authority.

The memorandum and articles of association of a company are a contract between the company and the members. They take effect:

> to the same extent as if they had respectively been signed and sealed by each member and contained covenants on the part of each member to observe all the provisions of the memorandum and the articles.
>
> (Companies Act 1985, s.14(1))

The consequences of there having been a purported agreement between the members in the formation or amendment of the memorandum and articles which means that they are inconsistent with the CR are difficult to predict (see *Chitty on Contracts* (28th ed), Chapter 17). Moneys paid over in reliance on illegal agreements (rather than merely void or voidable agreements) will probably not be recoverable; but there will always be a valid agreement, namely that imposed by the CR, to fall back on, and to which the courts can give effect.

7.3.1 Subsequent legislative amendment

The power given in paragraph 2(5) of Schedule 3 to the Act is extensive: it allows regulations to amend retrospectively contracts that are entered into by members of CAs, and relied on by others, including owners and mortgagees of units. There is a settled constitutional and judicial aversion to retrospective legislation, but in this case it may be thought desirable that the memorandum and articles of CAs should be kept on the same terms where required whenever they were incorporated or amended, and despite what the members may have agreed between themselves, or what may have been relied upon by people dealing with them.

7.3.2 Consensual amendment

Changes to the memorandum and articles are reserved by a special procedure under paragraph 3 of Schedule 3 to the Act, and alterations are to 'have no effect' until registered at the Land Registry – though this will not apply to changes in the form and content that may be prescribed by regulations. It will always be important to check registered documentation against that prescribed, and to bring the registered documentation up to date from time to time.

A company can change its memorandum or articles by special resolution, i.e. a resolution passed by three-quarters of those members who vote (Companies Act 1985, ss.4 or 9). A copy of the resolution must be lodged at Companies House within 15 days (Companies Act 1985, ss.378(2) and 380).

Within 21 days of the passing of such a resolution there is an opportunity for an application to be made to the Companies Court to alter or cancel the alteration of the memorandum. Any such application has to be made by at least 15 per cent of the members of the company, so long as they have not voted for or consented to the alterations (Companies Act 1985, s.5).

No change is to be registered at the Land Registry until the period of 21 days has elapsed, or the court has approved any alteration.

When an application is made to the Land Registry for registration of the altered memorandum and articles, the directors of the CA must certify that the altered memorandum or altered articles comply with the requirements of applicable regulations.

It is difficult to see the function of such a certificate, except to emphasise the need to comply with the requirements of the Act. Nobody will be able to rely on the memorandum and articles of a CA to the extent that they do not comply with regulations: everybody reading them is deemed to know the law, and thus to know the extent to which they may be of no effect. That being so, there can be no loss, and nothing against which the Land Registry needs protection.

In practice, directors will be cautious, and will be reluctant to give such certificates without relying on legal advice.

7.4 COMPANY LAW PRINCIPLES

The generality of companies law will apply to CAs: members enjoy the privileges of incorporation at the price of compliance with registration, filing and accountancy requirements.

7.5 DUAL REGISTRATION

The 'doubling-up' of registration between Companies House and the Land Registry is thought to be a small inconvenience in comparison to the creation of an entirely new kind of corporation for the purposes of commonhold land. It was thought that the standards of corporate governance, and of members' and public protection were best adopted wholesale, rather than recreated for a new species of corporation. Some of those requirements seem to lack real function: the guarantee from members is small, and the accounts should reveal restricted funds rather than moneys generally available to creditors. They will, in other words, be of little use to people proposing to deal with a CA.

The requirements for filing of accounts will vary with the size of the company, and it is thought that for small companies they may not be too onerous in practice, but the sanctions can be draconian, at least in theory. Many failures to comply with the proper procedures in the Companies Acts are technically criminal.

7.6 STRIKING OFF AT COMPANIES HOUSE

The Registrar of Companies has power to strike a company off the register if he has reasonable grounds for believing that it is not carrying on the business of the company (Companies Act 1985, s.652). The usual ground for such an inference is the non-filing of returns. It is difficult to see that evidence of mere non-filing would validly ground such an inference in the case of a CA registered with unit-holders after the transitional period (as defined in s.9 of the Act). The business of such a company is that of being a CA, and keeping land within the definition of commonhold land in section 1 of the Act. Its function is primarily owning the common parts and the rest could be argued to be mere mechanism.

On publication of 'striking off', the company is dissolved (Companies Act 1985, s.652(5)), and its property vests as *bona vacantia* in the Crown or in the

Duchy of Lancaster or of Cornwall as appropriate (Companies Act 1985, s.654). The property of the company is to be determined in accordance with usual principles, but will inevitably include the common parts, the benefit of insurance policies, balances of assessments not spent and reserve funds.

A more serious consequence for people interested in units is that the land ceases to be commonhold because it no longer satisfies the tests in section 1 of the Act. The sanction is a serious one for what may have been a minor failure on the part of the officers of the company to comply with administration or to reply to the Registrar's notice under section 652(1) of the Companies Act 1985. The officers themselves could face criminal penalties, albeit rarely invoked by the prosecuting authorities.

On dissolution of the CA as a body corporate, resulting from its striking off the Register of Companies, the association of the members will not itself come to an end. It will instead be transformed into an illegal association. It will not be a partnership – the rules will survive insofar as they can be made to apply to an unincorporated association, and they do not allow a view of profit, necessary for any partnership (Partnership Act 1890, s.1).

Section 653 of the Companies Act 1985 does give the court power during 20 years from the date of dissolution to restore the company to the Register and to corporate existence, and to make directions and provisions as seem just for placing the company and other persons in the same position (as nearly as may be) as if the company had not been struck off. Such an order has the effect of re-vesting in it property, which had vested as *bona vacantia*, but persons who have acquired an interest from the Crown or the appropriate Duchy are not to be prejudiced.

This power should be sufficient in most circumstances, and it must be expected that the Crown and the Duchies would not deal with the property of struck-off CAs without having tried to make sure that people with interests in units were informed and given the chance to apply for the restoration of the CA. The remedy may not always be available and is costly, perhaps disproportionately so, in comparison with the fault and any risk to the public.

The provisions of the Act as to termination (ss.50–56) do not apply in relation to striking-off under section 652 of the Companies Act 1985. There is no provision for successor CAs.

All CAs are required to have the words 'commonhold association' (or their Welsh equivalent) at the end of their names (CR, reg.12, made under Sched.3, para.16). It has been suggested, and is to be hoped, that the Registrar of Companies should agree to treat them differently, not exercising the power to strike them off without some better reason than non-filing or late filing of returns, but the response has not yet been made public.

It will have to be stressed to directors and secretaries of CAs that they must comply with the requirements of the Companies Acts and do what is necessary to keep their CA in being. The criminal sanctions for failure to file are, quite rightly, little used. It is to be hoped that the prosecuting authorities would not take action in circumstances where the failure resulted from inadvertence, or mere incompetence. The directors and secretary do, however, owe fiduciary duties to the members, and the members and unit-holders may incur serious loss if the CA is struck off. There may be costs of the striking off under section 652 of the Companies Act 1985; but there may also be lost sales (perhaps on advantageous terms). Unit-holders may look to recover such losses from the directors responsible, and they in turn may look to recover from professional advisers, perhaps if they were not adequately warned about the importance of regulatory compliance.

This illustrates the importance of competent management and insurance. It is also an argument in favour of professional management and company secretarial services. It must be remembered that the directors do not need to be members of a CA. Certainly with larger CAs, it may be appropriate to require the appointment of professional managers as directors.

7.7 MEMBERSHIP

Part 2 of Schedule 3 to the Act makes provision as to membership of CAs. The long-term intention is that only unit-holders should be members, but since at the commencement of a development there may be no units that goal may not be immediately achievable.

As discussed in **Chapters 3** and **4**, the structure of company formation means that initial members will be the subscribers, and paragraph 5 of Schedule 3 provides that until the land specified in the memorandum becomes commonhold land (i.e. on registration as such at the Land Registry) only the subscribers can be members of the CA. In practice, they will usually be the company formation agents, and will want to resign as soon as appropriate.

During the transitional period (defined at s.8; see also **Chapters 3** and **9**) the developer will be entitled to be a member of the CA (Sched.3, para.6). Whether or not the developer exercises that entitlement will depend on the particular circumstances. In many cases the developer will wish to do so, but since the subscribers will, in practice, inevitably hold their membership for the developer it may not be necessary for the developer to join. The rights of the developer under section 58 can be exercised whether or not the developer is a member.

The subscribers and the developer are entitled to resign from a CA only so long as they are not members as unit-holders (Sched.3, para.12). Members who are unit-holders cannot resign, but their membership only terminates when they cease to be unit-holders (Sched.3, para.13). The question of the replacement of one joint unit-holder as member by another is discussed in **Chapter 5**.

The subscribers will usually want to resign when they can, but it may be desirable (though not vital) to require their resignation once there are two members who are unit-holders.

The Act itself does not impose any obligation on unit-holders to join the CA. Paragraphs 7 and 8 of Schedule 3 use the language of entitlement, and a person who is entitled to membership only becomes a member when actually entered in the company's register of members in accordance with section 352 of the Companies Act 1985.

It is not, therefore, possible to rely on the registers publicly available at the Land Registry to find out who the unit-holders are: they are the persons entitled to be registered, not the persons actually registered as proprietors of the land.

It is also not possible to rely on the registers publicly available at Companies House to find out who the members of a CA are (nor even if it has any members). It is only possible to discover this by checking the company's own records, i.e. its register of members.

Whether or not a CA has any members may be important. This is because a company limited by guarantee and registered under the Companies Acts is a corporation aggregate, a collection of persons united into one body as a legal person. Section 1(3A) of the Companies Act 1985 (as amended by the Companies (Single Member Private Limited Companies) Regulations 1992, SI 1992/1699) does modify the common law so as to allow companies limited by shares or by guarantee to have only one member. It does not permit a corporation aggregate such as a CA to have no members.

Paragraph 12 of Schedule 3 to the Act means that whenever a person ceases to be a unit-holder (i.e. entitled to be registered as the proprietor of the freehold estate in the unit (s.12) he ceases to be a member of the CA. Thus people leave automatically, but join only on entry into the register of members.

If it ever happened that all the unit-holders who were members stopped being unit-holders, and thus members, before any new unit-holders were registered as members then the CA would cease to exist. Subsequent entry of applicants in the register of members is what would probably happen in practice; and it may be hoped that this would remedy the situation, and that the courts would take a benignant and indulgent approach if ever the question came before them. Acceptance of such a practice would, however, seem to have no foundation in law. The secretary of a CA does not have available to him an effective mechanism for making sure that the register of members is up to date and that the CA does not cease to exist as a legal person. Unit-holders will have obligations to notify the CA of changes, but that does not solve the problem. The prescribed forms seem to assume that notification of having become a unit-holder is tantamount to an application for membership, but are not explicit.

The consequences of a CA ceasing to exist as a legal person would, as a matter of pure law, be serious:

79

- the property of the company would vest in the Crown (or the Duchy of Cornwall or Lancaster as appropriate) as *bona vacantia* (on the assumption that ceasing to exist for lack of members is dissolution within the meaning of section 654 of the Companies Act 1985 – if not, then the freehold land would escheat, and it is almost impossible to predict what would be held to have happened to other property of the corporation);
- carrying on with the association of the people who would be members would be illegal, albeit that they might be associated together as members of an unincorporated association that was required by law to register as a company;
- the land would lose the legal characteristics of commonhold land, and thus unit-holders and others would not technically be bound by commonhold obligations.

Even though it cannot be conclusive, a purchaser of a unit should:

- check that no official action has been taken to dissolve the CA, and
- get a representation from it, if it exists, or from those who appear to be its officers, that it does exist in the commonhold unit information certificate, to be given under paragraph 4.7.2 of the CCS.

Certainly, it will not be in the interests of putative creditors, members or officers to argue that a CA does not exist for the reasons discussed above, and in many cases they may be estopped from doing so.

7.8 CHANGE OF UNIT-HOLDERS

Forms 10, 11, and 12 as prescribed in Schedule 4 to the CR are to be used for notification of changes of unit-holder, whether by transfer of whole or part, or by operation of law.

The notes on the forms suggest that the sanction for non-notification is that the CA may not, or will not (according to Form 12), register the new unit-holder as a member of the CA.

Nothing in the forms could sensibly be construed as being an application for membership, and there is no option offered of not joining the CA despite complying with the obligation to give notice of being a new unit-holder and thus entitled to membership.

The sanction of loss of entitlement to join the CA is not supported by the Act or the CR, or by the more substantive documents prescribed under them.

It would, accordingly, be rash of the secretary to enter people on the register of members merely because he had received formal notification of the new unit-holder.

It would be wrong to refuse membership when it had been applied for merely because that notification had not been given in time.

Paragraph 14 of Schedule 3 to the Act authorises the making of regulations that would deem notification of being a new unit-holder to be an application for membership. The CR do not, however, so provide. They simply prescribe articles of association at Schedule 2, a contract between the members of the CA that assume it, but cannot bind non-members. The prescribed CCS, (CR, Sched.3), which does have effect on unit-holders as such (see s.31(3)) does not contain a requirement to join the CA, or deem a notification to be an application. These matters should be added as additional provisions, local rules, in accordance with regulation 15(11) of the CR so that:

- joint unit-holders have a duty to provide a member of the CA; and
- notification of a new unit-holder will be deemed to be an application for membership; and
- notification of new joint unit-holders will be deemed to be an application for membership by the first named unless the joint unit-holders make an express nomination.

The provisions in Article 4(f) of the prescribed articles of association (CR, Sched.2), that allow joint unit-holders to replace as member a different one of their number are inconsistent with paragraph 13 of Schedule 3 to the Act, which allows resignation as a member only by the subscribers and the developer (if they are not also unit-holders); and inconsistent with paragraph 10, which allows membership only in accordance with Schedule 3. They are, however, sensible and practical, and it is to be hoped that the courts would find some way around the inconsistency.

7.9 DUTY TO MANAGE

Section 35 of the Act appears at first sight to be very helpful. It imposes on the directors of a CA a duty to manage the commonhold, the property of the company, so as to facilitate as far as possible the exercise of each unit-holder's rights and the enjoyment by each unit-holder of the freehold estate in his unit.

There is no ranking of these duties. The directors are to do what they can to make it easy for each unit-holder to enjoy his rights, presumably though only his rights as a unit-holder rather than the rights that arise by the operation of the general law (e.g. easements or profits appurtenant, or the benefit of restrictive covenants annexed, to units). If that exercise conflicts with the rights of the members of the CA (as well it could, since the statute does not require unit-holders to be members of the CA) then this statutory obligation will prevail over the normal fiduciary duty that directors owe to the members of the company.

The duty is imposed on the directors themselves, and not on the company as such. It is not to be thought that the qualification 'as far as possible' would

81

allow the company itself to restrict the discharge of this duty by directors, and it is thought that any resolution of the company that purported to do so would, to that extent, have no effect.

This seems to be the first occasion in English law when the directors of a company have been given duties to non-members (or non-creditors in insolvency) that override their duties to the members of the company as a whole. It may be a valuable precedent.

The term 'enjoyment' is not commonly used in English law in relation to a freehold estate; 'enjoyment' is much more commonly applied to leasehold estates, guarded by landlord's covenants for quiet enjoyment. All that enjoyment of an estate means is being able to exercise the bundle of rights that comprise it.

Unless there is careful drafting of the rights that unit-holders are to have over other units and over the common parts the directors might find themselves in breach of this duty. A CA has the right to deal with the common parts (s.27). This provision means that the directors would be personally liable if they caused the CA to do so in a way that interfered with a right given to any unit-holder to use any part of the common parts. Directors should therefore:

- give good notice of any proposed decision;
- consider representations carefully; and
- get reliable representations from each unit-holder that any interference will be accepted.

Such a representation from each person entitled to be registered as a member, but not so registered, would suffice, although the Act does not provide so explicitly.

Conveyancers must give close attention to the easements that benefit each unit, including those that may arise by implication.

Section 35 particularises the duty of the directors (not of the CA as such) to use all powers ('right, power or procedure') that they have under section 37 of the Act ('conferred or created') in order to require compliance with a requirement or duty, imposed by virtue of the CCS or the relevant part of the Act. This sub-section seems to be declaratory.

7.9.1 Directors' right to take no action

Section 35(3) qualifies the duty imposed on directors in the preceding subsection. It means that that in respect of any particular failure on the part of a unit-holder the directors need take no action in certain circumstances. The circumstances are that they reasonably think that inaction is in the best interests of establishing or maintaining harmonious relationships between all the unit-holders, and that inaction will not cause significant loss or significant disadvantage to any unit-holder who is not the defaulting unit-holder.

The test of reasonableness is applied to the directors' beliefs about establishing or maintaining harmonious relationships. It might be thought to mean that the directors should try to establish or maintain such relationships between all the unit-holders. That is probably going too far. They simply have an added discretion not to act if they reasonably think that it would help harmonious relationships. The relationships must be amongst all the unit-holders, and so the characteristics of a minority cannot be ignored, perhaps not even if there is nothing that would ever establish harmonious relationships with them.

The directors should be careful to be able to demonstrate that their beliefs were reasonable, and should, at least, have consulted those likely to be affected. They may be liable to those affected if they unreasonably decide to do nothing, or have not paid proper attention to complaints.

The directors' statutory discretion does not apply if inaction would cause significant loss or significant disadvantage to any non-defaulting unit-holder. 'Significant' here must mean 'important' rather than 'having a meaning' or 'expressive'.

There are no tests in the Act as to what would be significant.

The concept of 'disadvantage' is, in quite a few dictionaries, equivalent to that of loss. Lawyers often use pairs of words (often or frequently one from Anglo-Saxon roots and the other from Latin roots) where one would do. In this case, however, 'disadvantage' might introduce some idea of relative unfairness rather than actual loss. Inaction by the directors in a particular case might be treating one complainant unfairly by comparison with others in similar circumstances. The directors might have learnt from experience that action to remedy some defaults does nothing likely to maintain a harmonious relationship; and that itself might be to disadvantage one unit-holder as against the other, e.g. when any loss could be no more than merely nominal, or when advantages are given to some but not to others. The use of the disjunction 'or' suggests that 'loss' and 'disadvantage' bear the same meaning, but unfairness is important, and is to be avoided as well.

Directors already have a discretion about how to conduct the affairs of a company. It has been suggested that these provisions do nothing to extend that discretion, instead simply setting out expressly and in a declaratory manner what would anyway be implicit. Simply as a reminder to those managing property that it is not always sensible to insist on one's rights, it may be entirely wholesome.

Similar considerations apply to section 35(3)(b) by which the directors are enjoined to 'have regard' to the desirability of using arbitration, mediation or conciliation procedure, including any ombudsman scheme approved under section 42. The Act does not say how desirable the use of procedural arbitration as compared to legal proceeding is in any case – that cannot be decided in advance. The directors should consider whether alternative dispute resolution is preferable to legal proceedings in each case and should use it if it is preferable. These days the courts themselves will require no less.

7.9.2 Common parts and tenants

It should be noted that unit-holder in section 35 includes tenants of units. These provisions do not mention or apply to tenants of the common parts, when the directors must think about what to do in the light of their duties under section 35(1) and (2) and the common law without any assistance from the rest of section 35.

Directors may always have a discretion not to insist upon the rights of the company, but it is helpful to have something very clearly laid down in the Act that says so.

All potential litigants should consider alternative methods of resolving their disputes, but again it is helpful to have something plainly in the Act itself setting that out very clearly for all parties.

Practitioners, if not politicians and the public, know that they spend much of their time trying to stop the escalation of disputes and to encourage an amicable and low-key resolution. This will help, and the contrast with the in-built conflict in leasehold law is welcome.

CHAPTER 8

Lending on commonhold

Laurence Target

This chapter deals with transactions where commonhold land may be used as security for loans or other obligations.

8.1 INTRODUCTION

Commonhold land is freehold land, but subject to some peculiar legal characteristics that differ as to whether it forms part of the common part owned by a commonhold association (CA); or comprises a unit, owned by a unit-holder who will probably be a member of the CA.

Land of either category may be a valuable asset, and thus may be attractive to those doing business with unit-holders or with CAs as security for loans, credit or other obligations.

Commonhold land is freehold land, but it is governed by documentation that is largely standardised, and produced with statutory authority. It should thus be rather more easily acceptable to lenders than leasehold land. The most obvious advantage is that the asset does not waste: it is freehold and capable of lasting forever. It is not subject to the ever-present possibility of forfeiture (even though it is rarely actually carried out in practice, at least with leases that have a capital value). While that might make running a commonhold somewhat more difficult than would be running an estate subject to long leases for a landlord, it does mean that units must offer better security than leases. There is also comfort for the conveyancer in knowing that most of the governing documentation is standard and sanctioned by statute. Commonhold will not be inconsistent and unworkable, as leaseholds can be. The prescribed documentation is well drafted, and will not need such detailed investigation in each case as leases do.

The main transactions are these:

- lending on the security of a unit;
- lending on the security of the common parts;
- lending on other security from a CA;
- lending to a developer;

85

- lending to a landlord who wishes to convert to commonhold;
- lending to a tenant who wishes to convert to commonhold.

In all cases it is to be assumed that the potential or actual lender has been satisfied of the identity and creditworthiness of the borrower, since the security offered should never dominate the decision to lend. In the case of a CA the suitability of the borrower is absolutely inseparable for the functioning of the commonhold as a scheme, and lenders will need to develop their own standards and procedures for assessment.

Practitioners should always refer to the current requirements of the CML Lenders' Handbook and the specific requirements of the lender when taking security over commonhold land.

8.2 TERMINOLOGY

The terminology of secured lending helps to confuse an already difficult conceptual scheme. We are principally concerned with the legal mortgage as defined in section 205(1) of the Law of Property Act 1925. Despite the preservation of the legal mortgage by demise (in relation to unregistered land only, Land Registration Act 2002, s.23(1)) in practice that now means the familiar but ineptly named 'charge by way of legal mortgage', that was created by sections 85 and 87 of the Law of Property Act 1925. Because all commonhold land must be registered at the Land Registry (s.1) any charge by way of legal mortgage over commonhold land that is registered will be a 'registered charge'.

The Land Registration Act 2002 (LRA 2002) uses 'charge' to mean any mortgage, charge or lien for securing money or money's worth (s.132).

Section 51 of the LRA 2002 provides that on registration a charge created by a registrable disposition takes effect as a charge by deed by way of legal mortgage.

Section 69(3) of the Act applies to 'charge' the meaning from the LRA 2002.

The textbooks (Clark et al (2001) *Fisher and Lightwood Law of Mortgage* (11th ed), paras.1.3–1.6, 1.11; Cousins (2001) *Cousins: The Law of Mortgages* (2nd ed), Sweet & Maxwell, paras.1.13–1.17) and the cases cited there tell us that there are important differences between mortgages and charges.

- A *mortgage* is a conveyance of property subject to a proviso for re-conveyance on redemption.
- A *charge* is a mere appropriation of a fund out of which a debt is to be settled, and is governed by fewer formalities, and does not of itself create a proprietary interest in the fund identified.

The careful observance of distinctions and terminological exactness helps good practice and avoids disputes – but, as *Fisher and Lightwood* acknowledges, it is now perhaps too late to hope for consistent good usage of these terms.

The confusion is further exacerbated by the language of the Companies Acts, particularly the unsatisfactory section 395 of the Companies Act 1985, repealed prospectively by the Companies Act 1989, but still in force. This section is derived from the Companies Act 1902. Here 'charge' means any form of security interest 'over property' for financial indebtedness, and includes mortgages; however after much litigation there is little clarity. The practice of the profession is to register only mortgages and things that look like mortgages, but without too much scrupulosity about those that do not secure financial indebtedness; and not to register other interests such as options, even if in fact they do secure financial indebtedness, and thus must be regarded in equity as mortgages, since equity looks at the substance and not at the form.

Section 395 of the Companies Act 1985 will apply to charges created by CAs. The sanctions for non-compliance with section 395 are strict, and so it is better to err on the side of registration.

8.3 LENDING TO UNIT-HOLDERS

Unless a lender is willing to rely on the personal covenant of a person who is a unit-holder, or unless personal guarantees (e.g. from a bank or acceptable bondsman) are available and suitable, a lender will want to take a mortgage over the unit. In addition to the usual conveyancing investigation of title and searches, a lender will need to check that the CA exists, which will be verified principally by a search at Companies House. A lender will also want to check the functioning of the CA, and so will characteristically want to see three years' audited accounts, when they are available. The point is to ensure that the land actually is commonhold, and it cannot be so unless it meets the tests in section 1 of the Act, which requires there to be a CA in existence. The lender will also want to know that it is stable and well managed.

Rule 6 of the Solicitors' Practice Rules 1990 allows a solicitor acting for both borrower and lender to do these things.

A freehold of a flat, for example, without the mechanisms provided by the Act for the functioning of commonhold will not be satisfactory security except in special circumstances.

As a result of the need to keep the CA in existence and functioning properly, a lender would prudently require a unit-holder to be a member of the CA. A lender will almost invariably take an irrevocable power of attorney allowing the lender (and any receiver appointed by him) to exercise all rights of membership without being liable for loss. Lenders are reluctant, however, to act as agents or attorneys for borrowers, and so rarely use these powers.

Neither the Commonhold Regulations 2004 (CR) nor the documents prescribed under them have comprehensively addressed the rights of mortgagees and receivers whom they may have appointed. Lenders will need to have their own contractual arrangements with unit-holders and to incorporate them in their own standard documentation.

The provisions made under the Act are found in Articles 30 and 31 of the prescribed commonhold articles of association (CR, Sched.2). They have effect (whether adopted by the CA or not) by virtue of regulation 14 of the CR, made as authorised by paragraph 2 of Schedule 2 to, and section 34 of, the Act.

A receiver appointed by the court or by a mortgagee, an administrator, a trustee in bankruptcy, a commissioner in sequestration, or similar person may vote in place of a member. Such person must provide satisfactory evidence of his appointment to the directors before the meeting or vote.

A mortgagee in possession also has the right to vote in place of the member on providing to the directors a certificate of having taken possession and an official copy of the registered title to the unit showing the mortgagee as proprietor of the registered charge. The articles do not envisage a 'registration gap' or a mortgagee taking possession during it. Mortgagees will, therefore, continue to need a contractual security power of attorney, and possibly a separate proxy appointment.

Mortgage documentation should include provisions requiring a unit-holder to be a member of the CA, and stipulating how the unit-holder member is to exercise his rights of membership if the mortgagee does not go into possession.

Lenders will certainly want to ensure that notice is given to the CA of any mortgage in accordance with the CCS. A CA needs to keep a register of mortgages, and is not able simply to rely on registration at the Land Registry, though the latter is, of course, the only satisfactory evidence of there being a legal mortgage (registered charge) of registered land.

A mortgagee who has not gone into possession under the mortgage will not be personally liable to make payments of the assessment: he will not be a unit-holder, and so section 37 of the Act will not apply.

Mortgagees or chargees are not specifically included in sections 31 or 37 as being among the class of persons against whom the commonhold rights may be enforced. They have the right to go into possession. With other freehold land or leasehold land a mortgagee in possession is treated as being the landowner. That principle should also apply to commonhold land, and it would have been helpful if prescribed parts of the CCS made express provision to that effect. It would seem to have been within the scope of delegated legislation so to do.

There are no decided cases, and there is no provision in the Act or the CR, but the better view is that a mortgagee who has taken possession and who has not gone out of possession, whether by sale or returning possession to the mortgagor with the mortgagor's concurrence will be liable for assessment. He will be treated as an assignee of the unit (even though not apparently qualifying under section 12 of the Act). The corollary that a mortgagee in possession has the right to exercise membership of the CA is given effect by Article 31.

Members of CAs are allowed to use proxies. It is to be expected that such a power coupled with a security interest will be irrevocable. The principle is recognised in the Powers of Attorney Act 1971, which restates the common law rule (*Smart* v. *Sandars* (1848) 5 CB 895, 17 LJCP 258).

The forms of restriction imposed by rule 27 of the Commonhold (Land Registrations) Rules 2004 (CLRR) are not completely satisfactory. Form CB (CLRR, Sched.2) is required for the unit title, and reads as follows:

> No disposition *by* the proprietor of the registered estate (other than a transfer or charge of the whole of the land in the title) is to be registered without a certificate by a conveyancer or a director or secretary of the CA that the disposition is authorised by and made in accordance with the provisions of the Commonhold and Leasehold Reform Act 2002. [*Emphasis added.*]

This leaves open the possibility that dispositions of units or parts of units that are not authorised by and in accordance with the Act may be registered if they have been effected by persons other than the proprietor of the registered estate.

Mortgagees do have a power of sale, and exercise it quite frequently. They do not very often observe the direction given by section 7(4) of the Law of Property Act 1925 that where 'power for disposing of or creating a legal estate is exercisable by a person who is not the estate owner, the power shall, when practicable, be exercised in the name and on behalf of the estate owner'. It may, however, rarely be practicable – for such conveyances do not have the desirable and important effect of overreaching interests subsequent to the mortgage. That suggests that the restriction should not apply to them.

It might be thought that the power of sale *implied* into mortgages by section 101(1)(i) of the Law of Property Act 1925 is subject to section 21 of the Act (no disposition of part-units) (Law of Property Act 1925, s.1A), but this power of sale is in fact merely implied by the statute 'to the like extent as if [it] had been in terms conferred by the mortgage deed, but not further'. Thus strictly construed, the subjection imposed in section 1A of the Law of Property Act 1925 will not apply to any power of sale expressly conferred by the mortgage deed. Mortgages almost invariably have an *express* power of sale in addition to those implied by section 101 of the Law of Property Act 1925.

It may be argued that a mortgagor has no power to sell in breach of the conditions of the Act, and thus cannot convey it to the mortgagee. This argument is powerful, but has the awkward consequence of making section 1A of the Law of Property Act 1925 unnecessary, and it is a maxim of statutory interpretation that Parliament does nothing in vain. It also clashes with Land Registry practice, which is to reflect restrictions on powers of disposition that are imposed by statute in restrictions in the Register.

The practical conclusion is that mortgagees cannot sell except where the disposition is authorised by and made in accordance with the provisions of the Act. It is merely that there is no helpful restriction in the title to reflect that limitation in their powers, and no easy mechanism for ensuring that it is observed.

Mortgagees will not be obliged to discharge arrears of assessment on selling unless they have taken possession.

Purchasers will need to know what liabilities are outstanding. Section 16 of the Act means that liabilities will bind a new unit-holder in the same way as they bound the former unit-holder. Purchasers will be entitled to a statement of what is due, a 'commonhold information certificate' under Part 4 of the CCS, and will not be liable for more in respect of the period up to the date of the certificate. Unless mortgagees decide to pay off arrears as part of the marketing process they (like unit-holders themselves, and any other sellers) will need to negotiate an appropriate discount on the price. Where there are arrears mortgagees will require a covenant from the new unit-holder not to seek recovery from the former unit-holder in priority to or competition with the mortgagee.

As discussed above, mortgagees will not be able to sell part only of a unit without the agreement of the CA and observance of the procedure for amendment to the CCS. The same applies to any sale effected by a receiver, whether in the name of the mortgagee or of the mortgagor, or in his own capacity as receiver.

Article 30 of the prescribed articles of association gives receivers appointed by mortgagees the right to vote in the CA in the place of the unit-holder; Article 31 gives the same right to a mortgagee in possession. The usual rules of priority will apply when there is more than one mortgage.

Mortgage documentation should expressly regulate the exercise of rights of participation in the CA when no receiver has been appointed, or when the mortgagee is not in possession.

8.4 LENDING ON SECURITY OF COMMON PARTS

Section 29 of the Act allows the creation of a legal mortgage over the common parts, but subject to the safeguard that the charge must have been created following a resolution of the CA that was opposed by no members who voted. Such resolutions are called unanimous by the Act. In ordinary English a unanimous resolution is one that everybody who was at the meeting voted for.

In fact, the common parts are not likely to be the most valuable assets of the CA, and funders will develop more imaginative forms of security, but the presence of a mechanism that allows them to a mortgage will, no doubt, ensure that they do take mortgages over the common parts.

It will be worth analysing the rights and liabilities to which the common parts will be subject or which they may enjoy.

The Act does not exclude the operation of normal conveyancing principles, or the words that section 62 of the Law of Property Act 1925 (or *Wheeldon* v. *Burrows* (1879) LR 12 ChD 31) imply into conveyances of part of land out of single ownership.

The fact that land must be registered and that all subsisting estates on the creation of the commonhold are freehold estates means that at the moment of the creation of a commonhold there will have been one freehold estate out of which the units and the common parts spring. In the absence of some express provision each new parcel of freehold land will have appurtenant to it all the easements created by the conversion, quasi-easements, rights and privileges that apparently belonged to the unit or the common parts.

The setting up of a commonhold also satisfies the tests for the creation of a scheme of development, also called (though less appropriately) a building scheme. The tests are in the cases *Elliston* v. *Reacher* [1908] 2 Ch 374 and *Baxter* v. *Four Oaks Properties Ltd* [1965] Ch 816, [1965] 1 All ER 906. The consequence of a scheme of development is that the negative obligations, restrictive of the user of land, contained (explicitly or implicitly) in the commonhold documentation will bind each parcel of land in the commonhold and the successors in title of the original owners, who will inevitably have notice through the fact of registration.

Unless express provision to the contrary has been made in the commonhold documentation, the common parts will be subject to all sorts of easements and restrictive covenants, quite apart from express obligations in the commonhold documentation itself. It is expressly stated in the CCS that the rights and obligations that it creates are in addition to any that may exist as part of the general law (paragraph 1.1.3).

An unopposed resolution of the CA might just serve as an equitable release from the burden of easements or restrictive covenants on the part of those units whose unit-holders actually voted for the resolution. It would need annexed to it the consent of any mortgagees of the land benefiting from the covenants. It would be against all principles for it to be held that those who did not actually do something to divest themselves of their property rights (easements or the benefit of restrictive covenants) had nonetheless been stripped of them. To satisfy section 53 of the Law of Property Act 1925 and section 27 of the Land Registration Act 2002 any resolutions should be followed by deeds registered at the Land Registry.

The conclusion is that the common parts will be subject to easements and restrictive covenants enabling them to be used as the common parts of the commonhold even apart from the commonhold rights and duties that affect them. This must inevitably have a serious effect on their value in the event of their being removed from the commonhold or its having been terminated.

The exercise of the power of sale by a mortgagee of the whole of the common parts would have the effect of destroying the commonhold itself. Section 1 of the Act effectively requires a commonhold to have units and common parts since the CA is to have functions, and must have them in relation to common parts. This is a matter of logic, as well as of practicality. A mortgagee is not generally required to have regard to any interests but his own when exercising his powers, but the selling of assets which may be of limited or marginal value but whose sale would have such serious consequences on neighbouring owners might not be deemed to be an exercise of mortgagee's powers in good faith and for the proper purposes in order to recover the mortgage debt, and not in order to harm the mortgagee or others (*Downsview Nominees Ltd* v. *First City Corpn Ltd* [1993] AC 295, [1993] 3 All ER 626, PC).

A restriction in Form commonhold association (CLRR, Sched.2) will be entered in the proprietorship register of the CA's title and shall read:

> No charge by the proprietor of the registered estate is to be registered other than a legal mortgage which is accompanied by a certificate by a conveyancer or a director or secretary of the commonhold association that the creation of the mortgage was approved by a resolution complying with section 29(2) of the Commonhold and Leasehold Reform Act 2002.

There may be circumstances in which land that forms part of the common parts of a commonhold would be severable from it, and when severed would be valuable and sufficiently free from encumbrances as to be valuable, but it cannot be imagined that they will be many.

Lenders should, therefore, treat with great caution proposals for a mortgage of common parts as security for the debts of the CA. Lenders should take specialist advice as to valuation of the land to be mortgaged. They should ensure that it can be sold without remaining subject to encumbrances that would make it unusable for any other purpose. A legal mortgage would, of course, give some priority in a liquidation. The proceeds of sale of the mortgaged part would need to be paid to the mortgagee, and so a legal mortgage will not be altogether useless as part of a lender's security strategy – but lenders will be careful not to rely too much on this one device.

8.5 LENDING ON OTHER SECURITY FROM A COMMONHOLD ASSOCIATION

The legal vehicle chosen for CAs, the company limited by guarantee, means that CAs will not be heavily capitalised and will be likely to have few assets.

There is no paid up share capital. The obligation of members to contribute to the debts of the company in the event of its insolvency is £1 each, which would hardly cover the cost of collecting it.

Since CAs cannot distribute profit there will be pressure on the directors to run things as tightly as possible, not building up general reserves or otherwise accumulating property.

The common parts, all those parts of a scheme that are not parts of units, will be vested in the CA as its corporate property beneficially owned by it, but, as discussed in para.8.4, the common parts will be heavily encumbered by the rights of unit-holders, and are likely to be functional: mainly walls, foundations, roofs, sewers and cables, though perhaps gardens and car parks as well.

The value of participation in a well-resourced and well-managed commonhold should be reflected in the value of the units themselves.

The main asset of a CA is in fact its right to recover the assessment from unit-holders. It is their contributions that will fuel the operation of commonholds unless it is engaged in other business activities, such as letting out some of the common parts.

Section 38 provides that a CCS must make provision requiring the directors to make an annual estimate of the funds that the CA will need to raise and requiring each unit-holder to pay the percentage of the estimate allocated to his unit. There must be consultation, but the CCS does not require the members (or non-member unit-holders) to approve the annual estimate.

The power to raise an assessment is expressly conferred only on the directors by the Act.

There is an express power to appoint managing agents of the property, but the setting of an assessment is probably not the kind of thing that managing agents can do. The directors are authorised by Article 53 (with an ordinary resolution in favour) to delegate to committees, of which most members are members of the CA, and to individual directors. The role of such a committee could include setting an assessment. The delegation to anybody else of this power would be improper.

Section 38 provides that the CCS must make provision for the directors to raise estimates and serve notices and so on. It is possible, perhaps especially when the CA is in financial difficulty, that they may not have the wisdom to set sensible assessments when long-term expenditure is needed. It will not always be possible for reserves to have been built up in advance. There may be expenditure needed greater than can be funded from reserves and from the current year's assessment and additional assessments.

Assessments must be annual, which suggests on a cursory reading that they are restricted to the current year, and cannot cover expenditure for future years. If this were correct it would be difficult for a lender to be confident about his ability to lend on the security of a floating charge, or against an assignment of the right to recover against unit-holders. The power of directors to make estimates of additional income required does not give lenders all that they need.

In fact several assessments can be made for any year, and they can be made for future years. The CCS also has express provision for emergency assessments (paragraph 4.2). Lenders should require assessments to be made at the outset of the loan allowing amortisation of the loan over its lifetime. This relies on the rule that the singular includes the plural and vice versa (Law of Property Act 1925, s.61). It applies to all instruments. By section 17 of the Interpretation Act 1978 it applies to all legislation.

An alternative strategy involves the use of reserve funds under section 39 of the Act, with the CCS having specified the repayment of debt as the reserve fund activity.

There is little case law expressly about insolvency procedures in relation to companies limited by guarantee. It is not beyond doubt that the powers of administrators or liquidators (set out in Schedule 1 and Schedule 4 to the Insolvency Act 1986) are sufficiently widely-worded to confer on an administrator the power to raise an assessment when the directors have not done so, or in exclusion of the directors' rights, when he has been appointed.

The Schedules to the Insolvency Act 1986 are detailed and set out particular powers. The most probable power that would allow an insolvency practitioner to set the assessment is the general wording in paragraphs 14 and 23 of Schedule 1: 'Power to carry on the business of the company' and 'Power to do all other things incidental to the exercise of the foregoing powers'. In Schedule 4, in relation to liquidators, the wording is 'Power to carry on the business of the company so far as may be necessary for its beneficial winding up' and 'Power to do all such other things as may be necessary for winding up the company's affairs and distributing its assets'. The commonsense and practical approach is to interpret these words as allowing the insolvency office holders to raise the assessment as if they were the directors. It may strain the principles of statutory construction to do so, but avoids an absurd result.

It is not obvious either that the directors could hand over to an insolvency practitioner (or otherwise in security documentation) a power that has been conferred on them (and not on anybody else) by the statute. The principle remains that a delegate cannot delegate.

Lenders will prepare their own documentation addressing these issues; unfortunately each is likely to adopt its own solutions and procedural requirements. A prudent lender taking security for the right to collect under future assessments will require:

- an express power to do the things required of, and allowed to, the directors in Part 4.2 of the CSS;
- a directors' resolution; and
- a special resolution of the company.

8.6   LENDING TO A DEVELOPER

The difficulties involved in the release of mortgaged land and the flexibility desired by developers through the build process mean that large developers usually redeem mortgages on development land before carrying out the development and selling on to purchasers of completed units.

Aspects of the commonhold structure, notably the need to have the common parts and units defined on designation or registration of the freehold land as commonhold mean that some of these reasons will be less pressing. It will be much more difficult to re-designate units and reconfigure the development so plans are likely to be further worked out before commencement than is the case at present.

Thus it may be the case that more developments will be carried on mortgaged land.

The crucial stage will be the consent stage. A mortgagee lender, having already approved the borrower, the suitability of the land and the business plan, when taking a mortgage at all, will need to consent to registration of the land as commonhold.

On registration, with or without unit-holders, a subsisting mortgage will remain in place; but it is no longer possible for a mortgage to be granted over the common parts without following the detailed provisions of section 29 of the Act. While the developer retains control, before registration with unit-holders, that should not be too difficult.

It will be much more practical to replace a single mortgage with a series of mortgages over the units and to discharge the mortgage over the common parts. Thus purchasers of units could be entirely confident that their commonhold rights would cover the common parts. They do not only enjoy commonhold rights over the commonhold parts, but are allowed to gain easements and other rights as well. This means that in order to bind successors in title of the mortgage to the common parts, either the common parts must be free from any mortgage or the concurrence of the mortgagee to each first disposal of a unit must be procured. The latter course is costly and inconvenient. Better by far for the lender's interest to be secured on each unit, and an undertaking for discharge on receipt of a stipulated sum, or proportion of the sale proceeds given, in order to facilitate the sale process.

Section 59 of the Act allows succession to development rights, but may not allow for mortgagees selling under their mortgages (and overreaching subsequent encumbrances if they themselves exercise the power of sale) to pass on development rights. The section operates when the developer transfers the freehold of the common parts during the transitional period (s.59(1), (2) and (3)). In a post-1925 mortgage however, the freehold is not transferred to the mortgagee (Law of Property Act 1925, s.85), although a mortgagee in possession of freehold land is usually treated by the courts as the freehold owner. A receiver is (usually) deemed to be the agent of the mortgagor (Law of

Property Act 1925, s.109) and so a period of receivership will not cause a problem in this respect.

When a lender exercises its power of sale under a mortgage it is not, however, the freehold owner and is not the developer, and so on a strict and literal interpretation a purchaser of the freehold in such circumstances would not have development rights, and that would make a sale difficult.

Mortgagees can convey in the name and on behalf of the estate owner (Law of Property Act 1925, s.7(4)). They do not do so often, wanting to avoid any suspicion that they are acting 'on behalf of' the mortgagor, as its agent, with all of the onerous duties that would imply. (This is why lenders are unwilling to use the security powers of attorney that they invariably require to be granted to them in security documentation.) Mortgagees are properly governed by equitable rules, owing a duty to exercise their powers in good faith and for proper purposes, duties quite different from those of an agent at common law.

The courts may in fact disregard the idle stipulation that it must be the developer who transfers: any person to whom the freehold has been transferred and any mortgagee in possession ought to be able to enjoy the developer's rights.

8.7   LENDING TO A LANDLORD ON CONVERSION

The remedies of a landlord are extensive, including distraint and forfeiture, though they are not often exercised where leases have a capital value. Thus a reversion can be good security in a way that the common parts of a commonhold cannot be.

A mortgagee of a reversion will accordingly be unlikely to wish to consent to conversion but will be inclined to require redemption, or a restructuring of the debt so that it is assumed by the CA or the prospective unit-holders themselves. The mortgagee will need an acceptable undertaking for costs in the latter case, and the work involved will be likely to be extensive, and there may be difficulties in relation to priority where the prospective unit-holders already use mortgage finance.

8.8   LENDING TO A LEASEHOLDER ON CONVERSION

A secured lender should (on an undertaking for costs and substituted security) want to say yes to a conversion to commonhold, whether or not the present circumstances of the borrower would justify a new loan of the outstanding amount, whether or not the present value of the security would support the outstanding loan and whether or not the present leasehold and freehold are well run.

Commonhold land as freehold security will always be better than lease-hold security. It does not waste with time, and is not subject to forfeiture. A commonhold unit will have the advantage over a lease of the same land that it will be part of a statutory framework and thus will not be at risk of failing to work because of the bad drafting that is all too characteristic of leases, and will not be subject to the inevitable and institutionalised conflict of interest between landlord and tenant that so often makes management of leasehold properties so difficult.

There is, however, no compulsion, and there is a 100 per cent rule that means that the property cannot become commonhold unless all proprietors of registered charges do actually consent.

8.9 CONCLUSION

As freehold land, commonhold will offer attractive security to lenders. Commonhold units will not suffer the disadvantages of land held on long leases. Lending to a CA will not be the same as lending to a landlord company, whether owned by the tenants or not, but it will be possible to create security structures to support lending.

CHAPTER 9

Developer's rights

James Driscoll

9.1 INTRODUCTION

It is essential to the development of new commonholds that the developer has the necessary powers to complete the development. With the traditional leasehold form of development a developer can reserve rights in various ways from express terms in the draft leases to controlling votes in a management company, coupled with the power to appoint and remove directors. The purpose of this chapter is to show how, by using the different stages of a commonhold development such as the 'transitional period' and by reserving rights to complete the development, the developer can have ample powers to complete the development and to market and sell the commonhold units. These concerns and issues affect any commonhold development whether it is a commercial, residential or mixed-use development. They are not, of course, an issue for leasehold or freehold conversions to commonhold, which amounts to an application for a commonhold to be registered with unit-holders under section 9 of the Act. For new developments though there are three stages to consider: the 'pre-commonhold' period; the 'transitional period' and the remainder of the 'development period'.

In summary, the developer is in complete control at the pre-commonhold stage and during the transitional period.

9.2 PRE-COMMONHOLD

In the case of a new development there is no statutory requirement to apply for registration of the land as commonhold land prior to starting the development work, so the development work could be at an advanced stage before application to the Land Registry for commonhold registration.

Nor does the incorporation of the commonhold association (CA) (see **Chapter 7**) require such an application to the Land Registry in relation to the land to be made immediately.

9.3   TRANSITIONAL PERIOD

This is defined by section 8 of the Act as the period which starts with the registration of land as a freehold estate in commonhold land and ends with the date on which a purchaser of a commonhold unit becomes entitled to be registered as the proprietor of freehold estate in that unit. This is the stage at which the common parts are automatically registered in the name of the CA and the rules, rights and duties in the commonhold community statement (CCS) come into force (ss.7 and 8). It is also the date at which any leases relating to the land are automatically extinguished, an issue, it is thought, that will only usually arise in the case of a leasehold conversion to a commonhold with unit-holders.

As no one other than the developer owns an interest in the commonhold land during this period the developer is relatively free to alter the development so long as the alterations are within the general parameters of the commonhold legislation. For example, changes might have to be made to the memorandum of association of the CA to alter the reference to the land for which the commonhold has been established if land is removed or added. In common with any alteration to the constitution of the association, it has no effect until the altered version has been registered at the Land Registry (accompanied by a certificate from the CA's directors that the altered constitution is in accordance with the Commonhold Regulations 2004 (CR)). This is provided for in Schedule 3 to the Act.

Of course the developer may want or need to change other aspects of the development, such as changing some aspect or aspects of the commonhold's local rules or altering the number of the commonhold units or the common parts.

As, at this stage, the developer is the sole owner of the commonhold land and (with any subscribers to the CA) sole member of the CA he is again in complete control provided he proceeds in accordance with the principles of, and regulations made under, the Act.

In this context the general provisions regulating amendment of the CCS should be borne in mind.

9.4   AMENDING THE COMMONHOLD COMMUNITY STATEMENT

Under section 33 of the Act and subsequent regulations (the CR) each CCS must make provision about how it can be amended. An amended CCS has no effect until it has been registered at the Land Registry (s.33(3)). The application for the amended CCS to be registered must be accompanied by a certificate given by the directors of the CA that the amended document satisfies the provisions in the Act and the CR (s.33(5)). Further, should the amendment redefine the extent of a commonhold unit the application must also be accompanied by the consent of the owner of that unit and any chargee (s.33(6)). Similarly, where the change affects the common parts the consent of someone who has a charge over the land must be added (s.33(7)).

During the transitional stage no owner consents will be relevant unless the developer is adding land, in which case just the consent of any chargee is required.

Under regulation 15(1) of the CR, the CCS must be in the form prescribed by Schedule 3 to the CR (or a form to the same effect). It is to be expected then that any amendments to the CCS are similarly limited and prescribed. Under paragraph 4.8.2 of the prescribed CCS, amendment of 'local rules' in Parts 1–4 (defined in paragraph 1.4.5 as the 'provisions, including information contained in Annexes, inserted by the developer or the CA that are not prescribed by Regulations') require amendment by ordinary resolution. Paragraph 4.8.4 also restricts any changes to the format of the layout of the CCS. Further paragraphs state that other changes to the CCS require both a prior written consent and/or a special resolution depending on the type of change proposed.

The prior written consent of the unit-holder and registered proprietor of any charge is needed in order to:

- amend rights for, or over, a commonhold unit;
- amend who can be authorised users of limited use areas;
- redefine the extent of a unit; or
- take land forming part of a unit out of the title and add it to the common parts.

A special resolution is required in order to change:

- the percentages of assessment or reserve fund levies allocated to a partic-ular unit (subject to the unit-holder having the right conferred by para-graph 4.8.13 not to have such an alteration made if the effect would be to allocate a significantly disproportionate percentage); or
- the number of votes allocated to a member (subject to the unit-holder having a right conferred by paragraph 4.8.14 not to have such an alteration made if the effect would be to allocate a significantly disproportionate number of votes to him).

Both the prior written consent of the unit-holder and registered proprietor of any charge and a special resolution are required to change the:

- permitted use of unit specified in Annex.4, para.2 of the CCS; or
- boundaries following a transfer.

Note, however, that no prior resolution of a member is needed:

- to amend provisions which are inconsistent with the statutory scheme; or
- to remove any surrendered development rights.

The directors must apply for the registration of the amended CCS at the Land Registry 'as soon as practicable'.

Thus, as there are no unit holders at the transitional stage no special consents are required and the developer is free to change both the properties in the commonhold and the rules in the CCS, but the developer should use the procedures just described and then register the amended CCS at the Land Registry.

9.5 POST-TRANSITIONAL PERIOD (DEVELOPMENT PERIOD)

Once the first sale has taken place, the unit-holder is registered and the commonhold is under way, the statutory scheme under which commonhold operates may be in conflict with the developer's need for flexibility. However, under sections 57 and 58 of the Act the developer can reserve rights in the CCS. This is not, of course, automatic and the developer must ensure that such rights are reserved. As might be expected, these rights operate for the developer (and any successors) until the commonhold has been completed and the last unit has been sold. Under regulation 15(10) of the CR, the developer's rights must be set out in an additional Annex which must be the last one and must also be referred to in the table of contents of the CCS.

The Act defines who is a 'developer' for these purposes and how rights can be reserved to complete 'development business'. The Act also provides for these rights to be exercised by a successor developer. These points are now considered in turn.

A 'developer' is defined by section 58, as a person making an application for registration of a freehold estate in commonhold land. 'Development business' is widely defined in Schedule 4 to the Act as falling into 'works', 'marketing', 'variation' and 'appointment and removal of directors of the commonhold association' and summarised under the following categories:

- execution or completion of works on a commonhold; or
  - on land which is or may be added to a commonhold; or
  - on land which has been removed from a commonhold;
- advertising and other activities designed to promote transactions in commonhold units;
- the addition of land to a commonhold;
- the removal of land from a commonhold;
- the amendment of a CCS, including such amendment as would redefine the extent of a unit; and
- appointment and removal of directors of the CA.

Further provisions on developer's rights are contained in section 58(3). These allow the developer to include provisions in the CCS which:

- require the CA or unit-holders to co-operate with the developer for specified purposes connected with development business;
- make the exercise of development rights subject to terms and conditions specified or to be determined in accordance with express provisions;
- make provision about the effect of a breach of a requirement; and
- exclude the need for the CA to consent to an application to add land (s.41(2) and (3)).

In drafting the CR and in the consultation process that preceeded it, it was recognised that there was a challenge in balancing the interests of the initial unit-holders (who buy the first units when the development is still in its infancy) and the need for the greatest amount of flexibility achievable for developers who might otherwise be deterred from going down the common-hold route.

Overall the scheme in the Act and the CR is that the developers can reserve such rights as suit their requirements on the specific development in question, whilst giving protection to the first unit-holders whilst the development is being completed. In practical terms, the developer will also have to consider how the effects of reserving rights to complete the development may affect the marketability of the commonhold. After all, potential purchasers may be dissuaded from completing the purchase if the developer's rights could adversely affect enjoyment of their units whilst the development is being completed.

Assuming that the developer has reserved rights in the CCS does a unit-holder have any statutory protections against any exercise of these rights that adversely affects their use and enjoyment of the unit? The Act and the CR provide some recourse under regulation 18. First, a developer must not exercise development rights in a manner which would unreasonably interfere with either a unit-holder's enjoyment of the freehold interest in the commonhold unit or, the exercise by any unit-holder or tenant of rights under the CCS. Second, a developer must not reserve the right to remove parts of the common parts from the commonhold. Third, a developer may not remove land from the commonhold which has been transferred (that is sold) to a unit-holder unless the prior written consent of the unit-holder is obtained. Fourth, development rights cannot be exercised if works for which they were conferred have been completed although such work is permitted to carry out marketing (as defined in paragraph 3 of Schedule 4 to the Act) for such further period as is required.

9.6 APPOINTMENT AND REMOVAL OF DIRECTORS BY THE DEVELOPER

Another way in which the developer can retain controls over the development whilst is is being built and marketed is through the appointment and removal of directors. As has already been noted, the CCS must confer express rights on the developer to appoint and remove directors and where the CCS gives the developer the right to appoint and remove directors the provisions of regulation 1(8) of the CR have the following effects. First, during the transitional period the developer can appoint up to two directors in addition to those appointed by the subscriber(s) and may remove any so adopted. Second, after the end of the transitional period and for so long as the developer is the unit-holder of more than a quarter of the total number of units he may appoint up to one quarter of the directors of the CA and may remove or replace any so appointed. Third, if at any time the CA resolves to specify or reduce the maximum number of directors and in consequence the number of developer's directors exceeds what is permitted, the developer must immediately reduce the number as required and if this has not been done by the start of the next directors' meeting the longest in office of the developer's directors must cease to hold office immediately to the extent required to achieve the reduction in number. Fourth, if the developer ceases to be the unit-holder of more than one quarter of the total number of units he may no longer appoint, replace or remove a director and developer's directors previously appointed will cease to hold office immediately. In other words, the developer has significant influence over the appointment and the removal of directors of the CA, not only during the transitional period, but afterwards, until 75 per cent or more of the units are sold.

Further regulation of the right to appoint or remove directors is that whilst the developer has the power to appoint or remove directors the developer cannot vote on:

- a resolution which fixes the number of directors; or
- a resolution which involves the appointment or the removal of directors not appointed by him; or
- on any resolution governing remuneration of such directors.

Other points to bear in mind are that the the provisions in the prescribed articles of association dealing with retirement of directors by rotation (Arts.40 and 41) and remuneration (Art.54) do not apply to developer's directors. Also the quorum for directors' meetings is set at half of their number or two (whichever is the greater) by Article 61. Where the CCS confers rights on the developer to appoint and remove directors regulation 14(9)(b) of the CR requires that at least one of the directors at the meeting must not be a developer's director.

9.7 SURRENDER OF DEVELOPMENT RIGHTS

Development rights can be surrendered by the developer provided a notice is sent to the Land Registry. Rule 24 of the Commonhold (Land Registration)

Rules 2004 (CLRR), prescribes the forms and procedures which are to be used. An entry will appear in the property register of the common parts title. Once registered, rights cease to be exercisable and the Land Registry has a duty to inform the CA as soon as is reasonably practicable (s.58(6)).

9.8 PASSING DEVELOPMENT RIGHTS TO A SUCCESSOR

Under section 59 of the Act there is provision for the transfer of development rights to a purchaser of the whole of the commonhold. This can take place either during the transitional period or in the case where there is no transitional period (that is to say on a conversion) on the transfer of a whole or part of the development. The transfer must be expressed to be inclusive of development rights.

Other than during a transitional period no one may have the status of a developer with the consequential development rights unless that person has at some time been a registered owner of at least two or more units and is still the owner of at least one.

9.9 SUMMARY

There are various ways in which the developer can reserve the right to complete and market the commonhold development. First, by delaying (where this is feasible) the registration of the land as freehold commonhold land. Second, by noting that during the transitional period, the rules of the CCS are not in operation. Third, by noting that during the transitional period the CA does not own the common parts and is not responsible for them. Fourth, during the transitional period the developer is free to alter both the constitution of the CA and/or the CCS within, of course, the general parameters of the Act and the CR, or to apply for the commonhold registration to be rescinded. Finally, after the transitional period comes to an end and until the development has been completed and the units sold, the developer can exercise any developer's rights which have been reserved in the CCS.

CHAPTER 10

Managing a commonhold

Gary Cowen

10.1 INTRODUCTION

This chapter is intended to deal with aspects of management of a commonhold which are regulated by the Act or the Commonhold Regulations 2004 (CR) once the commonhold has been established and the freehold land registered as a freehold estate in commonhold.

It is intended to focus, therefore, upon the practical aspects of management of a commonhold including the financial affairs. The corporate aspects and requirements of managing and running a commonhold are dealt with in detail in **Chapter 7** on the commonhold association (CA) but these will be dealt with relatively briefly in this chapter. Reference should be made to **Chapter 7** for a more detailed explanation.

10.2 CORPORATE REQUIREMENTS

A CA is a company limited by guarantee (s.34(1)). Such a company has members but no shareholders as such. The company must apply its income solely to the objects specified in the memorandum of association and the premises. In the absence of a winding up of the CA, no dividend can be paid to members of the CA (CR, Sched.2, para.72). Hence, any profit made from the activities of the commonhold must effectively be ploughed back into the management of the commonhold.

The CA, like any other company, will have directors who will be responsible for its running. Directors may be drawn from the members of the CA but need not necessarily be so drawn. The articles of association of a commonhold make provision relating to the directors, details of which can be found in **Chapter 7**. In brief, the relevant provisions of the prescribed articles of association (CR, Sched.2) are the:

- number of directors – article 38;
- qualification of directors – article 39;
- retirement of directors by rotation – articles 40 to 42;

- appointment and re-appointment of directors at general meetings – article 43;
- notice of a proposed appointment of a director – article 44;
- appointment of a director by the members – article 45;
- appointment of a director by the directors – article 46;
- re-appointment of a director following retirement at an annual general meeting – article 47;
- disqualification and removal of directors – articles 48 to 49;
- powers of directors – articles 50 to 51;
- appointment of agents by directors – article 52;
- delegation of directors' powers – article 53;
- remuneration of directors – article 54;
- directors' expenses – article 55;
- appointment of executive directors – article 56;
- directors' interests – articles 57 to 59; and
- proceedings of the directors – articles 60 to 69.

The directors of the CA have a duty to manage the commonhold and in particular, a duty to use any right, power or procedure conferred or created by section 37 for the purpose of preventing, remedying, or curtailing a failure on the part of a unit-holder to comply with a requirement or duty placed upon him by virtue of the commonhold community statement (CCS) or by a provision of the Act (s.35(2)).

Other than preventing, remedying and curtailing failures on the part of the unit-holders, the Act is relatively vague about the extent of the duty of the directors of the CA.

However, in respect of their corporate responsibilities, the directors are responsible for:

- keeping adequate company records;
- holding Annual General Meetings; and
- ensuring that the functions of the commonhold are dealt with by adequate personnel.

Detailed discussion of these duties can be found in **Chapter 7**.

10.3 PROPERTY ISSUES

Whilst it was the intention of Parliament in creating commonhold as an estate in land to provide individual unit-holders with significantly more freedom than they would enjoy if they merely had leasehold title to their units, a balancing act would always be required to reflect the need to ensure that unit-holders, often living in very close proximity to one another in blocks of flats, are able to exercise such freedoms whilst not interfering with the freedoms of their neighbours. Each commonhold therefore has rules to regulate the behaviour of the unit-holders so that each unit-holder is protected from his neighbours. Because those rules are largely incorporated into the prescribed CCS, many of them are imposed upon every commonhold by Parliament. However, the ability to create 'local rules' gives the members of the commonhold a certain degree of flexibility in creating their own local law. The Department for Constitutional Affairs' Non-Statutory Guidance on the CR includes guidance on how to draft a CCS which in turn includes specimen local rules.

This part of this chapter will concentrate on five principal aspects of management of a commonhold. These are:

- repairs and maintenance;
- alterations;
- alienation;
- user; and
- insurance.

10.4   REPAIRS AND MAINTENANCE

The Act makes provision for obligations for repairs and maintenance of the commonhold land to be included within the CCS. First, in relation to commonhold units themselves, section 14 of the Act requires the CCS to make provision imposing duties in respect of the repair and maintenance of each commonhold unit (s.14(2)). Such a duty may be imposed on either the CA or on the unit-holder (s.14(3)).

So far as the common parts of the commonhold land are concerned, the Act provides that the CCS *must* make provision requiring the CA to maintain and repair the common parts (s.26(c)). Section 25 of the Act defines the common parts as 'every part of the commonhold which is not for the time being a commonhold unit in accordance with the commonhold community statement'.

The prescribed form of CCS deals with repairs and maintenance very shortly (CR, Sched.3, para.15). Paragraph 4.5.1 imposes an obligation on the CA to repair and maintain the common parts. This has been supplemented by the sentence 'this includes decorating them and putting them into sound condition'. This raises a number of issues that will be dealt with at **para.10.4.1** below.

The position in relation to commonhold units is even less well defined. The prescribed CCS merely states at paragraph 4.5.2 that the duties imposed by it in respect of the repair and maintenance of the commonhold units are specified in Paragraph 7 of Annex 4 to the CCS. This reference to Annex 4 is to the section of the CCS where the members of the CA can create their own local law.

10.4.1 Common parts

The common parts of the commonhold are every part of the commonhold which is not for the time being a commonhold unit in accordance with the CCS (s.25).

Whilst the obligation itself is strikingly plain, the legislation leaves unanswered the obvious question as to the standard of repair required. Notably, whilst an earlier draft of the CCS sought to set such a standard by reference to a notional specification or standard imposed by the CA, that requirement was dropped in favour of the general wording which now appears in the prescribed CCS.

It is suggested that in evaluating the standard of repair and maintenance required, the law relating to repairing obligations in the context of landlord and tenant law will be of some assistance. The scope of that topic is very wide and outside the remit of this work, but it is suggested that in determining whether the common parts of the commonhold are in disrepair or in need of maintenance and if so, what work is required to remedy the disrepair and/or maintain the common parts, the authorities relating to landlord and tenant situations will be of some use.

However, it should be borne in mind that there are significant differences between a straightforward landlord and tenant relationship and the relationship between the various parties involved in a commonhold which may have a bearing on the standard of repair and maintenance expected of the CA. In particular, by contrast with a landlord and tenant relationship, every party to a CCS will have a freehold interest in that part of the commonhold which he holds. In theory, therefore, every party to the CCS ought to have common cause in ensuring that the common parts are kept in repair and maintained on a long-term basis even where there has not yet been any deterioration in the fabric.

It might be suggested, therefore, that the repairing obligation placed upon the CA imposes, at least in theory, a higher standard of repair and maintenance than would be imposed in relation to a landlord and tenant relationship. Given that it is a freehold owner of the unit, the length of the unit-holder's 'term' which would be a factor to be borne in mind in a landlord and tenant scenario becomes irrelevant when one comes to consider a commonhold. Similarly, authorities which focus on the question of whether the tenant is being expected to 'hand back' something other than that which was let to him will be of only limited value given the freehold nature of commonhold ownership. It is submitted however, that it would be equally misguided simply to ignore the landlord and tenant law. A freehold interest in the unit might be treated in the same way as, for instance, a very long term of years in considering the appropriate standard of repair.

The additional sentence referred to in relation to repairs and maintenance above, 'this includes decorating them and putting them into sound condition', and added to the prescribed CCS at a relatively late stage in its emergence raises a number of points. The first is that it is expressly stated that the obligation to repair and to maintain 'includes' an obligation to decorate. Repair and redecoration have, in the context of landlord and tenant law, often been treated as two very separate obligations. Not least in relation to section 18(1) of the Landlord and Tenant Act 1927, which imposes a cap on damages recoverable for breaches of repairing obligations but which does not apply to obligations to decorate, yet it is clear that for the purposes of commonhold, decoration is to be treated as being included within the ambit of repair, or, at the very least, maintenance.

Once again, the obligation makes no reference to the standard of decoration required nor to the question of which elements of the common parts are required to be decorated. However, one would imagine that a degree of common sense will prevail. Those elements of the common parts which have formerly been decorated or which one might expect to be the subject of decoration would, it would seem, be the obvious elements of the common parts to be the subject of the obligation and one would hope that with all the owners seeking to achieve a common aesthetic appeal, the standard of decoration will not become contentious.

In addition, there is a requirement that the CA put the common parts into sound condition. Two points arise from this. First, it should be noted that the obligation to 'put' the common parts into sound condition clearly indicates that such an obligation exists notwithstanding that the common parts may not have been in such a condition at the start of the commonhold. Second, it is notable that the expression 'sound condition' is used. It would appear that it was intended by the draftsman that this expression should mean something distinct from the obligation to repair, maintain and decorate. In *Credit Suisse v. Beegas Nominees Limited* [1994] 1 EGLR 76, Lindsay J. held that a covenant to put a building into good and tenantable condition potentially went further than repairing it, saying that:

> ... whilst I accept the inevitability of the conclusion of the Court of Appeal in *Aquarius* [*Post Office* v. *Aquarius Properties Limited* [1987] 1 All ER 1055] that one cannot have an existing obligation to repair unless and until there is a disrepair, that reasoning does not apply to a covenant to keep (and put) into good and tenantable condition. One cannot sensibly proceed from 'No disrepair, ergo no need to repair' to 'no disrepair, ergo no need to put or keep in the required condition' ... all that is needed, in general terms, to trigger a need for activity under an obligation to keep in (and put into) a given condition is that the subject matter is out of that condition

It would seem, therefore, that the obligation to put the common parts into 'sound condition' will be triggered as soon as they are not in sound condition, even though there may be no physical deterioration sufficient to amount to disrepair.

10.4.2 Commonhold units

The prescribed CCS merely states in paragraph 4.5.2 that the duties imposed by it in respect of the repair and maintenance of the commonhold units are specified in Paragraph 7 of Annex 4 to the CCS.

In the initial stages of the legislative process, the draft CCS, attached to the consultation paper of October 2002, provided for a division of responsibility for commonhold units, with the CA being responsible for the repair and maintenance of the exterior of commonhold units whilst the unit-holders would be responsible for the interior. However, after consultation, that inflexible approach was dropped in favour of the present, more flexible approach.

Thus, the parties to the commonhold have complete flexibility in the manner in which they wish to cater for repair and maintenance of the commonhold units. It is suggested that this approach is a sensible one in the light of the fact that commonhold land may be made up of a number of different types of units. Whilst the members of a commonhold comprising a block of flats might well opt to replicate the former landlord and tenant position, whereby the owners of the flats were responsible for the repair and maintenance of the internal parts of their individual flats, such a position may be wholly inappropriate for a commonhold comprising, say, an industrial estate where the expectation might be that each unit-holder would be responsible for the repair and maintenance of the whole of the buildings comprising the units. The CA and unit-holders can draw up the repairing obligations to be attached to the commonhold units to reflect the peculiarities of the commonhold land.

It follows that the parties also have complete flexibility as to the standard of repair to be imposed on the parties who are responsible for repair and maintenance of the commonhold units.

Those who are drafting obligations in relation to commonhold units may also wish to consider whether to include obligations to decorate and to keep any commonhold unit clean.

10.4.3 Rights of access to repair

Because both the CA and the unit-holders are freehold owners of land within the commonhold, it is also desirable that they should make provision for access to the land owned by the other party in the event that maintenance or repairs cannot be carried out otherwise than from the other party's land. Access would be available in certain circumstances pursuant to the Access to Neighbouring Land Act 1992 but an application under this Act may not be open to a party.

The prescribed CCS makes provision at paragraph 2.4.3 both for the owners of commonhold units to have rights over the common parts and, at paragraph 2.4.4 for the CA to have rights over the commonhold units. Those rights are included at Paragraphs 6 and 7 respectively of Annex 2 to the CCS. The parties to the CCS may agree the extent of the rights to be granted to each other. However, it is envisaged, using the experience of the landlord and tenant model, that both the CA and unit-holders will be well advised to reserve rights to themselves to enter the land of the other to inspect their own land and to carry out any repairs, maintenance or decoration to their own land which can only reasonably be carried out from the land of the other party.

10.5 ALTERATIONS

The Act is, with one exception, silent on the question of the carrying out of alterations to commonhold land. It is provided in the Act that the amendment of a CCS to redefine the extent of a commonhold unit may not be made unless the unit-holder consents in writing before the amendment is made (s.23(1)). Section 23(2) provides that regulations may be made which would enable a court to dispense with such a consent in certain specified circumstances but the CR do not make any such provision. In addition, where the unit is charged, the consent of the charge-holder must also be obtained in writing prior to the amendment being made (s.24(1) and (2)). If land is added to the commonhold unit, the charge is deemed to be extended to apply to the unit in its extended form (s.24.(5)).

It should also be noted that an addition to a commonhold unit will often include the taking of land which would otherwise belong to the CA as part of the common parts. Clearly, in order to avoid a potential claim in trespass, the CA will additionally be required to consent to the alteration.

The standard form of CCS, at paragraph 4.6, places a restriction on alterations only upon the CA in relation to the common parts. No alteration may be made to the common parts unless the proposed alteration is approved by the CA by ordinary resolution.

There is nothing in the CCS which prevents a unit-holder from altering his unit. This may be a matter of concern to a CA and there are good grounds for a CA seeking to impose restrictions on unit-holders in Appendix 4 (which imposes local rules) of a CCS. First, a CA may be concerned to retain an aesthetic uniformity across a commonhold development. Second, where the commonhold units are dependent upon each other for support, for instance in the case of a block of flats, a mechanism for controlling alterations will be necessary. Finally, it may be necessary to control alterations if the commonhold environment is such that noisy works of alteration might be a disturbance to unit-holders, for instance in a sheltered housing scheme.

Clearly, it will be a matter for the CA in deciding how much latitude to allow unit-holders in altering their units. For instance, if aesthetic uniformity is the principal concern, it would be overly restrictive to prohibit any alteration to the commonhold units which would inadvertently restrict unseen internal alterations. Similarly, in the case of a block of flats, a blanket prohibition on alteration might catch internal alterations which have no structural significance whatsoever.

One suggested compromise is that the CCS could contain a provision requiring the consent of the CA for any alteration to a commonhold unit. A similar provision was suggested in the Government's first draft of the CCS (October 2002) whereby the consent of the Board of Directors of the CA was required (paragraph 27).

10.6 ALIENATION

The rules governing the alienation of commonhold units are detailed in **Chapter 12** but this section will provide an overview of the relevant provisions.

The Government made it very clear throughout the passage of the draft Bill through the legislative process that it was to be a feature of the commonhold estate in land that there would be no prohibition on the transfer of commonhold units. That principle is enshrined in section 15(2) of the Act in which it is provided that the CCS may not prevent or restrict the transfer of a commonhold unit. The provision applies to any transfer of a unit (s.15(1)):

- whether or not for consideration;
- whether or not subject to any reservations or other terms;
- whether or not by operation of law.

It follows that, unlike most situations in a leasehold system, the consent of the CA is not required prior to a transfer of a commonhold unit. The CA cannot, therefore, apply any leverage in respect of unpaid commonhold assessment.

When a unit is transferred, a right or obligation conferred or imposed by the CCS will apply to the new unit-holder in the same way as it applied to the former unit-holder (s.16(1)). A former unit-holder will not acquire any liability or any right arising from the CCS (s.16(2)) without prejudice to any rights or liabilities accruing prior to the relevant transfer (s.16(3)(b)). The parties may not vary or disapply that important provision by agreement (s.16(3)(a)).

Accordingly, a unit-holder who transfers his unit will not be liable for any future commonhold assessment though he will be liable for assessments already accrued at the date of the transfer. Upon the transfer, the transferee becomes liable for future commonhold assessments. However, notably, the transferee will also become liable for the debts of his predecessor.

The CA's consent in writing is required, however, where only part of a unit is proposed to be transferred (s.21(2)(c)). A transfer of part of a commonhold unit without first obtaining such a consent is of no effect (s.21). Such a consent requires a special resolution of the CA (s.21(8)). One important factor in deciding whether consent should be given to a transfer of part of a unit is the potential for changes to the percentages by which the commonhold assessments are levied. The division of the commonhold unit will inevitably lead to the creation of a new commonhold unit (s.21(9)(a)) or the addition of the divided unit to an existing commonhold unit (s.21(9)(b)). Either of those possibilities may well give rise to a variation in the appropriate percentages for commonhold assessment levies and presumably, consent might be made conditional upon the agreement of the revised percentages.

It is a further consequence of the fact that the consent of the CA is not required for a transfer of a unit, that a unit may be transferred without it necessarily coming to the attention of the CA. This would not aid the practical administration of the commonhold and consequently, the Act makes provision for the new unit-holder to notify the CA that the transfer has taken place. The new unit-holder must notify the CA of the transfer upon the transfer taking place (s.15(3)).

This statutory provision is expanded upon in the prescribed CCS which provides, at paragraph 4.7.8, that where a person becomes entitled to be registered as the proprietor of the freehold estate in any commonhold unit, he must notify the CA on Form 10 within 14 days, beginning with the date upon which he became entitled to be registered. Paragraph 4.7.9 provides that if the transfer takes effect by operation of law, the notification on Form 12 must take place within 14 days of the person becoming entitled to be registered becoming aware of that entitlement.

Following the transfer of the unit, the CA may require the new unit-holder to pay any commonhold assessment, reserve fund payment or interest due on either of those two sums which was outstanding from his predecessor (paragraph 4.7.3). The CA must give notice to the new unit-holder requiring him to pay those sums. The unit-holder then has 14 days within which to pay the outstanding sums (paragraph 4.7.5). If payment is not made, then interest must be paid on the outstanding sums at the prescribed rate (paragraph 4.7.6). The prescribed rate is the rate specified in Paragraph 1 of Annex 4 to the CCS. Once the new unit-holder has made payment of the outstanding debt, the right to collect the outstanding sums is deemed to have been assigned to him (paragraph 4.7.7).

A unit-holder may attempt to crystallise and to limit the extent of his liability to the CA by requesting information as to his liabilities in a commonhold unit information certificate (paragraph 4.7.1). If such a notice is served, the CA must then provide an information certificate to the unit-holder within 14 days of the date of service of the notice. The information must be in Form 9 which shows the amount outstanding and a breakdown of how that figure is calculated (paragraph 4.7.2).

If a commonhold unit information certificate has been provided to a unit-holder who then transfers his unit, the new unit-holder cannot be required to pay more than the amount specified in the certificate for the period covered by the certificate (paragraph 4.7.4). In this way, the unit-holder seeking to transfer his unit can provide comfort to a prospective purchaser that there are no 'hidden' expenses for which the prospective purchaser will be made liable.

It is a requirement of the CML Lenders' Handbook that mortgage lenders must ensure that they obtain a commonhold unit information certificate and ensure that all of the commonhold assessment in respect of the property has been paid up to the date of completion.

10.6.1 Letting of a commonhold unit

The commonhold regime was implemented, at least in part, to avoid the worst excesses of long leasehold tenure. Indeed, upon conversion of a freehold into a commonhold, existing leasehold interests are extinguished (s.7(3)(d) and s.9(3)(f)). Under the Act, the bare bones of a prohibition on letting is provided for. For a residential commonhold unit, no leasehold interest can be created in the unit unless certain conditions are satisfied (s.17(1)). A residential unit is defined in section 17(5) as a unit which, according to the CCS, can be used only for residential purposes or for residential and other incidental purposes.

The conditions themselves are to be found in regulation 11(1) of the CR, which provides that a tenancy in a residential unit may not be granted:

- for a premium;
- for a term of more than 7 years unless the conditions set out in regulation 11(2) are satisfied;
- under an option or agreement if:

  - the person to take the new lease has an existing term of years absolute of the premises to be let;
  - the new lease when added to the existing term will be more than 7 years; and
  - the option or agreement was entered into before or at the same time as the existing tenancy;

- which contains an option or agreement to renew the term which confers on either party to the tenancy an option or agreement for renewal of the tenancy which, together with the original term, amounts to more than 7 years;
- which contains an option or agreement to extend the existing tenancy beyond 7 years;

- which contains a provision requiring the tenant to make payments to the CA in discharge of payments which are due, in accordance with the CCS, from the unit-holder (reg.11(1)(f)).

It should be noted that each of these conditions is also set out in the prescribed form of CCS at paragraph 4.7.11.

The circumstances in which a term of more than 7 years may be granted are that a term of not more than 21 years may be granted to the holder of a lease which has been extinguished under section 11(2) if that new lease:

- is granted of the same premises as are comprised in the extinguished lease;
- is granted on the same terms as the extinguished lease except to the extent necessary to comply with the Act and the CR;
- is granted at the same rent as was payable under the extinguished lease as at the date of its extinguishment subject to the same rent review provisions as were contained in that lease;
- is granted for a term equivalent to the unexpired term of the lease immediately before it was extinguished or for 21 years, whichever is the shorter;
- takes effect immediately after the existing lease was extinguished;
- does not include any option or agreement which:

  - may create a term or an extension to a term which, together with the existing term, would amount to more than 21 years; or
  - may result in the grant of a lease containing an option or agreement to extend the term.

If a unit-holder purports to create a tenancy of a residential unit which does not comply with these requirements, the tenancy is of no effect (s.17(3)). However, section 17(4) does provide some relief for the 'tenant' in such a situation, providing that a party to an invalid instrument or agreement may apply to the court for an order:

- providing for the instrument or agreement to have effect as if it provided for the creation of a term of years of a specified kind;
- providing for the return or payment of money;
- making such other provision as the court thinks appropriate.

Presumably, using these provisions, the court may order that a lease of, say, 10 years which would be invalid under the Act, should take effect as if it was a lease of 7 years so as to comply with the Act.

The same regulatory regime does not apply to commonhold units which are not residential units (s.18). The only prohibitions relating to the letting of non-residential units are contained in the CCS.

Section 19 of the Act provides that regulations may impose wide-ranging obligations upon the tenants of units or may enable such regulations to be imposed by the CCS. However, notwithstanding the inclusion of such regulations in earlier drafts of the commonhold regulations, the CR make no provisions imposing obligations upon tenants. Such provisions are left to the CCS in paragraph 4.1.2 where the prescribed form makes it clear that the rules contained in the CCS will, where those rules so state, bind a tenant of a commonhold unit. A reference to a 'tenant', where there are joint tenants, is a reference to each of the joint tenants and also to the tenants together (paragraph 1.4.3).

The CCS also includes provision for the unit-holder to be responsible for the liabilities of his tenant. If a tenant fails to comply with a duty which, according to the CCS, is imposed both on the tenant and on the unit-holder, the CA may serve a notice on the unit-holder requiring him to reimburse the CA for its losses (paragraph 4.7.20). The unit-holder then has 14 days within which to comply (paragraph 4.7.21). Presumably, the unit-holder will then be entitled to seek redress from the tenant.

Prior to the grant of a tenancy of a commonhold unit, the prospective landlord must give two documents to the prospective tenant (paragraph 4.7.12). They are:

- a copy of the CCS including any plans which are relevant to that commonhold unit;
- a notice in Form 13 informing the prospective tenant that he will be required to comply with those paragraphs in the CCS which will impose duties upon him if he takes the tenancy.

If the prospective landlord fails to comply with these provisions and, as a result, the tenant suffers a loss as a result of obligations in the CCS being enforced against him, the tenant may serve a notice on the landlord requiring the landlord to reimburse him for that loss unless the relevant obligation is also reproduced in the tenancy agreement itself (paragraph 4.7.13). If such a notice is served, the landlord must reimburse the tenant within 14 days of the date of service of the notice (paragraph 4.7.14).

Notification of a letting

Because the tenant may have obligations under the CCS and because the consent of the CA is not required to a letting of a commonhold unit, it will be important for the CA to have notice of a letting of a commonhold unit. The prescribed CCS provides at paragraph 4.7.15, that within 14 days from the grant of a tenancy, the unit-holder or tenant (in the case of a sub-tenancy) who grants the tenancy must serve a notice in Form 14 on the CA and must provide a copy of any written tenancy agreement or give details of any oral tenancy.

Assignment of a tenancy

The CCS also makes provisions concerning the assignment of a tenancy of a commonhold unit. The provisions echo those relating to the initial grant of the tenancy. Paragraph 4.7.16 states that, prior to the assignment of the tenancy, the tenant must provide to the prospective assignee the same documentation as he was provided with by the unit-holder. Form 15 must be used. Similar provisions also apply relating to the consequences of a failure to serve the appropriate documents (paragraphs 4.7.17 and 4.7.18). Within 14 days of the date of the assignment, the new tenant must inform the CA using Form 16 that the assignment has been completed (paragraph 4.7.19).

10.7 USER

The Act makes provision for the prescribed CCS to contain restrictions upon the manner in which commonhold units (s.14(1)) and the common parts (s.26(a)) may be used. It is notable that these restrictions are very limited in their scope and are confined to prohibiting uses other than those specifically permitted by the CCS. This can be contrasted with the original draft version of the CCS which sought to impose a raft of restrictions on use. Most of these prohibitions had been abandoned by the time of the August 2003 draft and all had been abandoned in favour of a more flexible approach in the final prescribed CCS.

The CCS provides, at paragraph 4.3.1, that a commonhold unit may not be used other than in accordance with its permitted use as specified in Paragraph 2 of Annex 4 to the CCS. It is incumbent upon the parties to the commonhold, therefore, to set out in Annex 4 the uses which will be permitted in respect of each unit. The relevant form in Annex 4 does not provide any restriction on the manner in which the permitted use of a commonhold unit may be restricted. It will be a matter, therefore, for the relevant parties to the commonhold to decide whether they wish the restrictions to be wide, for instance specifying only that the units be residential or non-residential (which has implications for lettings, see above) or whether they wish to restrict user more severely, limiting specific units to very specific uses. In cases of commonholds containing a significant amount of commercial property, the CA might find it useful to attempt to restrict the user of each commonhold unit so as to encourage non-competing trades in a manner not unlike the landlord and tenant regime.

One question which might arise is whether it might be lawful to restrict the use of commonhold units to a particular class of persons, for instance, retired persons or persons over a certain age in the case of a sheltered housing commonhold. Whilst it is undoubtedly the case that it would be unlawful to discriminate against a group of persons on the grounds of race or religion, there is no reason contained in the commonhold legislation itself which would prevent such a restriction on use. However, there is a small possibility that such a restriction would fall foul of Article 14 in Part I of Schedule 1 to the Human Rights Act 1998 which might arguably prevent discrimination against the enjoyment of an individual's home based upon their 'status' as a person who must be older than a certain age.

The CCS also provides, at paragraph 4.3.2, that a unit-holder or tenant may not use the common parts other than in accordance with their permitted use as specified in Paragraphs 3 and 4 of Annex 4 or other than in accordance with the rights specified in Paragraph 6 of Annex 2. Notably, there is no restriction placed upon the use of the common parts by the CA.

Paragraph 3 of Annex 4 to the CCS provides for a general statement concerning the use of the common parts.

Paragraph 4 of Annex 4 provides for limited use areas. These areas are designed to be parts of the common parts in respect of which it is intended that there should be no general right of amenity. These might be, for instance, plant rooms, storage areas, parking spaces or garden areas. Paragraph 4 enables the CA to specify the limited use area in question both by describing it and by reference to the plan forming part of the CCS. The paragraph will then identify the authorised users of the particular area and the authorised use which they are entitled to make of the area. Plant rooms might be limited, for instance, to the CA itself for the purposes of security and maintenance. Storage areas and parking spaces might be allocated to particular unit-holders.

Paragraph 6 of Annex 2 to the CCS identifies the rights of the unit-holders over the common parts. Clearly, it is axiomatic that the unit-holders be entitled to use the common parts in such a manner as to be consistent with those rights. So, for instance, if the unit-holders have a right to park vehicles on a part of the common parts, their parking of vehicles on that area cannot be said to be an unlawful use of that part of the common parts.

It is a requirement of the CML Lenders' Handbook that mortgage lenders must ensure that the CCS does not include any material restrictions on occupation or use.

10.8 INSURANCE

The Act makes provision for the prescribed CCS to contain obligations in relation to the manner in which commonhold units (s.14(2)) and the common parts (s.26(b)) are to be insured. Clearly, it is in the interests of all members of the CA that each of the commonhold units and the common parts be adequately insured. However, a very different approach has been taken to the position relating to common parts and the position relating to commonhold units.

So far as the common parts are concerned, the prescribed CCS imposes, in paragraph 4.4.1, an obligation upon the CA to insure the common parts to their full rebuilding and reinstatement value against loss or damage by fire and such other risks as are specified in Paragraph 5 of Annex 4 of the CCS. The other risks against which the CA will insure will largely be dictated by the insurance market, the nature of the commonhold and the use to which the common parts might be put. It should be noted that, unlike the original draft CCS circulated by the government, the final version contains no provisions detailing the manner in which the full rebuilding and reinstatement value of the common parts is to be calculated. Presumably, it was felt that CAs would probably be sensible enough to adequately insure their own properties.

In the event of the destruction of, or damage, to the common parts as a result of an insured risk, the CA is under an obligation to use the proceeds of the insurance taken out for the purpose of rebuilding or reinstating the common parts (paragraph 4.4.2).

The CA is also under an obligation to keep details of the insurance of the common parts and evidence of the payment of the most recent insurance premium. The records may be kept at the registered office of the CA or at such other place as the directors of the CA shall think fit (paragraph 4.4.3). A unit-holder has the right to inspect the insurance policy for the common parts upon reasonable notice and at a reasonable time and place (paragraph 4.4.4). If the unit-holder pays the CA's reasonable charges, which might conceivably include copying and administration charges, the unit-holder is entitled to a copy of the insurance policy (paragraph 4.4.4). If a request is made to the CA for a copy of the insurance policy, then, as soon as reasonably practicable after the payment of the association's charges, the CA must provide a copy of the insurance policy to the unit-holder (paragraph 4.4.5).

This regulation of the CA's obligation to insure can be contrasted with the flexibility of the approach adopted in respect of the commonhold units themselves. In the original draft CCS and even in the later August 2003 draft, obligations were imposed upon unit-holders to insure their commonhold units (there were even requirements to take out contents insurance). In the final prescribed CCS, a flexible approach, similar to that adopted in relation to the user of the units, has been adopted instead (paragraph 4.4.6). The parties to the commonhold are free to impose whatever duties they see fit on the unit-holders concerning the insurance of their units. Those duties are to be set out at Paragraph 6 of Annex 4 to the CCS. It is likely that the CA will seek to impose an obligation upon the unit-holders to insure their units along very similar lines to the obligations imposed on the CA in respect of the common parts. It is quite possible that the CA might, particularly where units are within close proximity of each other, wish to reserve a right for the CA to insure units in default of the unit-holder insuring them.

119

It is a requirement of the CML Lenders' Handbook that mortgage lenders must ensure that the CA has obtained insurance for the common parts which complies with the CML's requirements.

10.9 FINANCIAL ISSUES

The CA is responsible for the management of the commonhold. In order to do so effectively, the CA requires the ability to recover funds from its members. The CA is responsible for the budgeting of the expenditure in operating the commonhold and for recovery of that expenditure, whether incurred or yet to be incurred.

The Act splits the costs of operating the commonhold into two parts. The day-to-day expenditure in running the commonhold including minor repairs, insurance, housekeeping and day-to-day administration, is referred to in section 38 as the 'commonhold assessment'. Major items of expenditure such as the renewal of the fabric of the common parts are dealt with and budgeted separately and are known as the 'reserve fund' in section 39.

The actual administration of the commonhold assessment and the reserve fund is placed in the hands of the directors of the CA. However, members of the CA have the ability to approve the commonhold's budgets and in this manner, will have a degree of direct control over the way in which their resources are utilised.

The commonhold assessment and reserve fund are, in many respects, similar to the landlord and tenant concept of service charges. However, unlike the way in which the law has developed in relation to service charges with a proliferation of legislation and regulation, mostly designed to protect the lessee from the unscrupulous lessor, the commonhold system of commonhold assessment and reserve fund are relatively untouched by regulation. This is because, as freeholders of their commonhold units, there is less scope for pressure to be exerted upon unit-holders by means of the potential for forfeiting their interests and because, as members of the CA which is the legal person responsible for the management of the commonhold, it is thought that it will be in the interests of all members of the CA to work together for the common good. Experience of lessee-owned or lessee-managed blocks of leasehold flats where all parties equally ought to be pulling together makes one sceptical about whether this faith in the system will be well founded.

10.10 COMMONHOLD ASSESSMENT

10.10.1 Budgeting

Section 38 of the Act requires the CCS to make provision for the budgeting and recovery of the commonhold assessment. In particular, section 38(1) requires the CCS to make provision:

- requiring the directors of the CA to make an annual estimate of the income required to be raised from unit-holders to meet the expenses of the CA;
- enabling the directors of the CA to make estimates from time to time of the income required to be raised from unit-holders in addition to the annual estimate;
- specifying the percentage of any estimate which is to be allocated to each unit;
- requiring each unit-holder to make payments in respect of the percentage of any estimate which is allocated to his unit;
- requiring the directors of the CA to serve notices on unit-holders specifying payments required to be made by them and the date on which each payment is due.

When specifying percentages to be allocated to each unit, the CA must ensure that the percentages allocated to the commonhold units must aggregate to 100 per cent (s.38(2)(a)). Notwithstanding that, section 38(2)(b) also makes it clear that the CA may choose to allocate a percentage of nil to a particular commonhold unit. The percentage allocated to each unit in respect of the commonhold assessment is set out in Paragraph 1 of Annex 3 to the CCS (paragraph 3.2.1).

The rules built into the prescribed CCS broadly follow section 38(1). Paragraph 4.2.1 provides that the directors of the CA must make an annual estimate of the income required to be raised from unit-holders to meet the expenses of the CA and may from time to time make estimates of the income required to be raised from unit-holders in addition to the annual estimate.

It will be incumbent upon the directors of the CA at an early stage to prepare a budget for each financial year that estimates the amount of routine expenditure anticipated for the next financial year and which takes into account income to meet such expenditure from sources other than the unit-holders. This income might derive from, for instance, investments or the letting of units retained by the CA. Because the budget must be prepared at an early stage and almost certainly at a time before the current financial year has come to an end, the directors will not know with certainty the expenditure for the current year nor whether the income generated from unit-holders and other sources has been sufficient to cover it. An element of estimation is inevitable but should be possible by using information accrued from previous years and expert advice.

Once the directors have completed the budget, if they consider that it is necessary to recover expenses from the unit-holders, they must serve each unit-holder with a notice containing details of the proposed commonhold assessment (paragraph 4.2.2). The notice must be in Form 1. The notice requires the CA to provide the proposed assessment for the commonhold – that is to say, the aggregate figure which the CA estimates will have to be recovered from the unit-holders, the percentage allocated to the unit-holder's unit and (in figures and words) the amount of the proposed assessment allocated to the unit-holder's unit. The notice then requires the CA to set out details of the amounts and dates of payments which the unit-holder will be required to make. CAs will no doubt have it in mind that they are more likely to be successful in recovering the assessment if its payment is made more palatable to the unit-holders by splitting into, say, two or four tranches over the course of the year.

Each unit-holder then has a period of one month from the date of service of the notice to make written representations to the CA regarding the amount of the proposed assessment (paragraph 4.2.3). Whilst that would theoretically include the percentage allocated to each individual unit, such a percentage will normally be fixed from the outset and it is unlikely, in the absence of changes to the composition of the commonhold, that percentages allocated will be the subject of any alteration. The notice on Form 1 must provide details of how the unit-holder may make representations (this might include fax numbers or email addresses to which representations can be sent) though representations must be in writing. The directors of the CA are then obliged to consider any representations made by a unit-holder (paragraph 4.2.4).

Having considered the representations, if the directors still require any unit-holder to make a contribution towards the assessment, a further notice requiring payment must be served on each unit-holder (paragraph 4.2.4). This notice must be on Form 2. The notice must once again specify the payments which are required and the date upon which each payment is due to be paid. The notice must not specify a date for payment to be made which is within 14 days of the date of service of the notice (paragraph 4.2.4).

The only exception to this procedure is where the CA requires income to meet its expenditure in an 'emergency'. In those circumstances, the directors of the CA may serve a notice on each unit-holder requiring payment of the commonhold assessment without seeking any representations from the unit-holders in advance (paragraph 4.2.5). Such a notice must be on Form 3. The word 'emergency' is not defined in the CCS. It is likely that the circumstances in which it will apply will be relatively narrow and will be confined to genuine emergencies rather than situations where, with better planning, contingencies could have been put in place to meet the situation. It is unlikely, therefore, that such a procedure could come to the aid of the CA if it merely required monies quickly to meet outstanding invoices.

10.10.2 Recovery

The CCS provides, at paragraph 4.2.16, that a unit-holder must pay to the CA the amount which is allocated to his unit in accordance with a notice given to him. Although it is not stated expressly, it is implicit in this provision that the payment must be made on or before the date specified for payment in the relevant notice.

If a payment which is due to the CA is not made on or before the date upon which it is due, the unit-holder is liable to pay interest at the prescribed rate on the unpaid sum for the period beginning with the date upon which the payment became due and ending on the date upon which payment is actually made (paragraph 4.2.17). The prescribed rate is the rate which has been prescribed by the CA in Paragraph 1 of Annex 4 to the CCS (paragraph 1.4.5). Unlike most leases, the CCS gives the unit-holder no leeway in paying the assessment otherwise than on time before the liability for interest arises.

Diversion of rent

If a unit-holder has failed to pay the commonhold assessment and his unit is let, the CCS makes provision for the CA to recover the sums due from the tenant. The tenant is defined for these purposes as the only immediate tenant of the unit-holder who has failed to pay (paragraph 4.2.17). The CA can recover the sums due from the tenant by diverting the rent due to the unit-holder from that tenant, a provision not unlike section 6 of the Law of Distress Amendment Act 1908. The CA may give a notice to the tenant (which must be on Form 6 and a copy of which must also be given to the unit-holder) requiring the tenant to divert to the CA all or part of the rent payable to the unit-holder from time to time until the CA has recovered an equivalent sum to the amount due from the unit-holder (paragraph 4.2.18).

The notice must specify the payments which the tenant is required to make. The notice cannot require the tenant to make a payment which is greater than the amount of the rent which he would otherwise be required to make under the tenancy agreement or to pay rent earlier than it is due under the tenancy agreement (paragraph 4.2.19). So, for instance, if the tenant pays £500 per month by way of rent, the notice of diversion cannot require the tenant to pay more than £500 in any month or to pay the sum earlier than it would fall due under the tenancy agreement. The CA will, of course, have received notification of the terms of the tenancy at the time of the letting (paragraph 4.7.15) but can also give notice to any party to a tenancy on Form 8 requesting details of the length of the tenancy and the rent payable under the tenancy. The details requested must be provided on Part B of Form 8 within 14 days of the date of service of the notice (paragraphs 4.2.41–4.2.42).

If a diversion notice is served on a tenant, he is obliged to make the payments required by the notice (see paragraph 4.2.20). If the notice does not specify a later date for the first payment to be made, the first payment must be made to the CA on the next date, after the diversion date, upon which rent would fall due to be paid to the unit-holder under the tenancy agreement (paragraph 4.2.21). The diversion date is defined as the date upon which a period of 14 days, beginning with the date upon which the diversion notice is served, comes to an end (paragraph 4.2.17).

Once all of the arrears of assessment have been recovered by the diversion of rent, the CA must, within a period of 14 days from the date upon which all of the payments required by the notice have been made, notify the tenant and the unit-holder that the diversion of rent has ended (paragraph 4.2.22). There is no prescribed form for this notification.

The CCS confirms the effect which payments made under such a diversion will have. A payment made by the tenant in accordance with a notice served upon him will discharge the liability of the unit-holder for the amount which he has failed to pay to the CA and the liability of the tenant to pay rent to the unit-holder under the tenancy agreement to the extent of the payment made (paragraph 4.2.24). The unit-holder is deemed to have received and accepted the rent paid under the notice and it is not open to him to forfeit the tenancy or to bring any claim for breach of covenant or condition in the tenancy agreement for non-payment of the rent deemed to have been paid (paragraph 4.2.25).

If the tenant fails to pay a sum due under the notice, the tenant is liable to the CA for interest on the unpaid sum at the prescribed rate for the period beginning with the date upon which the payment is due and ending on the date when the payment is made (paragraph 4.2.26). The prescribed rate is the rate which has been prescribed by the CA in Paragraph 1 of Annex 4 to the CCS (paragraph 1.4.5). It would appear that this interest becomes due over and above the sums payable under the notice and that the payments of interest will not be used to reduce the sum due from the tenant designed to reduce the arrears of assessment from the unit-holder.

The tenant is not entitled to rely upon any non-statutory right of deduction, set off or counterclaim which he has against the unit-holder to reduce the amount to be paid to the CA (paragraph 4.2.23). This seems harsh on the tenant who is obliged to make payment to the CA notwithstanding that he may have a perfectly legitimate counterclaim against the unit-holder. The unit-holder can have his liability to the CA extinguished by payments made by the tenant even though the tenant may have a good counterclaim against him which would outweigh the sums due to him under the lease.

These rules relating to diversion of the rent payable by the tenant to the unit-holder are then repeated, in almost identical terms, for a diversion of rent payable by a sub-tenant to the tenant where the tenant has failed to pay sums to the CA in the event of a diversion notice being served on the tenant (paragraphs 4.2.28–4.2.37).

If the tenant fails to pay sums which are due under the diversion notice (or interest due as discussed above), the CA may serve a notice on a sub-tenant requiring the sub-tenant to pay to the CA the rent which he would otherwise be liable to pay to the tenant pursuant to the terms of the sub-tenancy until such times as the sub-tenant has paid an amount equivalent to the sum due from the tenant (paragraph 4.2.28). This sum may be a different sum from the sum due from the unit-holder who is in default. Interest may also be due from the defaulting tenant pursuant to paragraph 4.2.26. The notice served by the CA must be in Form 7 and it must also be served on the unit-holder and the tenant. The sub-tenant is defined as meaning only the immediate tenant of the tenant who has failed to pay (paragraph 4.2.27).

Under paragraph 4.2.34 a payment made by a sub-tenant pursuant to such a notice therefore has the effect of discharging the liability of:

- the unit-holder for the amount he has failed to pay to the CA;
- the tenant for the payment which he ought to have made to the CA pursuant to the original diversion notice;
- the tenant for the payment of rent to the unit-holder which would otherwise have fallen due under the tenancy agreement;
- the sub-tenant for the payment of rent to the tenant which would otherwise have fallen due under the sub-tenancy.

Unsurprisingly, the same procedure can then be applied along a chain of sub-tenancies. A generic provision states that 'paragraphs 4.2.28 to 4.2.37 may be applied with necessary modifications as against the immediate tenant of that sub-tenant and so on' (paragraph 4.2.38). There is therefore no limit placed upon recovery of the commonhold assessment based upon the remoteness of the interest of the individual from whom payment may be sought from the CA.

If a tenant or sub-tenant (see the definition of 'tenant' in paragraph 1.4.5) suffers any loss as a result of a payment being made to the CA pursuant to a diversion notice, then he can serve a notice on the unit-holder requiring the unit-holder to reimburse him for that loss (paragraph 4.2.39). The unit-holder must reimburse the tenant or sub-tenant within 14 days of the date upon which that notice is served upon him (s.39). Ordinarily, of course, the tenant or sub-tenant will not suffer a loss as he cannot be made to pay any greater sum than that which he would be obliged to pay pursuant to his tenancy agreement in any event.

10.11   RESERVE FUND

The Act additionally provides that the CCS may make provision for the budgeting and recovery of a reserve fund (s.39). In particular, s.39(1) provides that the CCS may make provision:

- requiring the directors of the CA to establish and maintain one or more funds to finance the repair and maintenance of the common parts;
- requiring the directors of the CA to establish and maintain one or more funds to finance the repair and maintenance of the commonhold units.

Although the language used is permissory rather than mandatory, there is little doubt that every CCS will contain requirements for the establishment of reserve funds.

Where the CA chooses to make such provision in the CCS, it must also make provision (s.39(2)):

- requiring or enabling the directors of the CA to set a levy from time to time;
- specifying the percentage of any levy which is to be allocated to each unit;
- requiring each unit-holder to make payments in respect of the percentage of any levy which is allocated to his unit;
- requiring the directors of the CA to serve notices on unit-holders specifying payments required to be made by them and the date on which each payment is due.

When specifying percentages to be allocated to each unit, the CA must ensure that the percentages allocated to the commonhold units must aggregate to 100 per cent (s.39(3)(a)). Notwithstanding that, the Act also makes it clear that the CA may choose to allocate a percentage of nil to a particular commonhold unit (s.39(3)(b)). The percentage allocated to each commonhold unit in respect of the reserve fund levy is set out in Paragraph 2 of Annex 3 to the CCS (paragraph 3.3.1).

In the landlord and tenant regime, service charges including any reserve fund must be held by the landlord on trust for the lessees (Landlord and Tenant Act 1987, s.42). However, the Government decided that because the persons paying monies into the reserve fund will all be members of the CA, the monies paid into the reserve fund will be adequately protected by company law and that there was no need for a further statutory trust to be imposed although it would be open to the CA to introduce such a requirement as a local law.

The Act does include one safeguard, however, providing that the assets of a reserve fund shall not be used for the purpose of enforcement of any debt except a judgment debt referable to a reserve fund activity (s.39(4)). An asset is used for the purpose of enforcement of a debt if, in particular, it is taken in execution or is made the subject of a charging order under section 1 of the

Charging Orders Act 1979 (s.39(5)(b) of the Act). A reserve fund activity is defined as an activity which can be financed from a reserve fund in accordance with the CCS (s.39(5)(a)).

The prescribed CCS contains a regime for the reserve fund which differs from that in place for the commonhold assessment. The directors of the CA must consider whether to commission a reserve study by an appropriately qualified person in the first year in which the commonhold is registered (paragraph 4.2.6). A reserve study is an inspection of the common parts in order to advise the directors of the CA whether or not it is appropriate to establish or maintain a reserve fund (paragraph 1.4.5). Two points should be noted. First, there is no requirement placed upon the directors to have a reserve study in the first year of the commonhold. They must merely consider it as an option. For a new-built development where major (as opposed to routine) maintenance may not be countenanced for, say, 15 or 20 years, it may be felt that to carry out a reserve study and to establish a fund as early as the first year of the commonhold will be too early. Clearly, circumstances will vary from commonhold to commonhold. Second, the reserve study is a study of only the common parts and not the commonhold units. This is notwithstanding the fact that it is open to the CA to set up a reserve fund for the commonhold units (s.39(1)(b)).

Even if they decide not to have a reserve study carried out in the first year of the commonhold, the directors are required to commission such a study by an appropriately qualified person at least once in every 10 years (paragraph 4.2.7). Although the paragraph of the CCS does not say so, the period of 10 years would appear to be measured from the registration of the commonhold. There is nothing to stop the directors commissioning such studies more frequently if so desired.

Once a study has been commissioned and carried out, the directors are obliged to consider the results of the study with a view to deciding whether to establish a reserve fund and thereafter, whether to maintain such a fund. If they decide, having considered the matter, that it is appropriate to establish or maintain such a fund, then they are obliged to do so (paragraph 4.2.8). Further, the directors must then reconsider the position at 'appropriate intervals' in order to decide whether to establish or maintain an existing reserve fund. Again, if they consider that it is appropriate to do so, then they are obliged to do so (paragraph 4.2.9).

If the directors decide against the establishment of a reserve fund, the members of the CA can force their hand. The members may require the directors to set up such a fund by an ordinary resolution (paragraph 4.2.10).

Once a fund has been established, the directors are responsible for setting a levy to be imposed on the unit-holders according to the percentages set out in Paragraph 2 of Annex 3. When setting the levy, the directors must 'try to ensure' that unnecessary reserves are not accumulated (paragraph 4.2.11). This phrase is extraordinarily vague and it will be interesting to see whether members are able to challenge the directors of their CAs on the basis that they were not 'trying' hard enough to ensure that unnecessary revenues were not accumulated.

Notice of the proposed levy must then be given to each unit-holder on Form 4 (paragraph 4.2.12). In a similar fashion to the commonhold assessment, each unit-holder then has one month from the date of service of that notice to make written representations to the CA regarding the amount of the levy (paragraph 4.2.13). Whilst that would theoretically include the percentage allocated to each individual unit, such a percentage will normally be fixed from the outset and it is unlikely that, in the absence of changes to the composition of the commonhold, percentages allocated will be the subject of any alteration.

Having considered the representations, if the directors still require any unit-holder to make a payment towards the reserve fund, a further notice requiring payment must be served on each unit-holder (paragraph 4.2.14). This notice must be on Form 5. The notice must once again specify the payments which are required from the unit-holder and the date upon which each payment is due to be paid. The notice must not specify a date for payment to be made which is within 14 days of the date of service of the notice (paragraph 4.2.14).

Thereafter, the rules concerning payments of the levy towards the reserve fund are the same as the rules concerning payments of the commonhold assessment (paragraphs 4.2.15–4.2.42).

10.12 SUMMARY

By and large, Parliament's settled approach to management of commonhold developments has been to leave the vast majority of management issues to be determined by the parties to the commonhold itself, in stark contrast, it must be said, to earlier drafts of the legislation and associated prescribed documents. This attitude benefits from allowing the greatest flexibility to the parties but has the potential pitfalls of careless drafting of documents leaving lacunae in the regulation of the management of the commonhold and the potential for disputes concerning the construction of documents.

CHAPTER 11

Commonhold and taxes

Laurence Target

11.1 BACKGROUND

Taxation is a specialised area where it is always dangerous for the non-specialist to dabble. Involvement with commonhold will give rise to many occasions on which proper tax treatment of the persons, property and transactions involved will need to be decided. What follows can only be a rough guide to some of the questions that will need to be asked and answered. There is helpful commentary in the Land Registry's Practice Guide 60.

11.2 STAMP DUTY LAND TAX

11.2.1 Introduction

Stamp Duty Land Tax (SDLT) is a new tax which was introduced by the Finance Act 2003 (FA 2003) to replace stamp duty. Unlike stamp duty, it is not a tax on the documents by which transactions creating or dealing with estates and other interests in land are effected. It is instead a tax on the transactions themselves. SDLT cannot be regarded in any sense as a voluntary tax. It is not sanctioned by the inadmissibility of unstamped documents as evidence, but is backed by a positive requirement that the taxpayer should submit an SDLT return. When dealing with a freehold estate or a leasehold estate (regardless of whether it exists at law or only in equity) an SDLT return is compulsory if there has been any consideration in money or money's worth. When dealing with any other interest in land an SDLT return need only be made when the consideration given exceeds £120,000 in the case of residential property and £150,000 in the case of non-residential property.

There are many reliefs, and they will be applicable to commonhold land and to the estates and interests arising out of commonhold land in the same way as to dealings with other freehold land and dealings with estates and interests arising out of other freehold land. Practitioners should refer to specialist works for any detailed guidance.

Practitioners will also need to be alert to their duties in relation to money laundering. Since it is an offence not to make an SDLT return when one is required, and not to pay the tax when it is payable, it will be all too easy for practitioners to find themselves involved in arrangements which involve the retention of the proceeds of crime and thus put themselves at risk of committing criminal offences. Practitioners should either be sure that the returns will be made and that the SDLT will be paid, or notify the appropriate authorities, usually the National Criminal Intelligence Service (NCIS).

SDLT will arise on transactions with units and interests derivative from units in the same way as it will arise in relation to the common parts and transactions derivative from the common parts.

11.2.2   Registration without unit-holders

There should be no question of any liability for SDLT on conversion of land to commonhold and the Land Registry will not require any SDLT return certificate in relation to an application for conversion. It is only if there have been transactions that SDLT may need to be paid.

On registration without unit-holders the freehold both in the units and the common parts remains with the applicant, and thus there is no land transaction. On the sale of the first unit there clearly is a land transaction: the buyer of the first unit will have to notify and pay tax on his acquisition. There is also a land transaction effected by operation of law: the common parts are automatically transferred to the commonhold association (CA) on the registration of a unit with somebody new as the proprietor (s.7(3)). This is a land transaction as provided in section 43(2) and (3) of the FA 2003. There has been some concern amongst practitioners because at this stage the CA will still be controlled by the owner of all the units except the one that has been sold (Income and Corporation Taxes Act 1988, s.839). This means that the transaction will be covered by the deemed market value rule in section 53 of the FA 2003. The purchaser, the CA, is a company connected with the vendor – 'vendor' and 'purchaser' being as defined in section 43(4) of the FA 2003. Group relief under section 62 of and Schedule 7 to the FA 2003 will not be available because the CA is not a company with shares. There are no other reliefs and the transaction does not fall within the exceptions in section 54 of the FA 2003.

Importantly though, there will be no SDLT to be paid, and no notification to be made by the CA. It must be remembered that the rule in section 53 of the FA 2003 is a deemed market value rule. It requires the consideration to be taken to be not less than market value of the subject matter of the transaction.

'Market value' is defined by section 118 of the FA 2003 to be as provided in sections 272–274 of the Taxation of Chargeable Gains Act 1992. For any assets it is 'the price which those assets might reasonably be expected to fetch on a sale in the open market'.

What would it be reasonable to expect the commonhold land that forms the common parts of a commonhold to fetch on the open market? The answer is, in all cases, nothing. As commonhold land forming the common parts it cannot be sold: it is vested in the CA under the Act, and specified in accordance with section 1 as being land in relation to which it is to exercise functions. There could be no market for such land – there can only be a market for such land on its actually ceasing to be commonhold land and ceasing to be the common parts of a commonhold. There can be transactions in parts of the common parts (s.27), and on any such transactions the purchaser will have to pay any SDLT due. The whole can only be dealt with under the provisions for termination (ss.50–56; see also **Chapter 14**) when it has ceased to be commonhold land.

11.2.3 Registration with unit-holders

On registration with unit-holders the subject matter in the land transaction that is the acquisition of the common parts by the CA will not already be commonhold land, but it will become commonhold land on the acquisition. It will typically be the main structure and accessways of a building, subject to easements and quasi-easements in favour of the tenants and unit-holders, but without any right to recover contributions to maintenance. Thus the market value is exceedingly unlikely to be more than nil. The purchaser, the CA will have appropriate rights, but that does not affect the market value of the subject matter of the transaction.

11.2.4 Commonhold association connected with vendor

This will apply when the tenants either own the freehold, or own the company that owns the freehold (e.g. after enfranchisement) and then convert to commonhold.

The deemed market value rule in section 53 of the FA 2003 will apply, and the consideration must be taken to be not less than the price which the common parts might reasonably be expected to fetch on a sale in the open market. The valuer must remember that he is to value the subject matter of the transaction, and that it is not the freehold in all the land that is to become commonhold. The freeholds in each unit go to the unit-holders. The land acquired by the CA is what is left after the units have gone to the unit-holders. It is perhaps conceivable, for example with commonhold units of houses around common parts of a golf course and clubhouse, that the deemed market value of the land that forms the common parts could be so great as to mean that this structure may lead to the incidence of avoidable SDLT.

In registration with unit-holders there will be a number of transactions, but it is thought that they will be deemed to be 'in substance one bargain' (FA 2003, Sched.4, para.4(3)) so as to require a just and reasonable apportionment between all the elements, the acquisitions by unit-holders and the acquisition by the CA. In fact, the transfers of the freeholds are automatic on registration, and the consideration will have been given for the consent to registration as commonhold, which is discussed in **para.11.2.6**. No further SDLT will arise for unit-holders. If consideration was given for consent and it exceeded the relevant threshold then SDLT would be payable. A consent is a chargeable interest under section 48 of the FA 2003.

11.2.5   Commonhold association not connected with vendor

In such a case the deemed market value rule will not apply to the acquisition of the common parts by the CA. It would be liable to notify and to pay SDLT if the consideration that it gave exceeded the thresholds for non-residential property. In fact, however, the transfer is automatic on registration, and the consideration will already have been given for the consent to registration as commonhold, which is discussed in **para.11.2.6**. No separate consideration is given for the acquisitions of the freeholds, and any conceivable apportionment could only reduce the SDLT payable on the acquisition of the consent by ascribing it to units or the common parts. HM Revenue and Customs would not insist on such an apportionment, and as the risks on non-payment are so great it is not worth the CA even thinking about this.

11.2.6   Consents on conversion

Conversion itself must be distinguished from a freeholder's acquiring consent for conversion to commonhold from any of the persons whose consent is required under the Act (see **Chapter 3**). A consent is a chargeable interest, as provided in section 48 of the FA 2003, but is not a major interest in land, and so transactions involving consent will be notifiable only if the consideration exceeds the applicable tax threshold (£120,000 for residential land and £150,000 for non-residential – this will be rare in practice).

Where the tenants, or a company owned by the tenants, own the freehold the CA will be connected with the landlord, and thus the deemed market value rule in section 53 of the FA 2003 will apply. It will not yield any value, because consent from the freeholder to register land as commonhold is not the kind of thing that can be sold on the open market: it is usable only by the CA relevant to that particular land. There is thus no 'price which it might reasonably be expected to fetch on a sale in the open market' and the deemed market value will be nil.

11.2.7 Estates and interests extinguished on conversion to commonhold

Sections 7 and 9 of the Act provide that any lease of the whole or any part of the commonhold land is extinguished on registration, whether with or without unit-holders. The best construction of section 43 of the FA 2003 is that it is a deeming provision, and this means that the extinguishment of such a lease is going to be treated as an acquisition of the lease by the person whose land is benefited, i.e. the freeholder, and a disposal by the person losing the title to extinguished lease, the former tenant. Since the lease is classified as a major interest in land for purposes of SDLT it will be necessary for the freeholder to make an SDLT return if any consideration in money or money's-worth is given, and to pay SDLT on that consideration if it exceeds the appropriate threshold.

Almost always, 'self-certificates' (in the Form SDLT60) should be required on a substantive application for the removal of notice of registered leases. There could be no such certificate if the application to close the title were made by the registered proprietor of the leasehold title (the former tenant) and then the removal of any corresponding notice should be automatic. The extinguishment is effected by the statute, and so it may be questioned whether the requirement for an SDLT return certificate would be proper.

If a compensatory lease is granted in accordance with regulation 3 of the Commonhold Regulations 2004 (CR), then for purposes of SDLT this should fall within paragraph 16 of Schedule 17A to the FA 2003. Where the new lease is granted to the old tenant the grant of a new lease does not count as chargeable consideration for the surrender, and the surrender does not count as chargeable consideration for grant of the new lease. If the circumstances are such that a lease is granted to a different party then the transactions would fall to be dealt with as an exchange of land under paragraph 5 of Schedule 4 to the FA 2003. Each party would need to pay SDLT on the market value of the subject matter of the acquisition, i.e. the landlord on the market value of the extinguished lease, and the new tenant on the market value of the newly granted lease.

It will, accordingly, be important to ensure that compensatory leases are only granted to the persons whose leases are extinguished or there will be a risk that unnecessary SDLT will be incurred.

On an extinguished mortgage there will be no SDLT payable since security interests are exempt interests for SDLT under paragraph 1 of Schedule 3 to the FA 2003.

Any other interests extinguished will not be major interests in land. Arguably, the damages payable by the holder of the interest that was affected by the interest that was extinguished will not count as chargeable consideration for the interest that was extinguished. Schedule 4 to the FA 2003, dealing with what is to count as a chargeable consideration, does not include anything paid to discharge the liability for loss imposed by section 10 of the

Act. It is not at all in keeping with the traditions of the common law to treat damages as a purchase price or as consideration for the transaction that led to the arising of the liability for loss, and this would not be a good place to start doing so.

11.3 BUSINESS RATES AND COUNCIL TAX

11.3.1 Units

A person in rateable occupation of land for business purposes is liable to pay business rates on the rateable value of the hereditament as determined by the district valuer. This applies whether to land forming the whole or any part of a unit or land that forms the whole or any part of the common parts.

In practice, incidental business use of residential land is disregarded and it remains subject only to council tax. If the business use is more than incidental then the occupier of the land should report it to the district valuer who should assess the land as a composite hereditament, creating a liability for business rates as well as for council tax in the appropriate band.

11.3.2 Common parts

The extent of the common parts in a commonhold can vary very greatly. Common parts may just form the structural part of the building and access, and if merely the structural parts of the building then it would be very difficulty to imagine that the CA could be in rateable occupation of them.

If the common parts included merely access ways, sewers, drains, structural parts, and so forth, then even if the CA were in rateable occupation of them it is difficult to see that any particular value should be ascribed to them, since they would be subject to the easements and commonhold rights of the unit-holders in such a way that should leave them with little value. In other cases, however, the CA may find itself in rateable occupation of considerable and valuable premises, perhaps sporting facilities for which additional charges are made on the basis of use. In such a case the district valuer may allocate a rateable value that will lead to a real liability. In any particular case, the prudent course will be to discuss the matter with the district valuer and to instruct rating surveyors to negotiate the valuation if appropriate.

Council tax will be payable on residential units in the same way as with any other land.

It is a fundamental principle of company law that the CA is a distinct legal person from its members. In the case of CAs, they are clearly distinct from the unit-holders as such, only some of whom may be members of the CA. Commonhold associations are, accordingly, liable to pay corporation tax on their own profits, i.e. where their own income exceeds their allowable expenses.

Commonhold associations are not intended to be profit-making institutions, and are not allowed to distribute profit to their members. That does not, however, mean that they may not make a profit, and if they do they will need to pay corporation tax on it. It is entirely conceivable that CAs should have income other than that which arises by way of commonhold assessment, as for example if they let out facilities in the common parts, perhaps to specialist providers of services such as nurseries, crèches, sports facilities and so on.

11.4 COMMONHOLD ASSESSMENT

In the normal course of things the money raised by a CA so that it can discharge its liability to the unit-holders and raised by way of commonhold assessment will be its own money. There will be no question of there being a trust imposed by section 42 of the Landlord and Tenant Act 1987.

It will unquestionably be the case that the money raised by the CA through the assessment will be its own money. The CA will need the money in order to discharge its own liabilities, not those of the unit-holders. It would, accordingly, be wrong for a CA to declare any kind of trust over these monies in favour of the unit-holders.

So far as the annual assessment is concerned, then monies coming in that are spent within the year should not give rise to any corporation tax liability. The income should match the allowed-for expenditure, and might properly be held over until the next year when an adjusted assessment would allow things to balance out.

The case here is somewhat more difficult when considering the reserve funds which a CA may need to set up under section 39 of the Act and paragraph 4.2 of the prescribed CCS (CR, Sched.3).

Because of the absence of any kind of trust mechanism, Parliament has provided that reserve funds may only be spent on the purposes for which they were collected unless the company goes into insolvent liquidation (s.56). Insolvent liquidation is something that should happen very rarely. It could only arise where all of the unit-holders are actually unable to pay, and the units themselves, together with the common parts, are worth less than the debts of the CA.

HM Revenue and Customs has expressed the view orally that income that arises on reserve funds as they accumulate, and as unit-holders pay their assessments, will be liable to corporation tax.

It may, however, be strongly argued that the principle in *New York Life Insurance Co* v. *Styles (Surveyor of Taxes)* (1889) 14 App Cas 381 should be applied. The income of CAs as unit-holders pay their assessments, and as investment income mounts up on reserve funds, should fall within the 'self-trading' or 'mutual trading' rule because the overlap between members of the company and unit-holders is so close. The activities of the CA would be such that it should be regarded as several persons (the unit-holders) who combine together and contribute to a common fund for the financing of some venture or object. The particular form of a CA should be immaterial, merely a device to allow the property owners to deal with their own property in a collective way.

11.5 CAPITAL GAINS TAX

Capital gains tax will apply to commonhold land, whether part of a unit or the common parts, on a disposal, but subject to the usual extensions and reliefs. It may be that when CAs sell part of the common parts they will realise a gain and will need to pay this tax.

11.6 VALUE ADDED TAX

Value added tax arises on the supply of goods and services by a taxable person, and a business such as a CA will become taxable if its turnover exceeds the threshold, currently £60,000 per annum.

The discharge of its commonhold duties in accordance with the CCS will be a supply of services to non-residential unit-holders, and if the CA has elected to waive the exemption it will need to add VAT to assessments.

This will be different with residential unit-holders because there is an extra-statutory concession that covers the point (Customs Notice 742 Law & Property March 2002, para.12.2). VAT will not be chargeable, and this reflects the position where residential leaseholders pay mandatory service charges, though the legal analyses of the two positions are very different.

It may, however, be the case that the CA would need to charge VAT on rents and licence fees if it had elected to waive the exemption from VAT in relation to the common parts, and so careful thought should be given to that question.

An election to waive the exemption is, for most practical purposes, irrevocable and so it should not be done rashly. Specific expert advice should be taken.

CHAPTER 12

Purchasing and owning commonhold land

Laurence Target

12.1 BACKGROUND

A unit in a commonhold is held for a freehold estate – it is freehold land, though with particular incidents under the Act that make it work as commonhold. It has to be registered land because the Act requires all commonhold land to be registered at the Land Registry. There are certain qualifications as to the quality of the title of land in respect of which an application for registration at the Land Registry as commonhold can be made.

The Act requires all commonholds to have at least two units. Because commonhold land must have a commonhold association (CA) and because it must have functions (s.1(l)(c)) which must be relation to common parts, there must actually be common parts as well as units. Section 25 defines common parts as being every part of a commonhold that is not a unit. If a unit is part of a larger structure whose parts are interdependent then the structure and exterior must form part of the common parts, and amongst the functions of the CA will be their repair and insurance.

When anybody is considering the purchase of a unit these matters should already have been considered, and resolved satisfactorily, for the land will have been registered. The promoters of the company (i.e. the CA) and the Land Registry will need to have satisfied themselves that the land qualified, that the requirement documentation had been satisfactorily prepared and that all consents had been validly given, and remained in force.

Paragraph 7 of Schedule 1 to the Act requires the directors of each CA that applies for registration at the Land Registry to certify that:

- the memorandum and articles of association comply with the requirements of regulations under the Act;
- the CCS satisfies the requirements of the Act;
- the application is not made in relation to land that cannot be commonhold (e.g. agricultural land or land with a contingent title);
- the CA has not traded; and
- that the CA has not incurred any liability that has not been discharged.

This means that the directors and their professional advisers will need to have given careful attention to those matters, and thus it is certain in practice that the land will qualify. A buyer will be able to rely on the fact of registration at the Land Registry.

Because a unit will be freehold land it will be capable of being owned and dealt with in the same ways as other freehold land, although the Act does introduce some restrictions so as to ensure the proper functioning of commonhold, and to prevent the re-introduction of the long lease of residential property. There are restrictions that limit the ways in which units can be disposed of.

Nothing in the CCS can prevent or restrict the transfer of the freehold estate in a unit (s.15(2)), or in any part of the common parts (s.27(1)(a)). Practitioners should, however, be careful to ensure that there are no other documents or agreements that do so. A purchaser should not be affected by any such limitation or restriction that is not noted in the register of title at the Land Registry, but a unit-holder may have agreed to restrictions of his powers of disposition that go further than those imposed by or under the Act. A seller may be personally liable for breach of any such agreements even if they have not been protected at the Land Registry. There is nothing to prevent the making of agreements between the members of a CA on the analogy of a shareholders' agreement between the members of a private company limited by shares (which are commonly used, and are of great practical and commercial importance).

12.2   COMMONHOLD DOCUMENTATION

The registered title to a commonhold unit will clearly identify it as such, and refer to the rest of the land in the commonhold, both other units and the common parts. It will also refer to the other documents that are essential to the working of commonhold, the memorandum and articles of association of the CA, and the commonhold community statement (CCS). The Land Registry will (if nothing goes wrong) be able to supply official copies of these documents, and purchasers will need to check them against the current prescribed forms.

As discussed elsewhere, amendments to them are of no effect until they have been registered at the Land Registry, and so it will be part of the process of investigation of title to make sure that no amendments have been made but left unregistered, and to require the registration of any that have been.

Restrictions will appear in the title automatically when land is commonhold to reflect the limitations inherent in the scheme and flowing from the statute.

12.3 DEALING WITH ONLY PART OF A UNIT

The most important limitation on the way in which a commonhold unit can be dealt with is that the land can only be dealt with as a whole (certainly at law) unless the CA consents to the disposition of part only of a unit. Any agreement for a dealing with part of a unit that is intended to take effect at law should be expressly made subject to the consent of the CA. A unit-holder landlord and his tenant might, however, find that a lease of part that took effect only in equity was perfectly satisfactory for both of them, and so there can be appropriate flexibility despite these limitations.

Without written consent from the CA a unit may be transferred, mortgaged or leased only as a whole.

The transfer of part of a unit will entail one or more of these things:

- the creation of a new unit;
- the enlargement of an existing unit;
- the enlargement of the common parts; or
- the removal of land from the commonhold altogether.

As a mortgage carries a power of sale and a power of foreclosure (at least in theory) a mortgage of part implies the possibility that part only of the unit may permanently be severed from the rest and may remain in separate ownership. It thus needs the same careful thought as does an outright sale of part.

In any such case the dealing will not be valid unless the CA has joined in the disposition or given its written consent (s.20(3)). A prudent purchaser of a unit will want to ensure that the resolution has been passed with the necessary majority (75 per cent) required by section 20(4) rather than to rely on any presumption of the due observance of formalities from due execution or signature.

If there is a dealing with part of a unit that is not the grant of a permitted lease then the CCS will need to be amended. If the effect is to change the extent of the commonhold the memorandum will also need to be amended, for it needs to specify the land in relation to which the CA is to exercise its functions (s.1(1)(b)).

In these circumstances the directors of the CA will need to ensure that the costs of making these changes fall upon those who are to benefit from them rather than upon the rest of the unit-holders. Unless general provision has been made in the CCS, they will need an acceptable undertaking for costs or money on account at an early stage in the process of either deciding whether or not consent should be given, or actually implementing the changes.

12.4 DEALING WITH THE WHOLE OF A UNIT

If the purchase is simply of the whole of a unit then the purchaser will have few requirements additional to those relating to the purchase of the whole of the land in any other registered title.

The purchaser will need to check official copies of the memorandum, articles and the CCS, and that they match those filed at Companies House. He will need to ensure that the company has not been struck off, and is functioning properly (just as when purchasing a lease when the reversion is owned by a company that is itself owned by the tenants).

In order to advise properly, the conveyancer will need to check the position as against the currently prescribed forms: the latter will prevail, even if there being any difference is unlikely to cause any loss to the purchaser.

The task of understanding how the property is to work in relation to the other properties should be much easier than it is in relation to leasehold property. The documentation will be standardised to a very great extent, and the material peculiar to each commonhold will be clearly identified as such, and is thus likely to be more coherent.

12.5 COMMONHOLD UNIT INFORMATION CERTIFICATE

A purchaser will also require a commonhold unit information certificate from the CA which is to be supplied by the seller. It is to be given in Form 9, and it serves to limit the new unit-holder's liability in relation to the commonhold assessment, reserve fund levies and any interest for late payment of those amounts. A new unit-holder will not be liable to pay more than the amount certified up to the date of the certificate. It does not limit the former unit-holder's liability in relation to the period of his ownership. It has no function in relation to liabilities for other commonhold duties, which the new unit-holder will assume as provided by section 16 of the Act.

A buyer will want to ensure that the certificate is as up-to-date as possible, and there are no limits as to the frequency with which the CA may be required to produce such certificates. The directors will need to ensure that the CA is able to respond promptly with accurate information. The standard documentation is silent as to the costs of supplying such certificates, and so those drafting individual material for the CCS may wish to ensure that the persons who request such certificates are obliged to pay the costs of producing them so that those costs do not fall on other unit-holders.

Standard form preliminary enquiries should identify whether or not there are likely to be any areas of concern, and responsibility will be contractually allocated between buyer and seller, just as would be the case with the purchase of any other land subject to continuing obligations, or where there may be past breaches for which the buyer could find himself liable.

12.6   USE OF FORMS

The events in the cycle of ownership of a commonhold unit will be marked by the use of prescribed forms (Commonhold Regulations 2004, Sched.4), of a type familiar to conveyancers, but perhaps more unfamiliar to the lay person.

The CA must serve notice using prescribed forms (or forms to substantially the same effect) when exercising many of its functions.

These forms seem to be clearly written, unlike all too many statutory forms. They are designed with boxes, similar to many Land Registry Forms or Stamp Duty Land Tax returns. They are available online and with expandable fields through the usual commercial suppliers, and so are conveniently available to professionals. Non-professionals, such as are expected to be running many commonholds, may find it less convenient, and it may be difficult to put the appropriate details into 'hard copies' of the forms.

12.7   LEASING

Of particular importance may be some of the formal requirements in relation to letting units. There are no restrictions on the terms of leases that may be granted of non-residential units, though residential leases are limited as to length of term and the taking of a premium is not allowed.

In any case it is necessary for the prospective landlord to serve a notice on the prospective tenant telling him that the land is commonhold and informing him of the identity of the CA that manages the commonhold. It is not to be thought that non-observance will have any affect on the legal validity of the lease, whether as between landlord and tenant or between the CA and the tenant. It would, however, be a breach of the commonhold duties owed by the unit-holder landlord to the CA, and might leave him liable to it for any losses that it suffered in consequence of non-service of these notices. It is difficult to imagine that they could be large, or more than *de minimis* in any event. Similarly, a tenant on whom notice had not been served is not likely to suffer a real loss. He will be bound by certain commonhold obligations, but *caveat emptor* and the open register will do much to protect the landlord from liability.

The tenant may have an obligation to pay money to the CA if the unit-holder landlord does not, but that liability will be limited to the amount of rent that the tenant has not paid to the landlord before service of a rent diversion notice. With non-residential units there is a possibility of abuse. A tenant who has paid a premium for a long lease may not have any rent to pay, and the unit-holder may have become insolvent, or may not be easily found. A unit is not liable to forfeiture. In such circumstances it would be onerous property, and so the operation of section 16 will be limited by the fact that no well-advised purchaser will buy the freehold in the unit. A liquidator or trustee in bankruptcy would probably disclaim the unit; the *bona vacantia* authorities (The Treasury Solicitor, or the Duchy of Lancaster or Cornwall) will not become liable to pay unless they enter into possession, which is not to be expected, though disclaimer by them is. On such a disclaimer the land will escheat to the Crown, but the Crown will still not become liable to pay unless the Crown Estate Commissioners enter into possession, which is not to be expected. The burden will thus fall on the other unit-holders.

Pre-emptive solutions to this problem will have to be devised individually for each commonhold. Since any lease of a non-residential unit takes effect subject to any provision of the CCS (s.18) it would be possible to provide in the CCS that any tenant or undertenant had to pay the assessment to the extent that the unit-holder landlord or inferior landlord had not done so. There is no prescribed form for use in such circumstances.

12.8   TRUSTS OF LAND

A unit-holder does not have to be the legal and beneficial owner of the unit vested in him. He may hold it for others, in which case he will be a trustee under a trust of land. A sole trustee, or trustees who are not joint tenants in equity (i.e. where the beneficial interests will not pass to the survivor on death of the co-owner) must apply for entry of a restriction in the proprietorship register of the title at the Land Registry in Form A (Land Registration Rules 2003, Sched.4). The land will be held on trusts whose terms should be expressly set out, but will otherwise be implied in all the circumstances. This is just like any other freehold land, though the entitlement to be a member of the CA and the rights that it carries will, in some sense, also be part of the assets of the trust of land.

12.9   SOLICITORS' PRACTICE RULES

The Solicitors' Practice Rules 1990 were amended at the end of March 2005, and now make express mention of commonhold land, effectively allowing it to be dealt with by solicitors in conveyancing as other freehold land.

CHAPTER 13

Variation of a commonhold

Gary Cowen

13.1 GENERAL

It is envisaged that there are a number of ways in which a commonhold association (CA) might wish to alter an existing or proposed commonhold. This might be by way of a variation of the documents governing the existence of the commonhold, either by variation of the articles or memorandum of association of the CA or by variation of the commonhold community statement (CCS) itself. Additionally, the CA may wish to vary the extent of the land which is included in the commonhold.

13.2 ALTERATIONS TO THE CONSTITUTION

Because the CA is a company, its affairs are governed not only by the Act but also by the Companies Act 1985. It is therefore appropriate to look at the general requirements of the Companies Act 1985 as well as the further requirements of the Act.

13.3 ALTERATIONS TO THE MEMORANDUM AND ARTICLES OF ASSOCIATION UNDER THE COMPANIES ACT 1985

Any company may alter the statement of the company's objects in its memorandum by passing a special resolution to that effect (Companies Act 1985, s.4(1)). The company must then file a copy of the altered memorandum with the Registrar of Companies at Companies House (Companies Act 1985, s.18).

Similarly, a company may alter its articles of association by a special resolution of the company (Companies Act 1985, s.9). A copy of the amended articles of association must then be filed with the Registrar of Companies at Companies House (Companies Act, 1985, s.18).

There are no provisions in the Companies Act 1985 pursuant to which the members of the company or debenture holders may challenge an alteration of the articles of association.

The Companies Act 1985 provisions concerning the cancellation of a proposed alteration to the memorandum apply equally to the memorandum of a CA. Such an application must be made within 21 days of the special resolution confirming the amendment and must be made by not less than 15 per cent of the company's members who did not consent to or vote in favour of the amendment or not less than 15 per cent of the holders of the company's debentures.

A company may change its registered office by giving notice of the change to the Registrar of Companies (Companies Act 1985, s.287). Under the Companies Act 1985, the existing registered office address will remain a valid address for service of the company for 14 days after the new registered office address is registered with the Registrar of Companies. A CA must additionally comply with the requirements of the Act set out at **para.13.3** below

13.4 REQUIREMENTS OF THE ACT AND REGULATIONS

13.4.1 Memorandum of association

The Act imposes further restrictions upon the ability of the CA to alter its memorandum even though in all likelihood the only changes to be made will be to the name or address of the CA.

The alteration of the memorandum must be notified to, and registered with, the Land Registry. An application for registration of an amendment must be made on Form CM3 which must additionally be accompanied by a certificate from the directors of the CA certifying that the altered memorandum complies with the regulations concerning the form and content of the memorandum (Commonhold Regulations 2004 (CR), Sched.1) and two copies of the altered memorandum, one merely a printed copy and the other a certified copy for retention by the Land Registry.

The application to the Land Registry cannot be made until the period for any application to be made to the court for the cancellation of an amendment to the memorandum has expired without application having been made or, where such an application has been made, where the application has been finally determined by confirmation of the alteration by the court or by withdrawal.

Once the Land Registrar is satisfied that the application is in the correct form, he will register the amended memorandum, return one copy of the amended memorandum and make any consequential amendments to the register that he believes are appropriate. It should be noted that the amendment to the memorandum does not take effect until it is registered with the Land Registry even though it has already been filed with the Registrar of Companies and the time limit for an application to cancel the amendment has expired.

The CR impose further restrictions on the nature of the memorandum. Regulation 13 of the CR provides that the memorandum of the CA must be in a particular form set out in Schedule 1 to the CR or in a form to the same effect. It is not clear what is meant by the words 'in a form to the same effect' but it is suggested that very minor variations to the form of memorandum will be tolerated provided they do not result in variations of substance from the prescribed form. In any event, regulation 13 goes on to make it clear that further clauses may be added to the prescribed form of memorandum which would allow, it is submitted, a widening of the objects clause. It perhaps goes without saying that clauses may not be added which would contradict the prescribed form or infringe the CR themselves.

In order to change its registered address, a CA must comply with the Companies Act 1985 (see above). In addition, the CA must alter its memorandum and CCS (see **para.13.5**). The altered memorandum must be filed with the Land Registry and the change of registered office will not take effect until the registration at the Land Registry takes place (Sched.3, para.3).

13.4.2 Articles of association

In addition to the requirements of the Companies Act 1985, if the CA wishes to amend the articles of association, it must notify and register the alteration with the Land Registry. The application for registration follows an identical procedure to that described for alterations to the memorandum.

In addition, regulation 14 of the CR provides that the articles of association of the CA must be in a particular form set out in Schedule 2 to the CR or in a form to the same effect. It is not again clear what is meant by the words 'in a form to the same effect' but it is suggested that very minor variations to the form of articles of association will be tolerated provided they do not result in variations of substance from the prescribed form.

Regulation 14 also provides for various amendments to the standard articles of association to be permitted.

In general terms, a CA may add its own articles to the standard articles of association but must preface each additional article with a heading stating 'additional provision specific to this commonhold association' and the additional article must be given a number which fits in with the standard numbering sequence by the use of letters as suffixes. So, for instance, an additional article inserted between Articles 11 and 12 would be called 'Article 11A'.

More specifically, regulation 14 provides for specific permitted alterations to certain of the standard articles of association. In particular, the following may be altered:

- Articles 7, 18 and 48(f) may be altered to substitute a different time period provided that the substituted period is not shorter than the standard articles of association.

- Article 48(f) may additionally be altered to substitute a different number of meetings although the number specified can not be less than three.
- Article 13 may be altered to substitute different figures for the quorum of a meeting provided that the numbers are not reduced below those in the standard article. Different quorum figures may also be introduced for different purposes.
- Article 36 may be amended to introduce a specified time or date in substitution for 'at any time' for the delivery of proxies. Additionally, the CA may choose to omit the provision permitting the delivery of proxies at the meeting itself.
- Where the articles of association provide for the use of alternate directors, Article 38 concerning the number of directors is amended so as to exclude alternate directors from the count.
- Where the CA chooses to permit the developer to appoint or remove a director, Articles 45, 46 and 61 will also be varied. In addition, Articles 40, 41 and 54 do not apply to directors appointed by the developer.

It should be noted that regulation 14 also includes further regulations which will take effect where the CA chooses, in the CCS, to permit the developer to appoint and remove directors. These will take effect even if they are not subsequently adopted. The regulations cover the appointment and removal of developer's directors, the role of the developer during the period when he is entitled to appoint developer's directors and the liability of the CA to such a director upon his removal.

13.5 COMPELLING AN ALTERATION (SECTION 40 APPLICATION)

Section 40 of the Act introduces a provision whereby an individual unit-holder may apply to the court for a declaration that the memorandum or articles of association of the CA do not comply with regulations (s.40(1)(a). It should be noted that a provision in the memorandum or articles of association which is inconsistent with regulations is of no effect (Sched.3, para.2(4)). Accordingly, it would be open to a unit-holder confident of his position simply to do nothing, secure in the knowledge that the relevant provision of the memorandum or article is of no effect. In the case of a dispute, however, an application for a declaration under section 40 may be appropriate.

The unit-holder is under a time constraint if he does wish to make such an application. The application must be made within three months of the date upon which the proposed applicant became a unit-holder (s.40(4)(a)) or within three months of the date upon which an alteration is made to the memorandum or articles of association which does not comply with regulations (s.40(4)(b)). Section 40(4)(c) also provides the court with a discretion to extend these time limits by providing that such an application can be brought after the time limits have expired with the court's permission. It should be borne in mind that a person becomes a unit-holder upon the date upon which he becomes *entitled* to be registered as such at the Land Registry and not the date upon which he is actually registered.

If the court decides to grant a declaration that the memorandum or articles of association do not comply with regulations, the court has a discretion as to whether it should make any consequential directions and if so, what those directions should be (s.40(2)).

Section 40(3) suggests various potential directions which the Court may make, though it is clear from a reading of section 40(2) that the court is unfettered in its jurisdiction. The potential directions suggested by section 40(3) are:

(a) an order requiring a director or other specified officer of the CA to take steps to alter or amend a document;

(b) an order requiring a director or other specified officer of the CA to take specified steps;

(c) the making of an award of compensation to be paid by the CA to a specified person. (The order for payment of compensation may or may not be contingent upon the occurrence or non-occurrence of a specified event);

(d) the making of a provision for land to cease to be commonhold land.

It is thought to be unlikely that the court will ever be placed in a position whereby it thinks it appropriate to make an order that the land cease to be commonhold land. In most cases, the court will be able to remedy the defect in the memorandum or articles of association by means of an order under section 40(3)(a) or (b).

The reference in section 40(3)(c) to 'compensation' suggests that the jurisdiction of the court is limited to compensating actual losses sustained by a unit-holder by reason of the fact that the memorandum or articles do not comply with regulations. This would almost certainly include losses incurred as a result of actions taken by the CA in accordance with the unlawful memorandum or articles.

13.6 ALTERATION TO THE COMMONHOLD COMMUNITY STATEMENT

Regulation 15 of the CR requires the CCS to be in the form contained in Schedule 3 to the CR.

Paragraph 4.8 of the prescribed form of CCS is concerned with amendment of the statement itself.

The basic rule is that the body of the CCS itself may not be altered unless it is a local rule that any particular paragraph may be so altered (paragraph

4.8.2). A 'local rule' is defined as a provision, including information contained in the Annexes to the CCS, inserted by the developer or the CA which is not prescribed by regulations (paragraph 1.4.5). The developer or CA may therefore create local rules which enable the CCS to be altered.

Those local rules may only be altered where the CCS provides that they may be so altered (paragraph 4.8.3) or unless they are approved by ordinary resolution (defined in paragraph 1.4.5 as, in essence, a simple majority of those entitled to vote). Any alteration to local rules must additionally comply with the Companies Act 1985.

In addition, paragraph 4.8.4 provides that the format of the Annexes to the prescribed CCS 'cannot be amended'. Those Annexes provide information concerning the identity of the commonhold and the CA, the definition of the properties within the commonhold, the commonhold allocations and the local rules. It should be noted that it is the 'format' of the Annexes which may not be amended. It appears that provided the format of the Annexes is not tampered with, amendments may be made to the actual information provided (indeed, this is clarified by paragraphs 4.8.5 to 4.8.7). In the case of Annex 4 dealing with local rules, it would seem sensible for the CA to add any further local rules created by the developer or CA.

Further to those basic rules, there are more specific rules relating to specific situations which are as follows.

13.6.1 Amendment to rights in favour of, or over, a unit

An amendment to the rights in favour of, or over, a commonhold unit specified in Paragraphs 6 or 7 of Annex 2 may not be made 'unless the unit-holder and the registered proprietor of any charge over that commonhold unit have consented in writing to the proposed amendment before it is made' (paragraph 4.8.5).

13.6.2 Amendment to authorised user

An amendment to remove a reference to a particular unit-holder as an authorised user in Paragraph 4 of Annex 4 (which is concerned with areas where the user is limited) 'cannot be made unless the unit-holder and the registered proprietor of any charge over that commonhold unit have consented in writing to the proposed amendment before it is made' (paragraph 4.8.6).

13.6.3 Amendment to permitted use

An amendment to the permitted use of a commonhold unit specified in Paragraph 2 of Annex 4 cannot be made unless the proposed amendment is approved by a special resolution (defined in paragraph 1.4.5 of the CCS as, in essence, a resolution passed by a 75 per cent majority) and the unit-holder has consented in writing to the proposed amendment before it is made (paragraph 4.8.7).

13.6.4   Amendment to redefine extent of a unit

An amendment to the CCS which redefines the extent of a commonhold unit 'cannot be made unless the unit-holder and the registered proprietor of any charge over that commonhold unit have consented in writing to the proposed amendment before it is made' (paragraph 4.8.8).

13.6.5   Amendment to add to the common parts

An amendment to the CCS which specifies that land which forms part of a commonhold unit is to be added to the common parts 'cannot be made unless the unit-holder and the registered proprietor of any charge over that commonhold unit have consented in writing to the proposed amendment before it is made' (paragraph 4.8.9).

13.6.6   Amendment of the boundaries

The CCS cannot be amended so as to alter the boundaries of the commonhold, any commonhold unit or the common parts unless any relevant unit-holder and the registered proprietor of any charge over that commonhold unit have consented in writing to the proposed amendment before it is made, and the approval of the members of the CA has been given by special resolution (paragraph 4.8.10).

13.6.7   Amendments to commonhold assessment or levy and voting rights

A special resolution is also required (paragraph 4.8.11) to approve any proposed amendment which:

- amends the percentage of the commonhold assessment or levy allocated to a commonhold unit in Paragraphs 1 or 2 of Annex 3; or
- amends the number of votes allocated to a member of the CA in Paragraph 3 of Annex 3.

A unit holder does have a right not to have an amendment such as that referred to above whereby the percentage of commonhold assessment or levy allocated to his or any other commonhold unit is amended if the effect of the amendment, taking into account all of the circumstances of the case, would be to allocate a significantly disproportionate percentage of the commonhold assessment or levy to his commonhold unit (paragraph 4.8.12). This right would appear to supersede the will of the 75 per cent majority who may have approved such an amendment by special resolution provided, of course, that the condition referred to above can be proved.

Similarly, a unit-holder has a right not to have an amendment such as that referred to above whereby the number of votes allocated to him or any other member is amended if the effect of the amendment, taking into account all of the circumstances of the case, would be to allocate a significantly disproportionate number of votes to him (paragraph 4.8.13). This right would also appear to supersede the will of the 75 per cent majority who may have approved such an amendment by special resolution provided, again, that the condition referred to above can be proved.

Paragraph 4.8.14 of the CCS contains a provision authorising the directors of the CA to amend the CCS without any resolution of the members of the CA 'to include specified provisions, or provisions of a specified kind, for a specified purpose or about a specified matter required by the Act and regulations or to delete any provisions that are of no effect for the reasons set out in Paragraph 1.1.5'. It is suggested that the provision reflects two sides of the same coin. Paragraph 1.1.5 provides that a provision is of no effect to the extent that it is: inconsistent with a provision made by virtue of the Act; inconsistent with anything treated as included in the CCS by the regulations; inconsistent with the memorandum or articles of association; or prohibited by the regulations.

Thus, paragraph 4.8.14 of the CCS appears to be requiring the directors to remove any provisions of the CCS which are 'of no effect' for any of those reasons and to add provisions relating to specific matters required by the Act or regulations. In other words, the directors can replace a provision which is of no effect with one which replaces it. However, it is submitted that the wording of paragraph 4.8.14 is far from clear.

The amendment of the CCS must be notified to and registered with the Land Registry (s.33(3)). Paragraph 4.8.15 of the prescribed CCS imposes a duty upon the directors of the CA to apply to the Land Registry for registration of the amended CCS as soon as practicable. An application for registration of an amendment must be made on Form CM3 which must additionally be accompanied by a certificate from the directors of the CA certifying that the altered CCS satisfies the requirements of s.33(5), two copies of the altered CCS (one merely a printed copy and the other a certified copy for retention by the Land Registry) and any consents (or orders of the court dispensing with such consents) referred to above.

Once the Land Registrar is satisfied that the application is in the correct form, he will register the amended CCS (s.33(4)), return the original of the amended CCS and make any consequential amendments to the Register that he believes are appropriate (s.33(8)). It should be noted that the amendment does not take effect until it is registered with the Land Registry (paragraph 4.8.16).

It should be noted that the provisions of section 40 of the Act pursuant to which a unit-holder may make an application to the court to compel an alteration to a document applies equally to the CCS. The procedure is the same in relation to alterations to the CCS as it is in relation to the memorandum or articles of association and reference should be made to the discussion of section 40 in that context.

13.7   ALTERATION OF THE EXTENT OF THE COMMONHOLD

13.7.1   Addition of land to the commonhold

Section 41 of the Act provides a mechanism whereby land may be added to an existing commonhold. The mechanism presupposes that the transitional period has come to an end and that the CA has started to exercise its functions of management of the commonhold (s.41(1)). During the transitional period, therefore, there is no mechanism whereby land may be added to the proposed commonhold. In those circumstances, it would appear that the only option for the developer would be to effectively start again by cancelling the registration of the land as commonhold, redrafting the CCS to include the land which he wishes to add and apply for the registration of that commonhold with the additional land included.

Section 41(2) of the Act refers to the mechanism as an 'application to add land' and the land to which the application relates is referred to as the 'added land'.

Before any application can be made to add land to the commonhold, a resolution must be obtained of the CA (s.41(3)). The resolution must be passed unanimously (s.41(4)(b)) and must be passed prior to making the application to add land (s.41(4)(a)). The Act provides for a CCS to include a provision disapplying the requirement for a resolution of the CA so as to facilitate the developer's undertaking of development business (ss.58(2) and 58(3)(d)). Such a provision does not, however, appear in the prescribed CCS where an approach consistent with section 41 of the Act has been adopted, requiring a unanimous resolution of the CA (paragraph 4.7.10). Of course, it is possible to amend the CCS by means of local rules in the manner described earlier in this chapter.

An application to add land may then be made to the Land Registry. The application must be made on Form CM4 (Commonhold (Land Registration) Rules 2004 (CLRR), r.20(1)). The application must be accompanied by:

- any consents required in relation to the added land pursuant to section 3 of the Act. Hence, the freehold owner of the added land and any registered proprietor of a charge over that land will be required to provide written consents. Alternatively, an order of the court dispensing with such consents will suffice (s.41(5)(a); s.3; and Sched.1, para.6);

- an application pursuant to section 33 of the Act to alter the CCS to show the commonhold as including the added land (s.41(5)(b)). That application must be made on Form CM3 (CLRR, r.20(4)). The amended CCS will include an amended plan and will make it clear the extent to which the added land will form one or more commonhold units and the extent to which the added land will form part of the common parts. The application to add land must include the application to amend the CCS otherwise the Registrar has the power merely to reject the application to add land (CLRR, r.20(3));
- a certificate from the directors of the CA that the added land is not prohibited from being commonhold land by Schedule 2 to the Act and that the CA has given its approval to the addition of the land by unanimous resolution (s.41(5)(c));
- a statutory declaration complying with rule 6 of the CLRR relating to necessary consents, restrictions on the register and extinguishment of charges (CLRR, r.20(4)).

Once the Land Registrar is satisfied that the application is in the correct form, he will register the added land. If the added land is to form a commonhold unit, the unit will be registered in the name of the unit-holder in the usual way. If, on the other hand, the added land is to form part of the common parts, it will be registered in the name of the CA (s.41(7)(b)).

13.7.2 Removal of land from the commonhold

There are no provisions in the Act dealing with removal of land from the commonhold. Once land is included within the commonhold, there is no means of removing it without terminating the commonhold and starting again. In the case of the transitional period, that would require the developer to cancel the registration of the land as commonhold, redraft the CCS to omit the land which he wishes to remove and apply for the registration of that commonhold without the omitted land.

Once the transitional period is at an end, there is no means of removal of land from the commonhold other than by terminating the commonhold by a voluntary winding up.

13.7.3 Alterations to commonhold units

It might be that notwithstanding that there is no additional land to be included in the commonhold, the CA may wish to reassign parts of the land within the commonhold so as to alter the boundaries between units or to redesignate land which formed part of a commonhold unit as part of the common parts. This was touched upon when discussing alterations to the CCS at **para.13.5.**

Alteration to the size of a commonhold unit

An alteration to a CCS which has the effect of altering the size of a common-hold unit may not be made without the consent of the unit-holder which must be obtained prior to the alteration being made (s.23(1)).

Section 23 of the Act provides for regulations to be made which would enable a court to dispense with the requirement for consent on the application of a CA in prescribed circumstances (s.23(2)). The CR do not make any such provision.

An application to register an alteration to the CCS which has the effect of altering the extent of a commonhold unit must be made on Form CM3 and must be accompanied by an application to register any relevant transfer (CLRR, r.17(1)). If there is a relevant transfer and a copy of it does not accompany the application to register the alteration to the CCS, the Registrar is liable to reject the application to register (CLRR, r.17(2)).

Alteration where the commonhold unit is charged

If it is desired to change the extent of a commonhold unit where that unit is subject to a registered charge, then an alteration to the CCS which has the effect of altering the size of that commonhold unit may not be made without the consent of the registered proprietor of the charge which must be obtained prior to the alteration being made (s.24(2)).

The Act again provides for regulations to be made which would enable a court to dispense with the requirement for consent on the application of a CA in prescribed circumstances (s.24(3)). The CR do not make any such provision.

If the effect of the alteration is to remove land from the commonhold unit, then the effect of the amendment is to extinguish the charge to the extent that it relates to the land which is removed (s.24(4)). Conversely, if the effect of the alteration is to add land to the commonhold unit, then the effect of the amendment is to extend the charge so that it relates to the land which is added (s.24(5)).

13.7.4   Alteration to the common parts

Further provisions apply where it is desired to redesignate land which is part of a commonhold unit as part of the common parts of the commonhold (s.30).

In such a case, the amendment to the CCS may not be made without the consent of the registered proprietor of any charge over the added land (defined as the land to be added to the common parts, s.30(1)) which must be obtained prior to the alteration being made (s.30(2)).

Once again, the Act provides for regulations to be made which would enable a court to dispense with the requirement for consent on the application of a

CA in prescribed circumstances (s.30(3). Again, the CR do not make any such provision.

This provision seems to be unnecessary as the registered proprietor of any charge over a parcel of land which was to be removed from a commonhold unit and placed in the common parts would be required to provide its consent pursuant to s.24(2) of the Act in any event.

Once the amended CCS is filed under s.33, the CA is entitled to be registered as the proprietor of the added land and the Registrar is obliged to register the CA without any further application being made (s.30(4)).

An application to register an alteration to the CCS which has the effect of altering the extent of the common parts must be made on Form CM3 and must be accompanied by an application to register any relevant transfer (CLRR, r.18(1)). If there is a relevant transfer and a copy of it does not accompany the application to register the alteration to the CCS, the Registrar is liable to reject the application to register (CLRR, r.18(2)).

However, the provisions referred to above do not apply where s.30(4) of the Act applies (CLRR, r.18(1)). So, where the addition to the common parts derives from land which was formerly part of a commonhold unit, the application to register need not be accompanied by an application to register any relevant transfer.

13.8   SUMMARY

Before land is registered as commonhold land, the developer of the land may make alterations to the extent of the land which it is proposed to include within the commonhold and to the rules which he proposes will govern the commonhold. Once the land has been registered as commonhold, it is more difficult to make such alterations. In general terms, however, changes can be made with the consent of the relevant parties to the commonhold.

CHAPTER 14

Bringing a commonhold to an end

Gary Cowen

14.1 INTRODUCTION

This chapter will consider the ways in which a commonhold may be terminated. In particular, it will consider the procedures for winding up the commonhold association (CA) which has the effect of terminating the commonhold. However, there are two other possibilities which must be considered.

First, as has been discussed elsewhere, the commonhold can, in the case of a new development, be brought to an end prior to the end of the transitional period by the registered proprietor of the land by making an application to cancel the registration of the commonhold (s.8(4)).

Second, where the registration of the commonhold has been completed and where:

- the application for registration was not made in accordance with section 2 of the Act;
- the directors' certificate is inaccurate; or
- the registration is made other than in accordance with the provisions of the Act;

a person who has been adversely affected by the registration may apply to the court for a declaration that the land shall cease to be commonhold land (s.6(3)).

In addition to these methods, the principal ways in which a commonhold may be brought to an end are:

- the voluntary winding up of the CA;
- the compulsory winding up of the CA; and
- the compulsory purchase of the commonhold land.

14.2   VOLUNTARY WINDING UP

It might be that the members of a CA will wish to voluntarily wind up the commonhold. Such a situation might occur, for instance, where the CA wishes to sell the land comprising the commonhold for redevelopment and where such a sale might be advanced by the land being the subject of a single freehold title.

A CA is a company and as such, it is subject to the laws and regulations governing companies in England and Wales. Equally, the laws and regulations governing the winding up of companies also apply to a CA with the addition of further regulation under the Act.

So, the voluntary winding up of a CA is governed by the procedure set out in the Insolvency Act 1986 (IA 1986) with certain modifications.

The voluntary winding up of the CA is subject to three requirements set out in section 43(1) of the Act, i.e.:

- obtaining a declaration of solvency;
- passing a termination statement resolution; and
- passing a winding-up resolution.

14.2.1   Declaration of solvency

The first step in obtaining a voluntary winding up of the CA is the preparation of a declaration of solvency (s.43(1)(a)). A declaration of solvency is a statutory declaration made by the directors of the CA. The declaration must comply with section 89 of the IA 1986.

The declaration must be to the effect that the directors have made a full enquiry into the CA's affairs and that they are of the opinion, having made such an enquiry, that the CA would be able to pay its debts in full, with interest at the official rate, within such a period not exceeding 12 months from the date of the commencement of the winding up as shall be specified in the declaration (IA 1986, s.89(1)). The directors can specify any period provided the period does not exceed 12 months.

The official rate of interest is whichever is the higher of the current rate under the Judgment Act 1838 (eight per cent at the time of writing) and that rate which is contractually applicable to the debt (IA 1986, ss.251 and 189(4)).

There are further requirements (IA 1986, s.89(1)–(3)) in respect of the declaration of solvency, it:

- must be made by statutory declaration;
- must be made on Form 4.70 in Schedule 4 to the Insolvency Rules 1986;
- must be made at a directors' meeting of the CA;
- must be made within a period no greater than five weeks prior to the date upon which the winding-up resolution is passed. It may be made on the same date as the winding-up resolution;

- must be made by the majority of the directors if the CA has more than two directors or, if the CA has only two directors, it must be made by both of them;
- must include a statement of the CA's assets and liabilities at the last practical date before the making of the declaration;
- must be delivered to the Registrar of Companies no later than 15 days after the date upon which the winding-up resolution is passed.

A director who makes a declaration without having reasonable grounds for believing that it is true is guilty of a criminal offence and is liable to imprisonment, a fine or both. In addition, a CA and its directors are liable to be fined if they fail to deliver the declaration of solvency to the Registrar of Companies within 15 days of the date of the winding-up resolution (IA 1986, s.89(6)).

14.2.2 Termination-statement resolution

The next requirement which must be satisfied is the passing of a termination-statement resolution. A termination-statement resolution must be passed before a winding-up resolution is passed and a winding-up resolution will not take effect unless it is preceded by a termination-statement resolution (s.43(1)(b)). This resolution is a resolution approving a termination statement (s.43(2)).

The termination statement is designed to specify how the CA intends to deal with its assets upon the winding up. It is an important feature of the winding up of a CA that the freehold estate in each of the commonhold units becomes vested in the CA (s.49(3)). This may produce an anomalous result given that the commonhold units would formerly have been registered in the names of the individual unit-holders.

The termination statement is required to set out the CA's proposals for the transfer of commonhold land following the acquisition of the freehold of the commonhold units (s.47(1)(a)). It is thought likely that in practice, the CA would seek to revert to a more traditional long leasehold scheme of ownership; with individual unit-holders being granted long leases of individual units and a separate entity acquiring the reversionary interest of those long leaseholds together with the freehold of the common parts.

It is a requirement of the CML Lenders' Handbook that mortgage lenders must ensure that the commonhold community statement (CCS) provides that in the event of a voluntary termination of the commonhold, the termination statement provides that the unit-holders will ensure that any mortgage secured on their unit is repaid.

The termination statement must also set out the CA's proposals for the distribution of its other assets (s.47(1)(b)).

The Act provides for the CCS to make provision for any termination statement to include arrangements of a specified kind, or determined in a specified manner, concerning the rights of unit-holders in the event that the commonhold ceases to be a commonhold (s.47(2)). If any such provisions are made in the CCS, the termination statement must comply with them (s.47(3)). A member of the CA (s.47(5)) may apply to the court to disapply the requirement of the termination statement to comply with the provisions of the CCS generally, in respect of specified matters or for a specified purpose (s.47(4)). The prescribed form of CCS does not include any provisions relating to the termination statement. This is in contrast to the August 2003 draft of the CCS, which contained provisions requiring the termination statement to provide that a unit-holder was entitled to continue to occupy his unit until the CA transferred the commonhold land.

The termination-statement resolution must be passed by at least 80 per cent of the members of the CA (s.43(1)(c)).

14.2.3 Winding-up resolution

In order to wind up a CA, a winding-up resolution must be passed. The resolution must comply with section 84 of the IA 1986. Like the termination-statement resolution, the winding-up resolution must be passed by 80 per cent of the members of the CA (s.43(1)(c)). That can be contrasted with the usual position in Company Law whereby only 75 per cent support would be required for a resolution proposing the winding up of a solvent company.

A copy of the winding-up resolution must then be sent to the Registrar of Companies within 15 days of the date of the resolution being passed (IA 1986, s.84(3)). Section 85(1) of the IA 1986 also requires notice of the resolution to be given in the *Gazette* within 14 days of the date of the resolution being passed.

The procedure which then applies depends on whether both of the two resolutions previously referred to were passed by 100 per cent of the members of the CA or whether one or both were passed by less than 100 per cent.

14.2.4 Procedure in the case of unanimous passing of resolutions

In a case where the termination-statement resolution and the winding-up resolution are both passed by 100 per cent of the members of the CA, section 44 of the Act applies.

Once a winding-up resolution has been passed, a liquidator is appointed (IA 1986, s.91). The liquidator must be appointed by the CA in a general meeting (IA, 1986, s.91(1)). In advance of the meeting, the chosen liquidator must provide the chairman of the meeting with a written statement to the effect that he is an insolvency practitioner qualified under the IA 1986 to act as liquidator and that he consents to acting as liquidator (Insolvency Rules 1986 (IR 1986), r.4.139(1)–(2)).

If the liquidator is then appointed at the general meeting, the chairman of the meeting must certify the appointment. The certificate of appointment must be in the form prescribed by Schedule 4 to the IR 1986 (Form 4.27, or Form 4.28 in the case of more than one liquidator). The chairman of the meeting must immediately send the notice of appointment to the liquidator and the liquidator must then give notice of his appointment to the creditors (IR 1986, r.4.139(3)–(4)).

Between the winding-up resolution and the appointment of the liquidator, the directors of the CA may not exercise any of their powers except that the directors are empowered to do anything necessary to protect the assets of the CA (IA 1986, s.114). Once the liquidator is appointed, the powers of the directors cease immediately. The liquidator or the CA may sanction the continuation of the directors' powers in a general meeting (IA 1986, s.91(2)).

Within six months of the winding-up resolution, the liquidator must make an application to terminate the commonhold. If the liquidator fails to make the application within the six month period, it is open to a unit-holder to make the application to terminate (s.44(3)(a)). In addition, the Act makes provision for regulations to prescribe further classes of persons who may make the application to terminate in the event that the liquidator fails to do so within the prescribed period (s.44(3)(b)). However, the Commonhold Regulations 2004 (CR) make no such provision. An application to terminate the commonhold should be made to the Land Registrar and must be made on Form CM5 (Commonhold (Land Registration) Rules 2004 (CLRR), r.22(1)). The application must include the termination statement.

The liquidator must inform the Land Registrar that he has been appointed as liquidator (s.48(2)). In addition, the liquidator must, as soon as possible, under section 48(6), either:

- inform the Land Registrar that he is content with the terms of the termination statement which was submitted with the application to terminate (s.49(3)(a)); or
- make an application to the court to determine the terms of the termination statement (s.49(3)(b)). The order of the court determining the terms of the termination statement must then be sent to the Registrar of Companies (s.48(5)) and the Land Registrar (s.48(4)).

14.2.5   Procedure where less than unanimous passing of resolutions

In a case where either the termination-statement resolution or the winding-up resolution are passed by less than 100 per cent of the members of the CA, section 45 of the Act applies.

Once again, the first stage of the termination procedure is to appoint a liquidator. This is done in the same way as the procedure under section 44 described at **para.14.2.4**.

The liquidator must, within three months of the date of the winding-up resolution (s.45(3) and CR, reg.19(1)), make an application to the court to determine the terms pursuant to which an application to terminate the commonhold may be made and the terms of the termination statement which should accompany the application to terminate the commonhold (s.45(2)). If the liquidator fails to make the application within the three month period, it is open to a unit-holder to make the application to the court (s.45(4)(a)). In addition, the Act makes provision for regulations to prescribe further classes of persons who may make the application to the court in the event that the liquidator fails to do so within the prescribed period (s.45(4)(b)). However, the CR make no such provision.

Thereafter, the liquidator must, within three months of the date of the court's order (s.45(3)), apply to terminate the commonhold. The application must be made to the Land Registrar in accordance with the court's order. Once again, if the liquidator fails to make the application within the three month period, it is open to a unit-holder to make the application (s.45(3)(a)). In addition, the Act makes provision for regulations to prescribe further classes of persons who may make the application to the court in the event that the liquidator fails to do so within the prescribed period (s.45(3)(b)). Again, the CR make no such provision.

An application to terminate the commonhold is made to the Land Registrar and must be made on Form CM5 (CLRR, r.22(1)). The application must include a copy of the order made by the court and the certificate confirming the liquidator's appointment.

14.2.6 Effect of an application to terminate

Under either the section 44 or the section 45 procedure, the effect of the application to terminate is that the Land Registrar will register the CA as the proprietor of each of the commonhold units. In addition, the Registrar will cancel any entry on the Register of any unit which relates to the commonhold (CLRR, r.22(2)). The Registrar must also take any steps which are necessary to give effect to the termination statement (s.49(4)).

The liquidator may use the assets of the reserve fund to enforce a debt (s.56(a)). This applies only after a winding up and differs from the position prior to winding up where the assets may not be used for such a purpose except where the debt is a judgment debt which is specifically referable to a reserve fund activity (s.39(4)).

14.3 COMPULSORY WINDING UP

Because the CA is a company, the usual procedures for compulsory winding up of a company also apply. In addition, the Act provides for various additions and modifications to the usual procedure which are specific to CAs.

There are two principal modifications to the standard compulsory winding-up procedure. First, that the court has the power to order that the freehold interest in the common parts of the commonhold be transferred to a new CA, known as a succession order, and second, that the liquidator has certain additional duties in the case of a compulsory winding up of a CA.

14.3.1   Succession orders

The purpose of a succession order is to transfer the commonhold land owned by an insolvent CA into the hands of a new, or successor, CA (s.52(2)), which then adopts the rights and obligations of the insolvent CA (s.52(3)) so that the land owned by the insolvent CA is kept away from the CA's creditors. The wording of the Act imposes a duty on the court to make a succession order 'unless it thinks that the circumstances of the insolvent commonhold association make a succession order inappropriate' (s.51(4)). It is not clear what circumstances might have been envisaged and no guidance is given in the Act.

The Act provides for an application for a succession order to be made at the hearing of a winding-up petition (s.51(1)). There is no provision in the Act for such an application to be made at any other time.

An application for a succession order may be made by any person falling within any one of three categories and by no other person (s.51(2)). The categories are:

- the insolvent CA itself;
- one or more members of the CA;
- a provisional liquidator appointed for the CA pursuant to section 135 of the IA 1986.

The application for the succession order must be supported by:

- evidence of the formation of the successor CA (s.51(3)(a)). Regulation 19(2) of the CR provides that this evidence amounts to the certificate of incorporation of the successor CA (in accordance with Companies Act 1985, s.13) together with any altered certificates of incorporation (in accordance with the Companies Act 1985, s.28);
- a certificate given by the directors of the successor CA that its memorandum and articles of association comply with the requirements of paragraph 2(1) of Schedule 3 to the Act (s.51(3)(b)).

Section 52 of the Act contains various ancillary provisions relating to succession orders. The most important of these is that a succession order must make provision to deal with any charge over the common parts of the commonhold. Thus, the succession order will usually provide that the order is subject to the successor CA taking the transfer subject to the existing charge over the common parts, thus preserving the chargee's security (s.52(4)(a)). In addition, a succession order may (s.52(4)):

- require the Registrar to take action of a specified kind;
- enable the liquidator to require the Registrar to take action of a specified kind;
- make supplemental or incidental provisions.

If a succession order is made – and it is likely that in cases where an application is made that an order will be made – the consequences are that:

- the successor CA is entitled to be registered as the proprietor of the common parts of the commonhold (s.52(2));
- the insolvent CA shall for all purposes cease to be treated as the proprietor of the common parts of the commonhold (s.52(3));
- the successor CA is treated as the CA for the commonhold in respect of matters arising after the making of the winding-up order (s.53(2)). No new CCS is required and the successor CA and the unit-holders will be bound by the CCS of the previous CA;
- the successor CA is not liable for the debts of its predecessor or in respect of any claim made against its predecessor. However, it is likely that the successor CA will be required to take the freehold of the common parts of any commonhold subject to any existing charge over that land.

If a succession order is made, the court may require the liquidator of the predecessor CA to provide records, copies of records or information to the successor CA (s.53(3)). The court may also prescribe a time by which the documents or information must be provided and can provide that payment is to be made by the successor CA for the documents or information (s.53(4)).

14.3.2 Duties of the liquidator

If the court makes a compulsory winding-up order but does not make a succession order, then the liquidator of the insolvent CA has certain duties to provide information to the Land Registrar which arise under section 54 of the Act. These duties are in addition to the ordinary duties of the liquidator pursuant to the IA 1986.

The information which the liquidator must provide is (s.54(2)–(3)):

- that a winding-up order has been made and that a succession order has not been made;
- details of any directions made by the court on the winding up pursuant to section 168 of the IA 1986 together with a copy of any relevant court order;
- details of any notice given by the liquidator to the court or to the Registrar of Companies that a final meeting has been called by the

liquidator pursuant to section 172(8) of the IA 1986 together with a copy of the relevant notice;
- details of any notice given by the liquidator to the Secretary of State that a final meeting has been called by the liquidator pursuant to section 174(3) of the IA 1986 in a case where the liquidator is the Official Receiver;
- (in a case where the liquidator is the Official Receiver) details of any application made by the liquidator to the Registrar of Companies for early dissolution of the CA pursuant to section 202(2) of the IA 1986. (Such an application would be made where the assets of the CA were not sufficient to meet the costs of the winding up and where no further investigation of the CA's affairs is necessary. In such a case, a copy of the application must also be served.)
- (in a case where the liquidator is the Official Receiver) details of any notice given by the liquidator to the Registrar of Companies that the winding up has been completed pursuant to section 205(1)(b) of the IA 1986 together with a copy of any such notice;
- any other matter which, in the opinion of the liquidator, is relevant to the Land Registrar.

If the Land Registrar is informed by notification that the winding up of the CA has been completed, then he is obliged to terminate the commonhold by ensuring that the land formerly registered as commonhold land is no longer registered as a freehold estate in commonhold land as soon as reasonably practicable (s.54(4)(a)) and must take any other action which appears to him to be appropriate for the purposes of giving effect to a determination made by the liquidator in the exercise of his functions (s.54(4)(b)).

The liquidator may use the assets of the reserve fund to enforce a debt (s.56(a)). This applies only after a winding up and differs from the position prior to winding up where the assets may not be used for such a purpose except where the debt is a judgment debt which is specifically referable to a reserve fund activity (s.39(4)).

14.4   COMPULSORY PURCHASE OF THE COMMONHOLD LAND

Section 60 of the Act makes special provision for the compulsory purchase of commonhold land.

The compulsory purchaser of commonhold land must make a decision whether the land will continue as commonhold land after the compulsory purchase. If the compulsory purchaser wishes the land to continue as commonhold land, then he should indicate that desire to the Land Registrar. If the Land Registrar is satisfied that the compulsory purchaser has indicated such a desire, then the special provisions in section 60 will not apply (s.60(2)). If such a desire is not indicated, the compulsory purchase of the commonhold land will have the effect of terminating the commonhold (s.60(1)). It is thought likely that most compulsory purchasers will require the commonhold to be terminated.

It should be noted that s.60(7) extends the definition of a compulsory purchaser to a person who is entitled to exercise compulsory purchase powers but who, in fact, acquires the land by private treaty.

In the case of a compulsory purchase of part of a commonhold unit, the consent of the CA is not required (s.60(3)) notwithstanding that such a consent would be required in the case of a sale by private treaty (s.21(2)(c)).

Section 60 of the Act also provides for regulations to be made governing the manner in which commonhold land will be acquired by compulsory purchase. In particular, regulations may be made (s.60(5)–(6)) to deal with:

- the effect of the transfer of the commonhold land by compulsory purchase and in particular, the effect of the compulsory purchase being in respect of a part only of the commonhold land. These provisions may include provision for some or all of the commonhold land to cease to be commonhold land or for the Act to apply with specified modifications;
- any requirements regarding the service of notices;
- the powers of the court in relation to the purchase;
- provision for compensation;
- a power in favour of the CA requiring the compulsory purchaser to purchase the whole or a particular part of the commonhold land;
- the modification of any statutory provision relating to the compulsory purchase.

However, the CR do not contain any regulations dealing with any of these matters.

14.5 SUMMARY

The principal way in which a commonhold may be brought to an end is by winding up the CA which may take place either voluntarily, compulsorily or by the compulsory purchase of the commonhold land. The Act makes detailed provision for the winding up of a CA. If the CA is wound up, the liquidator must make an application to terminate the commonhold. Upon receipt of such an application, the Land Registry will terminate the commonhold and the commonhold units will vest in the CA subject to the proposals put forward by the CA in the termination statement.

CHAPTER 15

Commonhold: The alternative to the leasehold system

James Driscoll

15.1 INTRODUCTION

This book has examined the background to the commonhold legislation, how commonholds are created, how they are managed, and how they may be brought to an end. In this final chapter the potential of commonhold for property development in England and Wales is considered. This chapter examines first, the types of development where commonhold may appeal to developers and property owners; it then considers some of the criticisms that might be levelled at the commonhold legislation in its current form and concludes with a general assessment of the comparative advantages and disadvantages of commonhold over the traditional form of freehold and leasehold property development.

15.2 POTENTIAL OF COMMONHOLD

As has been seen, land can be registered as commonhold land under Part 1 of the Act for both new developments and for the conversion of existing leasehold and freehold properties.

15.3 LEASEHOLD AND FREEHOLD CONVERSIONS

15.3.1 Leasehold enfranchisement

It is possible that in the case of a smaller leasehold flat development, the leaseholders may choose to enfranchise and then convert to commonhold. In cases where leaseholders have already acquired the freehold through the medium of their nominee purchaser company they might also then decide to convert to commonhold. In this way they would exchange their leasehold flats for a freehold commonhold flat and the common parts to their building would be vested in a commonhold association (CA) in which all the flat owners would be members. The reason such conversions are only likely to take place in relation to smaller developments is the requirement that all those who hold an estate or interest in the land to be registered must unanimously agree before the land can be registered as commonhold land (s.3(1)).

Why would leaseholders who can enfranchise, or exercise the statutory right to manage under Part 2 of the Act choose to opt for commonhold? To begin with, some leaseholders may underestimate the fact that even when they have acquired the freehold (either voluntarily or through the statutory enfranchisement process under Part 1 of the Leasehold Reform, Housing and Urban Development Act 1993) and they collectively (or at least those who participate in the acquisition do) own the freehold, it still has to be managed under the terms of their leases which are themselves governed by other statutory provisions such as the Landlord and Tenant Act 1985, Landlord and Tenant Act 1987, and, of course, the major changes and reforms introduced by Part 2 of the Act. For example, leaseholders who are contemplating an enfranchisement need to consider how the building will be managed once they have acquired the freehold. In particular, attention has to be given to:

- estimating and obtaining where necessary, professional advice as to the works, repairs and maintenance that need to be carried out to the building as a whole;
- arranging the insurance of the exterior and common parts of the building; and
- consulting all of the leaseholders owning flats in the building over service and administration charges under the rules introduced under Part 2 of the Act.

The general business of managing residential leasehold premises has become extremely complex following the reforms made by legislation, in particular, by the most recent reform made by Part 2 of the Act. The revised consultation requirements for service charges, are complicated and failure to comply can be costly. This is one reason why leaseholders may consider converting to commonhold because, as explained in **Chapter 10**, the general business of making commonhold assessments and reserve funds contributions, and recovering these payments, is far more straightforward than it is under the residential leasehold system. Compare, for example, the new consultation requirements for setting leasehold service charges with the relative simplicity of setting commonhold assessments. On the issue of enforcement, recovery of an unpaid commonhold assessment by a unit-holder is also simpler: the unit-holder cannot refer any disputed assessment to a leasehold valuation tribunal (as leaseholders, of course, can) and recovery of the debt will usually be no more complicated that seeking a money judgment. True, forfeiture is not a remedy available to a CA, but many will consider that the reforms to forfeiture of residential leases, made under Part 2 of the Act now make forfeiture a weapon of last resort.

It is also likely that once commonhold becomes established in the market that a freehold commonhold unit may sell at a premium over a leasehold flat. This would simply be due to the fact that it is a freehold and not a wasting leasehold asset and also having regard to factors such as standard documentation which applies to the commonhold unit by comparison to what has often proved to be poorly drafted complex leasehold documentation.

Flat leaseholders in the small developments wishing to convert to commonhold who have not already acquired the freehold will obviously have to either use the statutory machinery for acquiring the freehold under Part 1 of the 1993 Act or negotiate with the current freeholder in order to acquire that interest.

15.3.2 Acquisition under the Landlord and Tenant Act 1987

Similar considerations apply where flat leaseholders have exercised rights under Part 1 of the Landlord and Tenant Act 1987 (the well known 'right of first refusal') and decided to acquire the freehold estate to the building where the landlord has offered them the right to purchase under the statutory revisions. However, conversion to commonhold is only likely again in the case of smaller leasehold developments which are exclusively residential as opposed to mixed-use developments.

Another possibility is that leaseholders who acquire the freehold by court order under the provisions in Part 3 of the Landlord and Tenant Act 1987 may decide to convert immediately to a commonhold. The Part 3 right is to compulsorily acquire the freehold from a landlord in cases where the landlord has failed to maintain the building properly and in other cases, such as where a leaseholder or group of leaseholders has procured the appointment of a manager by the Leasehold Valuation Tribunal under Part 2 of the 1987 Act and where such a management order has lasted for two years. There may sometimes be advantages to leaseholders proceeding in this way: to begin with, leaseholders who successfully acquire under Part 3 of the 1987 Act in county court proceedings could expect to have their costs paid by the former freeholder as 'costs follow the event'; secondly, the acquisition is on payment of the market value for the freehold with no 'marriage value' payable. In collective enfranchisement acquisitions under Part 1 of the 1993 Act, by contrast, the participating leaseholders have to pay the freeholder's reasonable professional costs and will also have to pay 50 per cent of any marriage value (except in relation to any leases which are longer than 80 years at the time of the enfranchisement claim).

15.3.3 Freehold flats

Another possible source of conversion is in the case of those who own freehold flats. One possible reason noted in **Chapter 1**, is that there can be immense difficulties in enforcing such positive covenants as the covenant to repair and to pay towards the cost of repairs and maintenance of the building in the case of freehold estates. In practice, freehold flats may be very difficult to market or to mortgage so conversion to a commonhold would seem to be an ideal solution for owners.

15.4 NEW PROPERTY DEVELOPMENTS

Turning to new developments, it is likely that investors in commercial property may be attracted by the opportunity of purchasing a freehold office, shop or other commercial units in either a commercial or mixed-used development. This might be thought by some to be a better form of investment than taking the traditional commercial lease.

Another factor for developers undertaking a new mixed-use development, where a feature of the development is the long term retention of the freehold in the hands of a management company, is that the current array of leaseholder's rights such as enfranchisement, the right to manage, service charge recovery, and so on, may militate against a development on the traditional freehold/leasehold basis. In such a case developing under a commonhold may be the way forward. Similar considerations apply to a mixed-use development too where the prospect of residential leaseholders in one part effectively opting out of the development (through the right to manage or the right to enfranchise) might make the long term goals of the development impossible.

15.5 SOME PROBLEMS OR ISSUES

The obvious difficulty is that commonhold is an entirely new concept in English property law and it will take some time for developers, property owners, investors and buyers, lawyers, surveyors and others to become familiar with the new legislation. There has so far been a very disappointing lack of publicity given by the government to the advantages of commonhold. This disappointment is all the more so as the government has stated that it considers commonhold to be the preferable long term alternative to the leasehold system.

Other concerns can be expressed as to the current drafting of the legislation. In particular, the legislation rules out multi-commonholds, that is to say a group of linked companies owning different commonhold developments under one commonhold umbrella. Reports and writings from other countries such as Australia and the United States show that more sophisticated commonhold laws can be developed to allow for more complex forms of development (see, for example, C. Baker and K. Fenn, 'Commonhold – A new system for land ownership', *Practical Law for Companies*, 16 (2005), 17–25).

Another issue is that at present the legislation only allows for land to be registered as commonhold land if the development is to be 'grounded', that is to say that the whole of the development is on freehold land. This precludes commonhold developments being built over a leasehold property, a type of development that is very familiar in Australia and which, it is reported, can work extremely well.

A related issue is that whilst the existing methods for setting and collecting the cost of commonholds have considerable merits the legislation does not, as currently drafted, allow easily for the setting of different types of assessments as may be necessary for mixed-use developments or any type of development of an interdependent building where different unit owners have different interests and responsibilities.

However, none of these concerns should of themselves inhibit the immediate spread of commonhold and it is entirely possible that the legislation will be recast in future so as to allow for more sophisticated types of development or, indeed, to deal with any practical problems that may emerge as the legislation and the regulations made under it are used.

Some concerns might be expressed over the insolvency provisions in the Act. Would a mortgagee of a commonhold unit lose its security if the unit-holders decided unanimously or on a 80 per cent majority vote to opt for a voluntary liquidation under sections 43–49 of the Act? One answer to this question is that the mortgagee would not automatically lose its security as under section 24 of the Land Registration Act 2002 a mortgage continues over land unless the land has been transferred for a valuable consideration and not, as is the case here, simply where the current unit-holders decide to opt for a voluntary liquidation. Other concerns might be expressed about the insolvency winding up provisions in the Act: is it possible, for example, that those contracting with the CA would be prejudiced if the CA became insolvent and some or all the unit-holders opted for a successor CA to take over the running of the commonhold, acquire the common parts in the insolvent CA and so on? As such, an application requires a court order under sections 50–56 of the Act and, even though there is statutory presumption that an order should be made in relation to the successor CA, it is thought extremely unlikely that the court would sanction the winding up of a CA and its replacement by a successor with some or all of the same unit-holders as owned under the auspices of the insolvent CA unless they are in a position to clear the debts and pay the premium or compensation for the acquisition of the common parts of the commonhold.

15.6 ADVANTAGES AND DISADVANTAGES OVER THE FREEHOLD/LEASEHOLD FORM OF DEVELOPMENT

15.6.1 Ownership

A lease is a time limited asset which, in consequence, is a wasting asset as a result of which someone investing in a lease finds its value gradually diminishes with time. Commonhold units, in contrast, are owned outright on a freehold basis. Moreover the freehold of the common parts of the development is owned by the CA whose members (post-completion of the commonhold development) are the owners of the commonhold units within the development.

15.6.2 Terminology

One of the many criticisms which is levelled at the leasehold system, particularly in the case of leasehold flats and leasehold houses, is that there is wide variation in the way in which leases are drafted and that in many cases lease terms are very poorly drafted and can put the parties to the lease to the expense of obtaining legal advice as to how problems can be rectified. In the case of a residential lease this might involve an application to the court or leasehold valuation tribunal for rectification of the terms of the lease (under Part 4 of the Landlord and Tenant Act 1987).

Here, again, there is a clear advantage of the commonhold development: as seen in **Chapter 6**, the rules of every commonhold are set out in a standard form commonhold community statement (CCS). A statutory instrument prescribes its basic form and although the details of the individual commonholds will vary quite considerably at times in relation to the local rules, the basic form of the rules is standardised. As commonhold becomes better known lawyers and other professional advisers should find it far easier to deal with the sale and transfer of mortgage of commonhold units than is the case with a leasehold unit.

15.6.3 Obligations of the parties

The obligations of the parties to a lease, as well as any third party to a lease, have often been expressed in unclear and confusing language. This leads to many uncertainties, leading to the need for the parties to obtain specialist legal advice on the meaning of the lease and the parties often have to resort to litigation for a determination of what some of the terms mean.

In contrast, the rules of every commonhold are not only prescribed by regulations but the drafting has been undertaken in plain straightforward language setting out the power, duties and responsibilities of the owner of the units and the CA.

15.6.4   Leasing units

In the case of a leasehold development it is usually the case that the lease-holder may only sub-let part or all of the premises with their landlord's consent. Although the landlord's consent can only be withheld on reasonable grounds, landlords are in a position to impose conditions which the lease-holder may find unacceptable.

In the case of a commonhold development the general principle is that the owner of the unit, as a freeholder, is placed in basically the same legal position as is the freehold owner of land. But, there are, in the case of residential units, such as commonhold flats or houses, statutory restrictions on leasing. These were examined in **Chapter 2**. However, these leasing restrictions do not in any way inhibit investment in residential units under buy-to-let arrangements since a unit-holder is free to let the unit under an assured shorthold or indeed a fully assured tenancy (as provided for in Part 1 of the Housing Act 1988). The policy for these restrictions is simply that the Government did not want what it considers to be the discredited leasehold system becoming established in commonhold. Another way of putting this is that residential commonhold unit-holders do have the statutory right to let their units provided that in doing so they comply with the terms of the CCS by, in particular, letting the prospective tenant have a copy of the CCS and ensuring that the lease complies with the conditions in the Act and in the Commonhold Regulations 2004.

Another advantage for both residential and commercial (or indeed mixed use) commonhold developments is that every CA has a statutory right to direct the tenant to pay his rent direct to the CA if the unit-holder is in default in paying assessments or reserve fund contributions.

15.6.5   Position of the parties

Under a lease the leaseholder stands in a very much hierarchical position and the landlord usually has a more or less complete say in how the leaseholder uses his unit and any common facilities. This is so even though the landlord may have a smaller financial stake in the building (such as a block of flats) than the individual leaseholders have collectively.

In contrast, there are, of course, no superior interests in the structure of any commonhold. Moreover the rules of the commonhold are written for the mutual benefit of the owners of the units and are enforced on their behalf by the CA which they own collectively. The statutory presumption in favour of using conciliation and mediation in solving disputes should also be borne in mind.

15.6.6 Legal complexity

In order to make the leasehold system work more effectively, and also in order to redress the imbalances of power between leaseholders, a considerable body of legislation has been passed as a result of Part 2 of the Act. Although these reforms improved the position of leaseholders (particularly residential leaseholders) it also introduced a degree of legal complexity which often requires parties to obtain legal advice. This legislation includes the Landlord and Tenant Acts of 1927, 1954, 1985, 1987, 1988, the Landlord and Tenant (Covenants) Act 1995 and other statutes and statutory instruments.

In contrast whilst every commonhold, of course, a subject of the general law of property, the basic law which governs and regulates commonholds, contained in Part 1 of the Act and in the regulations made under that Act, is overall a far less complicated area of property and leasehold law.

15.6.7 Forfeiture and termination of leases

Under previous law, the landlord usually had the power to re-enter and forfeit the lease in stated circumstances. Even though there were legal protections for leaseholders, particularly residential leaseholders, it was still possible in certain cases for a landlord to bring the leaseholder's estate interest or equity in the premises in question to an end. There are now major restrictions on forfeiting a residential lease introduced under Part 2 of the Act which effectively rule out the use of forfeiture for residential leases of flats and houses. This is likely to be just one part of a longer term programme to fundamentally reform forfeiture of leases under proposals which had been put forward by the Law Commission in a consultation paper on the termination of leases published in 2004.

None of these concerns applies a commonhold as it is not possible for a commonhold unit to be forfeited as it is a freehold estate in land. It is noted in **Chapter 10** that it would be possible to obtain a charging order in relation to a commonhold unit if the unit-holder had defaulted on payments of assignment or reserve funds.

15.6.8 Registered and unregistered title

Leases can be created in relation to both registered and unregistered land. In contrast the commonhold land can only be registered as commonhold land if the freehold estate is already registered.

15.6.9 Assignment

The right of a leaseholder to assign the lease is usually restricted by the terms of the lease, which in turn, invariably requires the agreement of the landlord.

Landlords usually reserve the power to impose conditions on such an assignment. In contrast, there are no statutory restrictions on the right of a commonhold unit-holder to assign, transfer or mortgage his unit and, in general terms, such restrictions cannot be imposed under the rules of the CCS.

15.6.10 Enforcement of obligations

Enforcement of obligations in a freehold/leasehold development is often adversarial and landlords are usually in a superior legal position in law. In practice issues relating to the enforcement of obligations between leaseholders themselves are sometimes difficult and in other cases impossible to resolve.

In contrast the policy underlying enforcement of obligations in a commonhold is based on co-operation between the commonhold unit-holders as well their mutual interest in running the commonhold effectively. In particular, every CA is required by statute to employ conciliation, mediation and other means short of litigation to secure compliance of the commonhold.

15.6.11 Service charges

Arguments over service charges and leases are very common whether one is examining a residential or a commercial lease. There are frequently complaints about the often poor drafting of service charge provisions in leases with the parties sometimes having to resort to litigation to get a determination as to the meaning and application of the service charge provisions. In the case of residential leases there are, as noted above, the complicated provisions allowing leaseholders to challenge service charges by reference to a leasehold valuation tribunal even though a service charge may have already been paid and even though the majority of the leaseholders might be perfectly happy with the level of expenditure, or the quality of work, or services that are being provided. In contrast, commonhold assignment is relatively straightforward and the enforcement of unit-holders' obligations to contribute towards the cost of the unit are set out in the rules of the CCS. These have been commented in detail in **Chapter 10**. It will be recalled that the statutory requirement to use conciliation is displaced if a CA is seeking to recover money against debts owing by a unit-holder and also in cases of emergencies.

APPENDIX A1

Commonhold and Leasehold Reform Act 2002, Part 1

Nature of commonhold

1   **Commonhold land**

(1)   Land is commonhold land if–
    (a)   the freehold estate in the land is registered as a freehold estate in commonhold land,
    (b)   the land is specified in the memorandum of association of a commonhold association as the land in relation to which the association is to exercise functions, and
    (c)   a commonhold community statement makes provision for rights and duties of the commonhold association and unit-holders (whether or not the statement has come into force).

(2)   In this Part a reference to a commonhold is a reference to land in relation to which a commonhold association exercises functions.

(3)   In this Part–
'commonhold association' has the meaning given by section 34,
'commonhold community statement' has the meaning given by section 31,
'commonhold unit' has the meaning given by section 11,
'common parts' has the meaning given by section 25, and
'unit-holder' has the meaning given by sections 12 and 13.

(4)   Sections 7 and 9 make provision for the vesting in the commonhold association of the fee simple in possession in the common parts of a commonhold.

Registration

2   **Application**

(1)   The Registrar shall register a freehold estate in land as a freehold estate in commonhold land if–
    (a)   the registered freeholder of the land makes an application under this section, and
    (b)   no part of the land is already commonhold land.

(2)   An application under this section must be accompanied by the documents listed in Schedule 1.

(3)   A person is the registered freeholder of land for the purposes of this Part if–
    (a)   he is registered as the proprietor of a freehold estate in the land with absolute title, or
    (b)   he has applied, and the Registrar is satisfied that he is entitled, to be registered as mentioned in paragraph (a).

3   Consent

(1)   An application under section 2 may not be made in respect of a freehold estate in land without the consent of anyone who–
    (a)   is the registered proprietor of the freehold estate in the whole or part of the land,
    (b)   is the registered proprietor of a leasehold estate in the whole or part of the land granted for a term of more than than 21 years,
    (c)   is the registered proprietor of a charge over the whole or part of the land, or
    (d)   falls within any other class of person which may be prescribed.

(2)   Regulations shall make provision about consent for the purposes of this section; in particular, the regulations may make provision–
    (a)   prescribing the form of consent;
    (b)   about the effect and duration of consent (including provision for consent to bind successors);
    (c)   about withdrawal of consent (including provision preventing withdrawal in specified circumstances);
    (d)   for consent given for the purpose of one application under section 2 to have effect for the purpose of another application;
    (e)   for consent to be deemed to have been given in specified circumstances;
    (f)   enabling a court to dispense with a requirement for consent in specified circumstances.

(3)   An order under subsection (2)(f) dispensing with a requirement for consent–
    (a)   may be absolute or conditional, and
    (b)   may make such other provision as the court thinks appropriate.

4   Land which may not be commonhold

Schedule 2 (which provides that an application under section 2 may not relate wholly or partly to land of certain kinds) shall have effect.

5   Registered details

(1)   The Registrar shall ensure that in respect of any commonhold land the following are kept in his custody and referred to in the register–
    (a)   the prescribed details of the commonhold association;
    (b)   the prescribed details of the registered freeholder of each commonhold unit;

(c)   a copy of the commonhold community statement;

(d)   a copy of the memorandum and articles of association of the commonhold association.

(2)   The Registrar may arrange for a document or information to be kept in his custody and referred to in the register in respect of commonhold land if the document or information–

(a)   is not mentioned in subsection (1), but

(b)   is submitted to the Registrar in accordance with a provision made by or by virtue of this Part.

(3)   Subsection (1)(b) shall not apply during a transitional period within the meaning of section 8.

6   Registration in error

(1)   This section applies where a freehold estate in land is registered as a freehold estate in commonhold land and–

(a)   the application for registration was not made in accordance with section 2,

(b)   the certificate under paragraph 7 of Schedule 1 was inaccurate, or

(c)   the registration contravened a provision made by or by virtue of this Part.

(2)   The register may not be altered by the Registrar under Schedule 4 to the Land Registration Act 2002 (c. 9) (alteration of register).

(3)   The court may grant a declaration that the freehold estate should not have been registered as a freehold estate in commonhold land.

(4)   A declaration under subsection (3) may be granted only on the application of a person who claims to be adversely affected by the registration.

(5)   On granting a declaration under subsection (3) the court may make any order which appears to it to be appropriate.

(6)   An order under subsection (5) may, in particular–

(a)   provide for the registration to be treated as valid for all purposes;

(b)   provide for alteration of the register;

(c)   provide for land to cease to be commonhold land;

(d)   require a director or other specified officer of a commonhold association to take steps to alter or amend a document;

(e)   require a director or other specified officer of a commonhold association to take specified steps;

(f)   make an award of compensation (whether or not contingent upon the occurrence or non-occurrence of a specified event) to be paid by one specified person to another;

(g)   apply, disapply or modify a provision of Schedule 8 to the Land Registration Act 2002 (c. 9) (indemnity).

Effect of registration

7   Registration without unit-holders

(1)   This section applies where –
    (a)   a freehold estate in land is registered as a freehold estate in commonhold land in pursuance of an application under section 2, and
    (b)   the application is not accompanied by a statement under section 9(1)(b).

(2)   On registration –
    (a)   the applicant shall continue to be registered as the proprietor of the freehold estate in the commonhold land, and
    (b)   the rights and duties conferred and imposed by the commonhold community statement shall not come into force (subject to section 8(2)(b)).

(3)   Where after registration a person other than the applicant becomes entitled to be registered as the proprietor of the freehold estate in one or more, but not all, of the commonhold units –
    (a)   the commonhold association shall be entitled to be registered as the proprietor of the freehold estate in the common parts,
    (b)   the Registrar shall register the commonhold association in accordance with paragraph (a) (without an application being made),
    (c)   the rights and duties conferred and imposed by the commonhold community statement shall come into force, and
    (d)   any lease of the whole or part of the commonhold land shall be extinguished by virtue of this section.

(4)   For the purpose of subsection (3)(d) 'lease' means a lease which –
    (a)   is granted for any term, and
    (b)   is granted before the commonhold association becomes entitled to be registered as the proprietor of the freehold estate in the common parts.

8   Transitional period

(1)   In this Part 'transitional period' means the period between registration of the freehold estate in land as a freehold estate in commonhold land and the event mentioned in section 7(3).

(2)   Regulations may provide that during a transitional period a relevant provision –
    (a)   shall not have effect, or
    (b)   shall have effect with specified modifications.

(3)   In subsection (2) 'relevant provision' means a provision made –
    (a)   by or by virtue of this Part,
    (b)   by a commonhold community statement, or
    (c)   by the memorandum or articles of the commonhold association.

(4)   The Registrar shall arrange for the freehold estate in land to cease to be registered as a freehold estate in commonhold land if the registered proprietor makes an application to the Registrar under this subsection during the transitional period.

(5)   The provisions about consent made by or under sections 2 and 3 and Schedule 1 shall apply in relation to an application under subsection (4) as they apply in relation to an application under section 2.

(6)   A reference in this Part to a commonhold association exercising functions in relation to commonhold land includes a reference to a case where a commonhold association would exercise functions in relation to commonhold land but for the fact that the time in question falls in a transitional period.

9   Registration with unit-holders

(1)   This section applies in relation to a freehold estate in commonhold land if–

    (a)   it is registered as a freehold estate in commonhold land in pursuance of an application under section 2, and

    (b)   the application is accompanied by a statement by the applicant requesting that this section should apply.

(2)   A statement under subsection (1)(b) must include a list of the commonhold units giving in relation to each one the prescribed details of the proposed initial unit-holder or joint unit-holders.

(3)   On registration–

    (a)   the commonhold association shall be entitled to be registered as the proprietor of the freehold estate in the common parts,

    (b)   a person specified by virtue of subsection (2) as the initial unit-holder of a commonhold unit shall be entitled to be registered as the proprietor of the freehold estate in the unit,

    (c)   a person specified by virtue of subsection (2) as an initial joint unit-holder of a commonhold unit shall be entitled to be registered as one of the proprietors of the freehold estate in the unit,

    (d)   the Registrar shall make entries in the register to reflect paragraphs (a) to (c) (without applications being made),

    (e)   the rights and duties conferred and imposed by the commonhold community statement shall come into force, and

    (f)   any lease of the whole or part of the commonhold land shall be extinguished by virtue of this section.

(4)   For the purpose of subsection (3)(f) 'lease' means a lease which–

    (a)   is granted for any term, and

    (b)   is granted before the commonhold association becomes entitled to be registered as the proprietor of the freehold estate in the common parts.

10   Extinguished lease: liability

(1)   This section applies where–

    (a)   a lease is extinguished by virtue of section 7(3)(d) or 9(3)(f), and

    (b)   the consent of the holder of that lease was not among the consents required by section 3 in respect of the application under section 2 for the land to become commonhold land.

(2)   If the holder of a lease superior to the extinguished lease gave consent under section 3, he shall be liable for loss suffered by the holder of the extinguished lease.

(3)   If the holders of a number of leases would be liable under subsection (2), liability shall attach only to the person whose lease was most proximate to the extinguished lease.

(4)   If no person is liable under subsection (2), the person who gave consent under section 3 as the holder of the freehold estate out of which the extinguished lease was granted shall be liable for loss suffered by the holder of the extinguished lease.

Commonhold unit

11   Definition

(1)   In this Part 'commonhold unit' means a commonhold unit specified in a commonhold community statement in accordance with this section.

(2)   A commonhold community statement must–
   (a)   specify at least two parcels of land as commonhold units, and
   (b)   define the extent of each commonhold unit.

(3)   In defining the extent of a commonhold unit a commonhold community statement–
   (a)   must refer to a plan which is included in the statement and which complies with prescribed requirements,
   (b)   may refer to an area subject to the exclusion of specified structures, fittings, apparatus or appurtenances within the area,
   (c)   may exclude the structures which delineate an area referred to, and
   (d)   may refer to two or more areas (whether or not contiguous).

(4)   A commonhold unit need not contain all or any part of a building.

12   Unit-holder

A person is the unit-holder of a commonhold unit if he is entitled to be registered as the proprietor of the freehold estate in the unit (whether or not he is registered).

13   Joint unit-holders

(1)   Two or more persons are joint unit-holders of a commonhold unit if they are entitled to be registered as proprietors of the freehold estate in the unit (whether or not they are registered).

(2)   In the application of the following provisions to a unit with joint unit-holders a reference to a unit-holder is a reference to the joint unit-holders together–
   (a)   section 14(3),
   (b)   section 15(1) and (3),
   (c)   section 19(2) and (3),
   (d)   section 20(1),
   (e)   section 23(1),
   (f)   section 35(1)(b),
   (g)   section 38(1),

(h)   section 39(2), and
(i)   section 47(2).

(3)   In the application of the following provisions to a unit with joint unit-holders a reference to a unit-holder includes a reference to each joint unit-holder and to the joint unit-holders together–
    (a)   section 1(1)(c),
    (b)   section 16,
    (c)   section 31(1)(b), (3)(b), (5)(j) and (7),
    (d)   section 32(4)(a) and (c),
    (e)   section 35(1)(a), (2) and (3),
    (f)   section 37(2),
    (g)   section 40(1), and
    (h)   section 58(3)(a).

(4)   Regulations under this Part which refer to a unit-holder shall make provision for the construction of the reference in the case of joint unit-holders.

(5)   Regulations may amend subsection (2) or (3).

(6)   Regulations may make provision for the construction in the case of joint unit-holders of a reference to a unit-holder in–
    (a)   an enactment,
    (b)   a commonhold community statement,
    (c)   the memorandum or articles of association of a commonhold association, or
    (d)   another document.

14   Use and maintenance

(1)   A commonhold community statement must make provision regulating the use of commonhold units.

(2)   A commonhold community statement must make provision imposing duties in respect of the insurance, repair and maintenance of each commonhold unit.

(3)   A duty under subsection (2) may be imposed on the commonhold association or the unit-holder.

15   Transfer

(1)   In this Part a reference to the transfer of a commonhold unit is a reference to the transfer of a unit-holder's freehold estate in a unit to another person–
    (a)   whether or not for consideration,
    (b)   whether or not subject to any reservation or other terms, and
    (c)   whether or not by operation of law.

(2)   A commonhold community statement may not prevent or restrict the transfer of a commonhold unit.

(3)   On the transfer of a commonhold unit the new unit-holder shall notify the commonhold association of the transfer.

(4)   Regulations may–
    (a)   prescribe the form and manner of notice under subsection (3);
    (b)   prescribe the time within which notice is to be given;

(c)   make provision (including provision requiring the payment of money) about the effect of failure to give notice.

16   Transfer: effect

(1)   A right or duty conferred or imposed –
(a)   by a commonhold community statement, or
(b)   in accordance with section 20,
shall affect a new unit-holder in the same way as it affected the former unit-holder.

(2)   A former unit-holder shall not incur a liability or acquire a right –
(a)   under or by virtue of the commonhold community statement, or
(b)   by virtue of anything done in accordance with section 20.

(3)   Subsection (2) –
(a)   shall not be capable of being disapplied or varied by agreement, and
(b)   is without prejudice to any liability or right incurred or acquired before a transfer takes effect.

(4)   In this section –
'former unit-holder' means a person from whom a commonhold unit has been transferred (whether or not he has ceased to be the registered proprietor), and
'new unit-holder' means a person to whom a commonhold unit is transferred (whether or not he has yet become the registered proprietor).

17   Leasing: residential

(1)   It shall not be possible to create a term of years absolute in a residential commonhold unit unless the term satisfies prescribed conditions.

(2)   The conditions may relate to –
(a)   length;
(b)   the circumstances in which the term is granted;
(c)   any other matter.

(3)   Subject to subsection (4), an instrument or agreement shall be of no effect to the extent that it purports to create a term of years in contravention of subsection (1).

(4)   Where an instrument or agreement purports to create a term of years in contravention of subsection (1) a party to the instrument or agreement may apply to the court for an order –
(a)   providing for the instrument or agreement to have effect as if it provided for the creation of a term of years of a specified kind;
(b)   providing for the return or payment of money;
(c)   making such other provision as the court thinks appropriate.

(5)   A commonhold unit is residential if provision made in the commonhold community statement by virtue of section 14(1) requires it to be used only –
(a)   for residential purposes, or
(b)   for residential and other incidental purposes.

18   Leasing: non-residential

An instrument or agreement which creates a term of years absolute in a commonhold unit which is not residential (within the meaning of section 17) shall have effect subject to any provision of the commonhold community statement.

19   Leasing: supplementary

(1)   Regulations may –
    (a)   impose obligations on a tenant of a commonhold unit;
    (b)   enable a commonhold community statement to impose obligations on a tenant of a commonhold unit.
(2)   Regulations under subsection (1) may, in particular, require a tenant of a commonhold unit to make payments to the commonhold association or a unit-holder in discharge of payments which –
    (a)   are due in accordance with the commonhold community statement to be made by the unit-holder, or
    (b)   are due in accordance with the commonhold community statement to be made by another tenant of the unit.
(3)   Regulations under subsection (1) may, in particular, provide –
    (a)   for the amount of payments under subsection (2) to be set against sums owed by the tenant (whether to the person by whom the payments were due to be made or to some other person);
    (b)   for the amount of payments under subsection (2) to be recovered from the unit-holder or another tenant of the unit.
(4)   Regulations may modify a rule of law about leasehold estates (whether deriving from the common law or from an enactment) in its application to a term of years in a commonhold unit.
(5)   Regulations under this section –
    (a)   may make provision generally or in relation to specified circumstances, and
    (b)   may make different provision for different descriptions of commonhold land or commonhold unit.

20   Other transactions

(1)   A commonhold community statement may not prevent or restrict the creation, grant or transfer by a unit-holder of –
    (a)   an interest in the whole or part of his unit, or
    (b)   a charge over his unit.
(2)   Subsection (1) is subject to sections 17 to 19 (which impose restrictions about leases).
(3)   It shall not be possible to create an interest of a prescribed kind in a commonhold unit unless the commonhold association –
    (a)   is a party to the creation of the interest, or
    (b)   consents in writing to the creation of the interest.
(4)   A commonhold association may act as described in subsection (3)(a) or (b) only if –

(a)   the association passes a resolution to take the action, and
(b)   at least 75 per cent. of those who vote on the resolution vote in favour.

(5)   An instrument or agreement shall be of no effect to the extent that it purports to create an interest in contravention of subsection (3).
(6)   In this section 'interest' does not include–
(a)   a charge, or
(b)   an interest which arises by virtue of a charge.

21   Part-unit: interests

(1)   It shall not be possible to create an interest in part only of a commonhold unit.
(2)   But subsection (1) shall not prevent–
(a)   the creation of a term of years absolute in part only of a residential commonhold unit where the term satisfies prescribed conditions,
(b)   the creation of a term of years absolute in part only of a non-residential commonhold unit, or
(c)   the transfer of the freehold estate in part only of a commonhold unit where the commonhold association consents in writing to the transfer.
(3)   An instrument or agreement shall be of no effect to the extent that it purports to create an interest in contravention of subsection (1).
(4)   Subsection (5) applies where–
(a)   land becomes commonhold land or is added to a commonhold unit, and
(b)   immediately before that event there is an interest in the land which could not be created after that event by reason of subsection (1).
(5)   The interest shall be extinguished by virtue of this subsection to the extent that it could not be created by reason of subsection (1).
(6)   Section 17(2) and (4) shall apply (with any necessary modifications) in relation to subsection (2)(a) and (b) above.
(7)   Where part only of a unit is held under a lease, regulations may modify the application of a provision which–
(a)   is made by or by virtue of this Part, and
(b)   applies to a unit-holder or a tenant or both.
(8)   Section 20(4) shall apply in relation to subsection (2)(c) above.
(9)   Where the freehold interest in part only of a commonhold unit is transferred, the part transferred–
(a)   becomes a new commonhold unit by virtue of this subsection, or
(b)   in a case where the request for consent under subsection (2)(c) states that this paragraph is to apply, becomes part of a commonhold unit specified in the request.
(10)   Regulations may make provision, or may require a commonhold community statement to make provision, about–
(a)   registration of units created by virtue of subsection (9);
(b)   the adaptation of provision made by or by virtue of this Part or by or by virtue of a commonhold community statement to a case where units are created or modified by virtue of subsection (9).

22   Part-unit: charging

(1)   It shall not be possible to create a charge over part only of an interest in a commonhold unit.

(2)   An instrument or agreement shall be of no effect to the extent that it purports to create a charge in contravention of subsection (1).

(3)   Subsection (4) applies where–

    (a)   land becomes commonhold land or is added to a commonhold unit, and

    (b)   immediately before that event there is a charge over the land which could not be created after that event by reason of subsection (1).

(4)   The charge shall be extinguished by virtue of this subsection to the extent that it could not be created by reason of subsection (1).

23   Changing size

(1)   An amendment of a commonhold community statement which redefines the extent of a commonhold unit may not be made unless the unit-holder consents–

    (a)   in writing, and

    (b)   before the amendment is made.

(2)   But regulations may enable a court to dispense with the requirement for consent on the application of a commonhold association in prescribed circumstances.

24   Changing size: charged unit

(1)   This section applies to an amendment of a commonhold community statement which redefines the extent of a commonhold unit over which there is a registered charge.

(2)   The amendment may not be made unless the registered proprietor of the charge consents–

    (a)   in writing, and

    (b)   before the amendment is made.

(3)   But regulations may enable a court to dispense with the requirement for consent on the application of a commonhold association in prescribed circumstances.

(4)   If the amendment removes land from the commonhold unit, the charge shall by virtue of this subsection be extinguished to the extent that it relates to the land which is removed.

(5)   If the amendment adds land to the unit, the charge shall by virtue of this subsection be extended so as to relate to the land which is added.

(6)   Regulations may make provision–

    (a)   requiring notice to be given to the Registrar in circumstances to which this section applies;

    (b)   requiring the Registrar to alter the register to reflect the application of subsection (4) or (5).

Common parts

25   Definition

(1)   In this Part 'common parts' in relation to a commonhold means every part of the commonhold which is not for the time being a commonhold unit in accordance with the commonhold community statement.

(2)   A commonhold community statement may make provision in respect of a specified part of the common parts (a 'limited use area') restricting–
(a)   the classes of person who may use it;
(b)   the kind of use to which it may be put.

(3)   A commonhold community statement–
(a)   may make provision which has effect only in relation to a limited use area, and
(b)   may make different provision for different limited use areas.

26   Use and maintenance

A commonhold community statement must make provision–
(a)   regulating the use of the common parts;
(b)   requiring the commonhold association to insure the common parts;
(c)   requiring the commonhold association to repair and maintain the common parts.

27   Transactions

(1)   Nothing in a commonhold community statement shall prevent or restrict–
(a)   the transfer by the commonhold association of its freehold estate in any part of the common parts, or
(b)   the creation by the commonhold association of an interest in any part of the common parts.

(2)   In this section 'interest' does not include–
(a)   a charge, or
(b)   an interest which arises by virtue of a charge.

28   Charges: general prohibition

(1)   It shall not be possible to create a charge over common parts.

(2)   An instrument or agreement shall be of no effect to the extent that it purports to create a charge over common parts.

(3)   Where by virtue of section 7 or 9 a commonhold association is registered as the proprietor of common parts, a charge which relates wholly or partly to the common parts shall be extinguished by virtue of this subsection to the extent that it relates to the common parts.

(4)   Where by virtue of section 30 land vests in a commonhold association following an amendment to a commonhold community statement which has

the effect of adding land to the common parts, a charge which relates wholly or partly to the land added shall be extinguished by virtue of this subsection to the extent that it relates to that land.

(5) This section is subject to section 29 (which permits certain mortgages).

29 New legal mortgages

(1) Section 28 shall not apply in relation to a legal mortgage if the creation of the mortgage is approved by a resolution of the commonhold association.

(2) A resolution for the purposes of subsection (1) must be passed –
    (a) before the mortgage is created, and
    (b) unanimously.

(3) In this section 'legal mortgage' has the meaning given by section 205(1)(xvi) of the Law of Property Act 1925 (c. 20) (interpretation).

30 Additions to common parts

(1) This section applies where an amendment of a commonhold community statement –
    (a) specifies land which forms part of a commonhold unit, and
    (b) provides for that land (the 'added land') to be added to the common parts.

(2) The amendment may not be made unless the registered proprietor of any charge over the added land consents –
    (a) in writing, and
    (b) before the amendment is made.

(3) But regulations may enable a court to dispense with the requirement for consent on the application of a commonhold association in specified circumstances.

(4) On the filing of the amended statement under section 33 –
    (a) the commonhold association shall be entitled to be registered as the proprietor of the freehold estate in the added land, and
    (b) the Registrar shall register the commonhold association in accordance with paragraph (a) (without an application being made).

Commonhold community statement

31 Form and content: general

(1) A commonhold community statement is a document which makes provision in relation to specified land for –
    (a) the rights and duties of the commonhold association, and
    (b) the rights and duties of the unit-holders.

(2) A commonhold community statement must be in the prescribed form.

(3) A commonhold community statement may –
    (a) impose a duty on the commonhold association;
    (b) impose a duty on a unit-holder;

(c)   make provision about the taking of decisions in connection with the management of the commonhold or any other matter concerning it.

(4)   Subsection (3) is subject to –

(a)   any provision made by or by virtue of this Part, and

(b)   any provision of the memorandum or articles of the commonhold association.

(5)   In subsection (3)(a) and (b) 'duty' includes, in particular, a duty –

(a)   to pay money;

(b)   to undertake works;

(c)   to grant access;

(d)   to give notice;

(e)   to refrain from entering into transactions of a specified kind in relation to a commonhold unit;

(f)   to refrain from using the whole or part of a commonhold unit for a specified purpose or for anything other than a specified purpose;

(g)   to refrain from undertaking works (including alterations) of a specified kind;

(h)   to refrain from causing nuisance or annoyance;

(i)   to refrain from specified behaviour;

(j)   to indemnify the commonhold association or a unit-holder in respect of costs arising from the breach of a statutory requirement.

(6)   Provision in a commonhold community statement imposing a duty to pay money (whether in pursuance of subsection (5)(a) or any other provision made by or by virtue of this Part) may include provision for the payment of interest in the case of late payment.

(7)   A duty conferred by a commonhold community statement on a commonhold association or a unit-holder shall not require any other formality.

(8)   A commonhold community statement may not provide for the transfer or loss of an interest in land on the occurrence or non-occurrence of a specified event.

(9)   Provision made by a commonhold community statement shall be of no effect to the extent that –

(a)   it is prohibited by virtue of section 32,

(b)   it is inconsistent with any provision made by or by virtue of this Part,

(c)   it is inconsistent with anything which is treated as included in the statement by virtue of section 32, or

(d)   it is inconsistent with the memorandum or articles of association of the commonhold association.

32   Regulations

(1)   Regulations shall make provision about the content of a commonhold community statement.

(2)   The regulations may permit, require or prohibit the inclusion in a statement of –

(a)   specified provision, or

(b)   provision of a specified kind, for a specified purpose or about a specified matter.

(3)   The regulations may–
    (a)   provide for a statement to be treated as including provision pre-
scribed by or determined in accordance with the regulations;
    (b)   permit a statement to make provision in place of provision which
would otherwise be treated as included by virtue of paragraph (a).
(4)   The regulations may–
    (a)   make different provision for different descriptions of commonhold
association or unit-holder;
    (b)   make different provision for different circumstances;
    (c)   make provision about the extent to which a commonhold commu-
nity statement may make different provision for different descrip-
tions of unit-holder or common parts.
(5)   The matters to which regulations under this section may relate include, but
are not limited to–
    (a)   the matters mentioned in sections 11, 14, 15, 20, 21, 25, 26, 27, 38,
39 and 58, and
    (b)   any matter for which regulations under section 37 may make
provision.

33   Amendment

(1)   Regulations under section 32 shall require a commonhold community statement to make provision about how it can be amended.
(2)   The regulations shall, in particular, make provision under section 32(3)(a)
(whether or not subject to provision under section 32(3)(b)).
(3)   An amendment of a commonhold community statement shall have no effect
unless and until the amended statement is registered in accordance with this
section.
(4)   If the commonhold association makes an application under this subsection
the Registrar shall arrange for an amended commonhold community statement to be kept in his custody, and referred to in the register, in place of the
unamended statement.
(5)   An application under subsection (4) must be accompanied by a certificate
given by the directors of the commonhold association that the amended
commonhold community statement satisfies the requirements of this Part.
(6)   Where an amendment of a commonhold community statement redefines the
extent of a commonhold unit, an application under subsection (4) must be
accompanied by any consent required by section 23(1) or 24(2) (or an order
of a court dispensing with consent).
(7)   Where an amendment of a commonhold community statement has the
effect of changing the extent of the common parts, an application under
subsection (4) must be accompanied by any consent required by section
30(2) (or an order of a court dispensing with consent).
(8)   Where the Registrar amends the register on an application under subsection
(4) he shall make any consequential amendments to the register which he
thinks appropriate.

Commonhold association

34   Constitution

(1)   A commonhold association is a private company limited by guarantee the memorandum of which –
      (a)   states that an object of the company is to exercise the functions of a commonhold association in relation to specified commonhold land, and
      (b)   specifies £1 as the amount required to be specified in pursuance of section 2(4) of the Companies Act 1985 (c. 6) (members' guarantee).
(2)   Schedule 3 (which makes provision about the constitution of a commonhold association) shall have effect.

35   Duty to manage

(1)   The directors of a commonhold association shall exercise their powers so as to permit or facilitate so far as possible –
      (a)   the exercise by each unit-holder of his rights, and
      (b)   the enjoyment by each unit-holder of the freehold estate in his unit.
(2)   The directors of a commonhold association shall, in particular, use any right, power or procedure conferred or created by virtue of section 37 for the purpose of preventing, remedying or curtailing a failure on the part of a unit-holder to comply with a requirement or duty imposed on him by virtue of the commonhold community statement or a provision of this Part.
(3)   But in respect of a particular failure on the part of a unit-holder (the 'defaulter') the directors of a commonhold association –
      (a)   need not take action if they reasonably think that inaction is in the best interests of establishing or maintaining harmonious relationships between all the unit-holders, and that it will not cause any unit-holder (other than the defaulter) significant loss or significant disadvantage, and
      (b)   shall have regard to the desirability of using arbitration, mediation or conciliation procedures (including referral under a scheme approved under section 42) instead of legal proceedings wherever possible.
(4)   A reference in this section to a unit-holder includes a reference to a tenant of a unit.

36   Voting

(1)   This section applies in relation to any provision of this Part (a 'voting provision') which refers to the passing of a resolution by a commonhold association.
(2)   A voting provision is satisfied only if every member is given an opportunity to vote in accordance with any relevant provision of the memorandum or articles of association or the commonhold community statement.

(3)   A vote is cast for the purposes of a voting provision whether it is cast in person or in accordance with a provision which –
  (a)   provides for voting by post, by proxy or in some other manner, and
  (b)   is contained in the memorandum or articles of association or the commonhold community statement.

(4)   A resolution is passed unanimously if every member who casts a vote votes in favour.

Operation of commonhold

37   Enforcement and compensation

(1)   Regulations may make provision (including provision conferring jurisdiction on a court) about the exercise or enforcement of a right or duty imposed or conferred by or by virtue of –
  (a)   a commonhold community statement;
  (b)   the memorandum or articles of a commonhold association;
  (c)   a provision made by or by virtue of this Part.

(2)   The regulations may, in particular, make provision –
  (a)   requiring compensation to be paid where a right is exercised in specified cases or circumstances;
  (b)   requiring compensation to be paid where a duty is not complied with;
  (c)   enabling recovery of costs where work is carried out for the purpose of enforcing a right or duty;
  (d)   enabling recovery of costs where work is carried out in consequence of the failure to perform a duty;
  (e)   permitting a unit-holder to enforce a duty imposed on another unit-holder, on a commonhold association or on a tenant;
  (f)   permitting a commonhold association to enforce a duty imposed on a unit-holder or a tenant;
  (g)   permitting a tenant to enforce a duty imposed on another tenant, a unit-holder or a commonhold association;
  (h)   permitting the enforcement of terms or conditions to which a right is subject;
  (i)   requiring the use of a specified form of arbitration, mediation or conciliation procedure before legal proceedings may be brought.

(3)   Provision about compensation made by virtue of this section shall include –
  (a)   provision (which may include provision conferring jurisdiction on a court) for determining the amount of compensation;
  (b)   provision for the payment of interest in the case of late payment.

(4)   Regulations under this section shall be subject to any provision included in a commonhold community statement in accordance with regulations made by virtue of section 32(5)(b).

38   Commonhold assessment

(1)   A commonhold community statement must make provision –
    (a)   requiring the directors of the commonhold association to make an annual estimate of the income required to be raised from unit-holders to meet the expenses of the association,
    (b)   enabling the directors of the commonhold association to make estimates from time to time of income required to be raised from unit-holders in addition to the annual estimate,
    (c)   specifying the percentage of any estimate made under paragraph (a) or (b) which is to be allocated to each unit,
    (d)   requiring each unit-holder to make payments in respect of the percentage of any estimate which is allocated to his unit, and
    (e)   requiring the directors of the commonhold association to serve notices on unit-holders specifying payments required to be made by them and the date on which each payment is due.

(2)   For the purpose of subsection (1)(c) –
    (a)   the percentages allocated by a commonhold community statement to the commonhold units must amount in aggregate to 100;
    (b)   a commonhold community statement may specify 0 per cent. in relation to a unit.

39   Reserve fund

(1)   Regulations under section 32 may, in particular, require a commonhold community statement to make provision –
    (a)   requiring the directors of the commonhold association to establish and maintain one or more funds to finance the repair and maintenance of common parts;
    (b)   requiring the directors of the commonhold association to establish and maintain one or more funds to finance the repair and maintenance of commonhold units.

(2)   Where a commonhold community statement provides for the establishment and maintenance of a fund in accordance with subsection (1) it must also make provision –
    (a)   requiring or enabling the directors of the commonhold association to set a levy from time to time,
    (b)   specifying the percentage of any levy set under paragraph (a) which is to be allocated to each unit,
    (c)   requiring each unit-holder to make payments in respect of the percentage of any levy set under paragraph (a) which is allocated to his unit, and
    (d)   requiring the directors of the commonhold association to serve notices on unit-holders specifying payments required to be made by them and the date on which each payment is due.

(3)   For the purpose of subsection (2)(b) –
    (a)   the percentages allocated by a commonhold community statement to the commonhold units must amount in aggregate to 100;
    (b)   a commonhold community statement may specify 0 per cent. in relation to a unit.

(4) The assets of a fund established and maintained by virtue of this section shall not be used for the purpose of enforcement of any debt except a judgment debt referable to a reserve fund activity.

(5) For the purpose of subsection (4)–

(a) 'reserve fund activity' means an activity which in accordance with the commonhold community statement can or may be financed from a fund established and maintained by virtue of this section,

(b) assets are used for the purpose of enforcement of a debt if, in particular, they are taken in execution or are made the subject of a charging order under section 1 of the Charging Orders Act 1979 (c. 53), and

(c) the reference to a judgment debt includes a reference to any interest payable on a judgment debt.

40   Rectification of documents

(1) A unit-holder may apply to the court for a declaration that–

(a) the memorandum or articles of association of the relevant commonhold association do not comply with regulations under paragraph 2(1) of Schedule 3;

(b) the relevant commonhold community statement does not comply with a requirement imposed by or by virtue of this Part.

(2) On granting a declaration under this section the court may make any order which appears to it to be appropriate.

(3) An order under subsection (2) may, in particular–

(a) require a director or other specified officer of a commonhold association to take steps to alter or amend a document;

(b) require a director or other specified officer of a commonhold association to take specified steps;

(c) make an award of compensation (whether or not contingent upon the occurrence or non-occurrence of a specified event) to be paid by the commonhold association to a specified person;

(d) make provision for land to cease to be commonhold land.

(4) An application under subsection (1) must be made–

(a) within the period of three months beginning with the day on which the applicant became a unit-holder,

(b) within three months of the commencement of the alleged failure to comply, or

(c) with the permission of the court.

41   Enlargement

(1) This section applies to an application under section 2 if the commonhold association for the purposes of the application already exercises functions in relation to commonhold land.

(2) In this section–

(a) the application is referred to as an 'application to add land', and

(b) the land to which the application relates is referred to as the 'added land'.

192

(3) An application to add land may not be made unless it is approved by a resolution of the commonhold association.

(4) A resolution for the purposes of subsection (3) must be passed –
    (a) before the application to add land is made, and
    (b) unanimously.

(5) Section 2(2) shall not apply to an application to add land; but the application must be accompanied by –
    (a) the documents specified in paragraph 6 of Schedule 1,
    (b) an application under section 33 for the registration of an amended commonhold community statement which makes provision for the existing commonhold and the added land, and
    (c) a certificate given by the directors of the commonhold association that the application to add land satisfies Schedule 2 and subsection (3).

(6) Where sections 7 and 9 have effect following an application to add land –
    (a) the references to 'the commonhold land' in sections 7(2)(a) and (3)(d) and 9(3)(f) shall be treated as references to the added land, and
    (b) the references in sections 7(2)(b) and (3)(c) and 9(3)(e) to the rights and duties conferred and imposed by the commonhold community statement shall be treated as a reference to rights and duties only in so far as they affect the added land.

(7) In the case of an application to add land where the whole of the added land is to form part of the common parts of a commonhold –
    (a) section 7 shall not apply,
    (b) on registration the commonhold association shall be entitled to be registered (if it is not already) as the proprietor of the freehold estate in the added land,
    (c) the Registrar shall make any registration required by paragraph (b) (without an application being made), and
    (d) the rights and duties conferred and imposed by the commonhold community statement shall, in so far as they affect the added land, come into force on registration.

42   Ombudsman

(1) Regulations may provide that a commonhold association shall be a member of an approved ombudsman scheme.

(2) An 'approved ombudsman scheme' is a scheme which is approved by the Lord Chancellor and which –
    (a) provides for the appointment of one or more persons as ombudsman,
    (b) provides for a person to be appointed as ombudsman only if the Lord Chancellor approves the appointment in advance,
    (c) enables a unit-holder to refer to the ombudsman a dispute between the unit-holder and a commonhold association which is a member of the scheme,
    (d) enables a commonhold association which is a member of the scheme to refer to the ombudsman a dispute between the association and a unit-holder,

(e)   requires the ombudsman to investigate and determine a dispute referred to him,

(f)   requires a commonhold association which is a member of the scheme to cooperate with the ombudsman in investigating or determining a dispute, and

(g)   requires a commonhold association which is a member of the scheme to comply with any decision of the ombudsman (including any decision requiring the payment of money).

(3)   In addition to the matters specified in subsection (2) an approved ombudsman scheme—

(a)   may contain other provision, and

(b)   shall contain such provision, or provision of such a kind, as may be prescribed.

(4)   If a commonhold association fails to comply with regulations under subsection (1) a unit-holder may apply to the High Court for an order requiring the directors of the commonhold association to ensure that the association complies with the regulations.

(5)   A reference in this section to a unit-holder includes a reference to a tenant of a unit.

Termination: voluntary winding-up

43   **Winding-up resolution**

(1)   A winding-up resolution in respect of a commonhold association shall be of no effect unless—

(a)   the resolution is preceded by a declaration of solvency,

(b)   the commonhold association passes a termination-statement resolution before it passes the winding-up resolution, and

(c)   each resolution is passed with at least 80 per cent. of the members of the association voting in favour.

(2)   In this Part—

'declaration of solvency' means a directors' statutory declaration made in accordance with section 89 of the Insolvency Act 1986 (c. 45),

'termination-statement resolution' means a resolution approving the terms of a termination statement (within the meaning of section 47), and

'winding-up resolution' means a resolution for voluntary winding-up within the meaning of section 84 of that Act.

44   **100 per cent. agreement**

(1)   This section applies where a commonhold association—

(a)   has passed a winding-up resolution and a termination-statement resolution with 100 per cent. of the members of the association voting in favour, and

(b)   has appointed a liquidator under section 91 of the Insolvency Act 1986 (c. 45).

(2)   The liquidator shall make a termination application within the period of six months beginning with the day on which the winding-up resolution is passed.

(3)   If the liquidator fails to make a termination application within the period specified in subsection (2) a termination application may be made by –
      (a)   a unit-holder, or
      (b)   a person falling within a class prescribed for the purposes of this subsection.

45   80 per cent. agreement

(1)   This section applies where a commonhold association –
      (a)   has passed a winding-up resolution and a termination-statement resolution with at least 80 per cent. of the members of the association voting in favour, and
      (b)   has appointed a liquidator under section 91 of the Insolvency Act 1986.
(2)   The liquidator shall within the prescribed period apply to the court for an order determining –
      (a)   the terms and conditions on which a termination application may be made, and
      (b)   the terms of the termination statement to accompany a termination application.
(3)   The liquidator shall make a termination application within the period of three months starting with the date on which an order under subsection (2) is made.
(4)   If the liquidator fails to make an application under subsection (2) or (3) within the period specified in that subsection an application of the same kind may be made by –
      (a)   a unit-holder, or
      (b)   a person falling within a class prescribed for the purposes of this subsection.

46   Termination application

(1)   A 'termination application' is an application to the Registrar that all the land in relation to which a particular commonhold association exercises functions should cease to be commonhold land.
(2)   A termination application must be accompanied by a termination statement.
(3)   On receipt of a termination application the Registrar shall note it in the register.

47   Termination statement

(1)   A termination statement must specify –
      (a)   the commonhold association's proposals for the transfer of the commonhold land following acquisition of the freehold estate in accordance with section 49(3), and
      (b)   how the assets of the commonhold association will be distributed.
(2)   A commonhold community statement may make provision requiring any termination statement to make arrangements –

(a)   of a specified kind, or

(b)   determined in a specified manner,

about the rights of unit-holders in the event of all the land to which the statement relates ceasing to be commonhold land.

(3)   A termination statement must comply with a provision made by the commonhold community statement in reliance on subsection (2).

(4)   Subsection (3) may be disapplied by an order of the court –

(a)   generally,

(b)   in respect of specified matters, or

(c)   for a specified purpose.

(5)   An application for an order under subsection (4) may be made by any member of the commonhold association.

48   The liquidator

(1)   This section applies where a termination application has been made in respect of particular commonhold land.

(2)   The liquidator shall notify the Registrar of his appointment.

(3)   In the case of a termination application made under section 44 the liquidator shall either –

(a)   notify the Registrar that the liquidator is content with the termination statement submitted with the termination application, or

(b)   apply to the court under section 112 of the Insolvency Act 1986 (c. 45) to determine the terms of the termination statement.

(4)   The liquidator shall send to the Registrar a copy of a determination made by virtue of subsection (3)(b).

(5)   Subsection (4) is in addition to any requirement under section 112(3) of the Insolvency Act 1986.

(6)   A duty imposed on the liquidator by this section is to be performed as soon as possible.

(7)   In this section a reference to the liquidator is a reference –

(a)   to the person who is appointed as liquidator under section 91 of the Insolvency Act 1986, or

(b)   in the case of a members' voluntary winding up which becomes a creditors' voluntary winding up by virtue of sections 95 and 96 of that Act, to the person acting as liquidator in accordance with section 100 of that Act.

49   Termination

(1)   This section applies where a termination application is made under section 44 and –

(a)   a liquidator notifies the Registrar under section 48(3)(a) that he is content with a termination statement, or

(b)   a determination is made under section 112 of the Insolvency Act 1986 (c. 45) by virtue of section 48(3)(b).

(2)   This section also applies where a termination application is made under section 45.

(3)   The commonhold association shall by virtue of this subsection be entitled to be registered as the proprietor of the freehold estate in each commonhold unit.

(4)   The Registrar shall take such action as appears to him to be appropriate for the purpose of giving effect to the termination statement.

Termination: winding-up by court

50   Introduction

(1)   Section 51 applies where a petition is presented under section 124 of the Insolvency Act 1986 for the winding up of a commonhold association by the court.

(2)   For the purposes of this Part –
  (a)   an 'insolvent commonhold association' is one in relation to which a winding-up petition has been presented under section 124 of the Insolvency Act 1986,
  (b)   a commonhold association is the 'successor commonhold association' to an insolvent commonhold association if the land specified for the purpose of section 34(1)(a) is the same for both associations, and
  (c)   a 'winding-up order' is an order under section 125 of the Insolvency Act 1986 for the winding up of a commonhold association.

51   Succession order

(1)   At the hearing of the winding-up petition an application may be made to the court for an order under this section (a 'succession order') in relation to the insolvent commonhold association.

(2)   An application under subsection (1) may be made only by –
  (a)   the insolvent commonhold association,
  (b)   one or more members of the insolvent commonhold association, or
  (c)   a provisional liquidator for the insolvent commonhold association appointed under section 135 of the Insolvency Act 1986.

(3)   An application under subsection (1) must be accompanied by –
  (a)   prescribed evidence of the formation of a successor commonhold association, and
  (b)   a certificate given by the directors of the successor commonhold association that its memorandum and articles of association comply with regulations under paragraph 2(1) of Schedule 3.

(4)   The court shall grant an application under subsection (1) unless it thinks that the circumstances of the insolvent commonhold association make a succession order inappropriate.

52   Assets and liabilities

(1)   Where a succession order is made in relation to an insolvent commonhold association this section applies on the making of a winding-up order in respect of the association.

(2)   The successor commonhold association shall be entitled to be registered as the proprietor of the freehold estate in the common parts.

(3)   The insolvent commonhold association shall for all purposes cease to be treated as the proprietor of the freehold estate in the common parts.

(4)   The succession order –
        (a)   shall make provision as to the treatment of any charge over all or any part of the common parts;
        (b)   may require the Registrar to take action of a specified kind;
        (c)   may enable the liquidator to require the Registrar to take action of a specified kind;
        (d)   may make supplemental or incidental provision.

53   Transfer of responsibility

(1)   Where a succession order is made in relation to an insolvent commonhold association this section applies on the making of a winding-up order in respect of the association.

(2)   The successor commonhold association shall be treated as the commonhold association for the commonhold in respect of any matter which relates to a time after the making of the winding-up order.

(3)   On the making of the winding-up order the court may make an order requiring the liquidator to make available to the successor commonhold association specified –
        (a)   records;
        (b)   copies of records;
        (c)   information.

(4)   An order under subsection (3) may include terms as to –
        (a)   timing;
        (b)   payment.

54   Termination of commonhold

(1)   This section applies where the court –
        (a)   makes a winding-up order in respect of a commonhold association, and
        (b)   has not made a succession order in respect of the commonhold association.

(2)   The liquidator of a commonhold association shall as soon as possible notify the Registrar of –
        (a)   the fact that this section applies,
        (b)   any directions given under section 168 of the Insolvency Act 1986 (c. 45) (liquidator: supplementary powers),
        (c)   any notice given to the court and the registrar of companies in

accordance with section 172(8) of that Act (liquidator vacating office after final meeting),

(d) any notice given to the Secretary of State under section 174(3) of that Act (completion of winding-up),

(e) any application made to the registrar of companies under section 202(2) of that Act (insufficient assets: early dissolution),

(f) any notice given to the registrar of companies under section 205(1)(b) of that Act (completion of winding-up), and

(g) any other matter which in the liquidator's opinion is relevant to the Registrar.

(3) Notification under subsection (2)(b) to (f) must be accompanied by a copy of the directions, notice or application concerned.

(4) The Registrar shall—

(a) make such arrangements as appear to him to be appropriate for ensuring that the freehold estate in land in respect of which a commonhold association exercises functions ceases to be registered as a freehold estate in commonhold land as soon as is reasonably practicable after he receives notification under subsection (2)(c) to (f), and

(b) take such action as appears to him to be appropriate for the purpose of giving effect to a determination made by the liquidator in the exercise of his functions.

Termination: miscellaneous

55   Termination by court

(1) This section applies where the court makes an order by virtue of section 6(6)(c) or 40(3)(d) for all the land in relation to which a commonhold association exercises functions to cease to be commonhold land.

(2) The court shall have the powers which it would have if it were making a winding-up order in respect of the commonhold association.

(3) A person appointed as liquidator by virtue of subsection (2) shall have the powers and duties of a liquidator following the making of a winding-up order by the court in respect of a commonhold association.

(4) But the order of the court by virtue of section 6(6)(c) or 40(3)(d) may—

(a) require the liquidator to exercise his functions in a particular way;

(b) impose additional rights or duties on the liquidator;

(c) modify or remove a right or duty of the liquidator.

56   Release of reserve fund

Section 39(4) shall cease to have effect in relation to a commonhold association (in respect of debts and liabilities accruing at any time) if—

(a) the court makes a winding-up order in respect of the association,

(b) the association passes a voluntary winding-up resolution, or

(c) the court makes an order by virtue of section 6(6)(c) or 40(3)(d) for all the land in relation to which the association exercises functions to cease to be commonhold land.

Miscellaneous

57   Multiple site commonholds

(1)   A commonhold may include two or more parcels of land, whether or not contiguous.

(2)   But section 1(1) of this Act is not satisfied in relation to land specified in the memorandum of association of a commonhold association unless a single commonhold community statement makes provision for all the land.

(3)   Regulations may make provision about an application under section 2 made jointly by two or more persons, each of whom is the registered freeholder of part of the land to which the application relates.

(4)   The regulations may, in particular–

    (a)   modify the application of a provision made by or by virtue of this Part;

    (b)   disapply the application of a provision made by or by virtue of this Part;

    (c)   impose additional requirements.

58   Development rights

(1)   In this Part–

'the developer' means a person who makes an application under section 2, and

'development business' has the meaning given by Schedule 4.

(2)   A commonhold community statement may confer rights on the developer which are designed–

    (a)   to permit him to undertake development business, or

    (b)   to facilitate his undertaking of development business.

(3)   Provision made by a commonhold community statement in reliance on subsection (2) may include provision–

    (a)   requiring the commonhold association or a unit-holder to co-operate with the developer for a specified purpose connected with development business;

    (b)   making the exercise of a right conferred by virtue of subsection (2) subject to terms and conditions specified in or to be determined in accordance with the commonhold community statement;

    (c)   making provision about the effect of breach of a requirement by virtue of paragraph (a) or a term or condition imposed by virtue of paragraph (b);

    (d)   disapplying section 41(2) and (3).

(4)   Subsection (2) is subject–

    (a)   to regulations under section 32, and

    (b)   in the case of development business of the kind referred to in paragraph 7 of Schedule 4, to the memorandum and articles of association of the commonhold association.

(5)   Regulations may make provision regulating or restricting the exercise of rights conferred by virtue of subsection (2).

(6)   Where a right is conferred on a developer by virtue of subsection (2), if he sends to the Registrar a notice surrendering the right–

(a)   the Registrar shall arrange for the notice to be kept in his custody and referred to in the register,

(b)   the right shall cease to be exercisable from the time when the notice is registered under paragraph (a), and

(c)   the Registrar shall inform the commonhold association as soon as is reasonably practicable.

59   Development rights: succession

(1)   If during a transitional period the developer transfers to another person the freehold estate in the whole of the commonhold, the successor in title shall be treated as the developer in relation to any matter arising after the transfer.

(2)   If during a transitional period the developer transfers to another person the freehold estate in part of the commonhold, the successor in title shall be treated as the developer for the purpose of any matter which–

(a)   arises after the transfer, and

(b)   affects the estate transferred.

(3)   If after a transitional period or in a case where there is no transitional period–

(a)   the developer transfers to another person the freehold estate in the whole or part of the commonhold (other than by the transfer of the freehold estate in a single commonhold unit), and

(b)   the transfer is expressed to be inclusive of development rights,

the successor in title shall be treated as the developer for the purpose of any matter which arises after the transfer and affects the estate transferred.

(4)   Other than during a transitional period, a person shall not be treated as the developer in relation to commonhold land for any purpose unless he–

(a)   is, or has been at a particular time, the registered proprietor of the freehold estate in more than one of the commonhold units, and

(b)   is the registered proprietor of the freehold estate in at least one of the commonhold units.

60   Compulsory purchase

(1)   Where a freehold estate in commonhold land is transferred to a compulsory purchaser the land shall cease to be commonhold land.

(2)   But subsection (1) does not apply to a transfer if the Registrar is satisfied that the compulsory purchaser has indicated a desire for the land transferred to continue to be commonhold land.

(3)   The requirement of consent under section 21(2)(c) shall not apply to transfer to a compulsory purchaser.

(4)   Regulations may make provision about the transfer of a freehold estate in commonhold land to a compulsory purchaser.

(5)   The regulations may, in particular–

(a)   make provision about the effect of subsections (1) and (2) (including provision about that part of the commonhold which is not transferred);

(b)   require the service of notice;

(c)   confer power on a court;

(d)   make provision about compensation;

(e)   make provision enabling a commonhold association to require a compulsory purchaser to acquire the freehold estate in the whole, or a particular part, of the commonhold;

(f)   provide for an enactment relating to compulsory purchase not to apply or to apply with modifications.

(6)   Provision made by virtue of subsection (5)(a) in respect of land which is not transferred may include provision –

(a)   for some or all of the land to cease to be commonhold land;

(b)   for a provision of this Part to apply with specified modifications.

(7)   In this section 'compulsory purchaser' means –

(a)   a person acquiring land in respect of which he is authorised to exercise a power of compulsory purchase by virtue of an enactment, and

(b)   a person acquiring land which he is obliged to acquire by virtue of a prescribed enactment or in prescribed circumstances.

61   Matrimonial rights

In the following provisions of this Part a reference to a tenant includes a reference to a person who has matrimonial home rights (within the meaning of section 30(2) of the Family Law Act 1996 (c. 27) (matrimonial home)) in respect of a commonhold unit –

(a)   section 19,

(b)   section 35, and

(c)   section 37.

62   Advice

(1)   The Lord Chancellor may give financial assistance to a person in relation to the provision by that person of general advice about an aspect of the law of commonhold land, so far as relating to residential matters.

(2)   Financial assistance under this section may be given in such form and on such terms as the Lord Chancellor thinks appropriate.

(3)   The terms may, in particular, require repayment in specified circumstances.

63   The Crown

This Part binds the Crown.

General

64   Orders and regulations

(1)   In this Part 'prescribed' means prescribed by regulations.

(2)   Regulations under this Part shall be made by the Lord Chancellor.

(3)   Regulations under this Part–
        (a)   shall be made by statutory instrument,
        (b)   may include incidental, supplemental, consequential and transi-
                tional provision,
        (c)   may make provision generally or only in relation to specified cases,
        (d)   may make different provision for different purposes, and
        (e)   shall be subject to annulment in pursuance of a resolution of
                either House of Parliament.

65   Registration procedure

(1)   The Lord Chancellor may make rules about–
        (a)   the procedure to be followed on or in respect of commonhold reg-
                istration documents, and
        (b)   the registration of freehold estates in commonhold land.
(2)   Rules under this section–
        (a)   shall be made by statutory instrument in the same manner as land
                registration rules within the meaning of the Land Registration Act
                2002 (c. 9),
        (b)   may make provision for any matter for which provision is or may
                be made by land registration rules, and
        (c)   may provide for land registration rules to have effect in relation to
                anything done by virtue of or for the purposes of this Part as they
                have effect in relation to anything done by virtue of or for the
                purposes of that Act.
(3)   Rules under this section may, in particular, make provision–
        (a)   about the form and content of a commonhold registration
                document;
        (b)   enabling the Registrar to cancel an application by virtue of this
                Part in specified circumstances;
        (c)   enabling the Registrar, in particular, to cancel an application by
                virtue of this Part if he thinks that plans submitted with it
                (whether as part of a commonhold community statement or
                otherwise) are insufficiently clear or accurate;
        (d)   about the order in which commonhold registration documents
                and general registration documents are to be dealt with by the
                Registrar;
        (e)   for registration to take effect (whether or not retrospectively) as
                from a date or time determined in accordance with the rules.
(4)   The rules may also make provision about satisfaction of a requirement for
        an application by virtue of this Part to be accompanied by a document; in
        particular the rules may–
        (a)   permit or require a copy of a document to be submitted in place
                of or in addition to the original;
        (b)   require a copy to be certified in a specified manner;
        (c)   permit or require the submission of a document in electronic form.
(5)   A commonhold registration document must be accompanied by such fee (if
        any) as is specified for that purpose by order under section 102 of the Land
        Registration Act 2002 (c. 9)(fee orders).
(6)   In this section–

'commonhold registration document' means an application or other document sent to the Registrar by virtue of this Part, and

'general registration document' means a document sent to the Registrar under a provision of the Land Registration Act 2002.

66   Jurisdiction

(1)   In this Part 'the court' means the High Court or a county court.

(2)   Provision made by or under this Part conferring jurisdiction on a court shall be subject to provision made under section 1 of the Courts and Legal Services Act 1990 (c. 41) (allocation of business between High Court and county courts).

(3)   A power under this Part to confer jurisdiction on a court includes power to confer jurisdiction on a tribunal established under an enactment.

(4)   Rules of court or rules of procedure for a tribunal may make provision about proceedings brought–

(a)   under or by virtue of any provision of this Part, or

(b)   in relation to commonhold land.

67   The register

(1)   In this Part–

'the register' means the register of title to freehold and leasehold land kept under section 1 of the Land Registration Act 2002,

'registered' means registered in the register, and

'the Registrar' means the Chief Land Registrar.

(2)   Regulations under any provision of this Part may confer functions on the Registrar (including discretionary functions).

(3)   The Registrar shall comply with any direction or requirement given to him or imposed on him under or by virtue of this Part.

(4)   Where the Registrar thinks it appropriate in consequence of or for the purpose of anything done or proposed to be done in connection with this Part, he may–

(a)   make or cancel an entry on the register;

(b)   take any other action.

(5)   Subsection (4) is subject to section 6(2).

68   Amendments

Schedule 5 (consequential amendments) shall have effect.

69   Interpretation

(1)   In this Part–

'instrument' includes any document, and

'object' in relation to a commonhold association means an object stated in the association's memorandum of association in accordance with section 2(1)(c) of the Companies Act 1985 (c. 6).

(2)　In this Part –

    (a)　a reference to a duty to insure includes a reference to a duty to use the proceeds of insurance for the purpose of rebuilding or reinstating, and

    (b)　a reference to maintaining property includes a reference to decorating it and to putting it into sound condition.

(3)　A provision of the Law of Property Act 1925 (c. 20), the Companies Act 1985 (c. 6) or the Land Registration Act 2002 (c.9) defining an expression shall apply to the use of the expression in this Part unless the contrary intention appears.

70　Index of defined expressions

In this Part the expressions listed below are defined by the provisions specified.

Expression	Interpretation provision
Common parts	Section 25
A commonhold	Section 1
Commonhold association	Section 34
Commonhold community statement	Section 31
Commonhold land	Section 1
Commonhold unit	Section 11
Court	Section 66
Declaration of solvency	Section 43
Developer	Section 58
Development business	Section 58
Exercising functions	Section 8
Insolvent commonhold association	Section 50
Instrument	Section 69
Insure	Section 69
Joint unit-holder	Section 13
Liquidator (sections 44 to 49)	Section 44
Maintenance	Section 69
Object	Section 69
Prescribed	Section 64
The register	Section 67
Registered	Section 67
Registered freeholder	Section 2
The Registrar	Section 67
Regulations	Section 64
Residential commonhold unit	Section 17
Succession order	Section 51
Successor commonhold association	Section 50
Termination application	Section 46
Termination-statement resolution	Section 43
Transfer (of unit)	Section 15
Transitional period	Section 8
Unit-holder	Section 12
Winding-up resolution	Section 43

Commonhold and Leasehold Reform Act 2002, Schedules 1–5

SCHEDULE 1

APPLICATION FOR REGISTRATION: DOCUMENTS

Introduction

1   This Schedule lists the documents which are required by section 2 to accompany an application for the registration of a freehold estate as a freehold estate in commonhold land.

Commonhold association documents

2   The commonhold association's certificate of incorporation under section 13 of the Companies Act 1985 (c. 6).

3   Any altered certificate of incorporation issued under section 28 of that Act.

4   The memorandum and articles of association of the commonhold association.

Commonhold community statement

5   The commonhold community statement.

Consent

6   (1)   Where consent is required under or by virtue of section 3–
        (a)   the consent,
        (b)   an order of a court by virtue of section 3(2)(f) dispensing with the requirement for consent, or
        (c)   evidence of deemed consent by virtue of section 3(2)(e).
    (2)   In the case of a conditional order under section 3(2)(f), the order must be accompanied by evidence that the condition has been complied with.

Certificate

7   A certificate given by the directors of the commonhold association that–

    (a)   the memorandum and articles of association submitted with the application comply with regulations under paragraph 2(1) of Schedule 3,

    (b)   the commonhold community statement submitted with the application satisfies the requirements of this Part,

    (c)   the application satisfies Schedule 2,

    (d)   the commonhold association has not traded, and

    (e)   the commonhold association has not incurred any liability which has not been discharged.

SCHEDULE 2
LAND WHICH MAY NOT BE COMMONHOLD LAND

'Flying freehold'

1   (1)   Subject to sub-paragraph (2), an application may not be made under section 2 wholly or partly in relation to land above ground level ('raised land') unless all the land between the ground and the raised land is the subject of the same application.

    (2)   An application for the addition of land to a commonhold in accordance with section 41 may be made wholly or partly in relation to raised land if all the land between the ground and the raised land forms part of the commonhold to which the raised land is to be added.

Agricultural land

2   An application may not be made under section 2 wholly or partly in relation to land if–

    (a)   it is agricultural land within the meaning of the Agriculture Act 1947 (c. 48),

    (b)   it is comprised in a tenancy of an agricultural holding within the meaning of the Agricultural Holdings Act 1986 (c. 5), or

    (c)   it is comprised in a farm business tenancy for the purposes of the Agricultural Tenancies Act 1995 (c. 8).

Contingent title

3   (1)   An application may not be made under section 2 if an estate in the whole or part of the land to which the application relates is a contingent estate.

    (2)   An estate is contingent for the purposes of this paragraph if (and only if)–

(a)   it is liable to revert to or vest in a person other than the present registered proprietor on the occurrence or non-occurrence of a particular event, and

(b)   the reverter or vesting would occur by operation of law as a result of an enactment listed in sub-paragraph (3).

(3)   The enactments are–

(a)   the School Sites Act 1841 (c. 38) (conveyance for use as school),

(b)   the Lands Clauses Acts (compulsory purchase),

(c)   the Literary and Scientific Institutions Act 1854 (c. 112) (sites for institutions), and

(d)   the Places of Worship Sites Act 1873 (c. 50) (sites for places of worship).

(4)   Regulations may amend sub-paragraph (3) so as to–

(a)   add an enactment to the list, or

(b)   remove an enactment from the list.

SCHEDULE 3

COMMONHOLD ASSOCIATION

PART 1

MEMORANDUM AND ARTICLES OF ASSOCIATION

Introduction

1   In this Schedule–

(a)   'memorandum' means the memorandum of association of a commonhold association, and

(b)   'articles' means the articles of association of a commonhold association.

Form and content

2   (1)   Regulations shall make provision about the form and content of the memorandum and articles.

(2)   A commonhold association may adopt provisions of the regulations for its memorandum or articles.

(3)   The regulations may include provision which is to have effect for a commonhold association whether or not it is adopted under sub-paragraph (2).

(4)   A provision of the memorandum or articles shall have no effect to the extent that it is inconsistent with the regulations.

(5)   Regulations under this paragraph shall have effect in relation to a memorandum or articles–

(a)   irrespective of the date of the memorandum or articles, but

(b)   subject to any transitional provision of the regulations.

Alteration

3 (1) An alteration of the memorandum or articles of association shall have no effect until the altered version is registered in accordance with this paragraph.

(2) If the commonhold association makes an application under this sub-paragraph the Registrar shall arrange for an altered memorandum or altered articles to be kept in his custody, and referred to in the register, in place of the unaltered version.

(3) An application under sub-paragraph (2) must be accompanied by a certificate given by the directors of the commonhold association that the altered memorandum or articles comply with regulations under paragraph 2(1).

(4) Where the Registrar amends the register on an application under sub-paragraph (2) he shall make any consequential amendments to the register which he thinks appropriate.

Disapplication of Companies Act 1985

4 (1) The following provisions of the Companies Act 1985 (c. 6) shall not apply to a commonhold association –
(a) sections 2(7) and 3 (memorandum), and
(b) section 8 (articles of association).

(2) No application may be made under paragraph 3(2) for the registration of a memorandum altered by special resolution in accordance with section 4(1) of the Companies Act 1985 (objects) unless –
(a) the period during which an application for cancellation of the alteration may be made under section 5(1) of that Act has expired without an application being made,
(b) any application made under that section has been withdrawn, or
(c) the alteration has been confirmed by the court under that section.

PART 2
MEMBERSHIP

Pre-commonhold period

5 During the period beginning with incorporation of a commonhold association and ending when land specified in its memorandum becomes commonhold land, the subscribers (or subscriber) to the memorandum shall be the sole members (or member) of the association.

Transitional period

6   (1)   This paragraph applies to a commonhold association during a transitional period.

        (2)   The subscribers (or subscriber) to the memorandum shall continue to be members (or the member) of the association.

        (3)   A person who for the time being is the developer in respect of all or part of the commonhold is entitled to be entered in the register of members of the association.

Unit-holders

7   A person is entitled to be entered in the register of members of a commonhold association if he becomes the unit-holder of a commonhold unit in relation to which the association exercises functions–

        (a)   on the unit becoming commonhold land by registration with unit-holders under section 9, or

        (b)   on the transfer of the unit.

Joint unit-holders

8   (1)   This paragraph applies where two or more persons become joint unit-holders of a commonhold unit–

            (a)   on the unit becoming commonhold land by registration with unit-holders under section 9, or

            (b)   on the transfer of the unit.

        (2)   If the joint unit-holders nominate one of themselves for the purpose of this sub-paragraph, he is entitled to be entered in the register of members of the commonhold association which exercises functions in relation to the unit.

        (3)   A nomination under sub-paragraph (2) must–

            (a)   be made in writing to the commonhold association, and

            (b)   be received by the association before the end of the prescribed period.

        (4)   If no nomination is received by the association before the end of the prescribed period the person whose name appears first in the proprietorship register is on the expiry of that period entitled to be entered in the register of members of the association.

        (5)   On the application of a joint unit-holder the court may order that a joint unit-holder is entitled to be entered in the register of members of a commonhold association in place of a person who is or would be entitled to be registered by virtue of sub-paragraph (4).

        (6)   If joint unit-holders nominate one of themselves for the purpose of this sub-paragraph, the nominated person is entitled to be entered in the register of members of the commonhold association in place of the person entered by virtue of–

            (a)   sub-paragraph (2),

(b)   sub-paragraph (5), or
(c)   this sub-paragraph.

Self-membership

9   A commonhold association may not be a member of itself.

No other members

10   A person may not become a member of a commonhold association otherwise than by virtue of a provision of this Schedule.

Effect of registration

11   A person who is entitled to be entered in the register of members of a commonhold association becomes a member when the company registers him in pursuance of its duty under section 352 of the Companies Act 1985 (c. 6) (duty to maintain register of members).

Termination of membership

12   Where a member of a commonhold association ceases to be a unit-holder or joint unit-holder of a commonhold unit in relation to which the association exercises functions–
(a)   he shall cease to be a member of the commonhold association, but
(b)   paragraph (a) does not affect any right or liability already acquired or incurred in respect of a matter relating to a time when he was a unit-holder or joint unit-holder.

13   A member of a commonhold association may resign by notice in writing to the association if (and only if) he is a member by virtue of paragraph 5 or 6 of this Schedule (and not also by virtue of any other paragraph).

Register of members

14   (1)   Regulations may make provision about the performance by a commonhold association of its duty under section 352 of the Companies Act 1985 (c. 6) (duty to maintain register of members) where a person–
(a)   becomes entitled to be entered in the register by virtue of paragraphs 5 to 8, or
(b)   ceases to be a member by virtue of paragraph 12 or on resignation.
(2)   The regulations may in particular require entries in the register to be made within a specified period.

(3)   A period specified under sub-paragraph (2) may be expressed to begin from–

    (a)   the date of a notification under section 15(3),

    (b)   the date on which the directors of the commonhold association first become aware of a specified matter, or

    (c)   some other time.

(4)   A requirement by virtue of this paragraph shall be treated as a requirement of section 352 for the purposes of section 352(5) (fines).

Companies Act 1985

15   (1)   Section 22(1) of the Companies Act 1985 (initial members) shall apply to a commonhold association subject to this Schedule.

    (2)   Sections 22(2) and 23 of that Act (members: new members and holding company) shall not apply to a commonhold association.

PART 3
MISCELLANEOUS

Name

16   Regulations may provide–

    (a)   that the name by which a commonhold association is registered under the Companies Act 1985 must satisfy specified requirements;

    (b)   that the name by which a company other than a commonhold association is registered may not include a specified word or expression.

Statutory declaration

17   For the purposes of section 12 of the Companies Act 1985 (registration: compliance with Act) as it applies to a commonhold association, a reference to the requirements of that Act shall be treated as including a reference to a provision of or made under this Schedule.

SCHEDULE 4
DEVELOPMENT RIGHTS

Introductory

1   This Schedule sets out the matters which are development business for the purposes of section 58.

Works

2   The completion or execution of works on–
    (a)   a commonhold,
    (b)   land which is or may be added to a commonhold, or
    (c)   land which has been removed from a commonhold.

Marketing

3   (1)   Transactions in commonhold units.
    (2)   Advertising and other activities designed to promote transactions in commonhold units.

Variation

4   The addition of land to a commonhold.

5   The removal of land from a commonhold.

6   Amendment of a commonhold community statement (including amendment to redefine the extent of a commonhold unit).

Commonhold association

7   Appointment and removal of directors of a commonhold association.

SCHEDULE 5

COMMONHOLD: CONSEQUENTIAL AMENDMENTS

Law of Property Act 1922 (c. 16)

1   At the end of paragraph 5 of Schedule 15 to the Law of Property Act 1922 (perpetually renewable leases) (which becomes sub-paragraph (1)) there shall be added–
    '(2)   Sub-paragraph (3) applies where a grant–
        (a)   relates to commonhold land, and
        (b)   would take effect by virtue of sub-paragraph (1) as a demise for a term of two thousand years or a subdemise for a fixed term.
    (3)   The grant shall be treated as if it purported to be a grant of the term referred to in sub-paragraph (2)(b) (and sections 17 and 18 of the Commonhold and Leasehold Reform Act 2002 (residential and non-residential leases) shall apply accordingly).'

Law of Property Act 1925 (c. 20)

2   After section 101(1) of the Law of Property Act 1925 (mortgagee's powers)
         there shall be added–
         '(1A)   Subsection (1)(i) is subject to section 21 of the Commonhold and
                  Leasehold Reform Act 2002 (no disposition of part-units)'.

3   At the end of section 149 of that Act (90-year term in place of certain deter-
         minable terms) there shall be added–
         '(7)   Subsection (8) applies where a lease, underlease or contract–
                  (a)   relates to commonhold land, and
                  (b)   would take effect by virtue of subsection (6) as a lease,
                           underlease or contract of the kind mentioned in that sub-
                           section.
         (8)   The lease, underlease or contract shall be treated as if it purported
                  to be a lease, underlease or contract of the kind referred to in sub-
                  section (7)(b) (and sections 17 and 18 of the Commonhold and
                  Leasehold Reform Act 2002 (residential and non-residential
                  leases) shall apply accordingly).'

Limitation Act 1980 (c. 58)

4   After section 19 of the Limitation Act 1980 (actions for rent) there shall be
         inserted–

'Commonhold

19A   Actions for breach of commonhold duty

An action in respect of a right or duty of a kind referred to in section 37(1) of the
Commonhold and Leasehold Reform Act 2002 (enforcement) shall not be brought
after the expiration of six years from the date on which the cause of action accrued.'

Housing Act 1985 (c. 68)

5   At the end of section 118 of the Housing Act 1985 (the right to buy) there
         shall be added–
         '(3)   For the purposes of this Part, a dwelling-house which is a com-
                  monhold unit (within the meaning of the Commonhold and
                  Leasehold Reform Act 2002) shall be treated as a house and not as
                  a flat.'

Insolvency Act 1986 (c. 45)

6   At the end of section 84 of the Insolvency Act 1986 (voluntary winding-up)
         there shall be added–

'(4)   This section has effect subject to section 43 of the Commonhold and Leasehold Reform Act 2002.'

Law of Property (Miscellaneous Provisions) Act 1994 (c. 36)

7   (1)   Section 5 of the Law of Property (Miscellaneous Provisions) Act 1994 (discharge of obligations) shall be amended as follows.

(2)   In subsection (1) for the words 'or of leasehold land' substitute 'of leasehold land or of a commonhold unit'.

(3)   After subsection (3) insert –

'(3A)   If the property is a commonhold unit, there shall be implied a covenant that the mortgagor will fully and promptly observe and perform all the obligations under the commonhold community statement that are for the time being imposed on him in his capacity as a unit-holder or as a joint unit-holder.'

(4)   For subsection (4) substitute –

'(4)   In this section –

(a)   'commonhold community statement', 'commonhold unit', 'joint unit-holder' and 'unit-holder' have the same meanings as in the Commonhold and Leasehold Reform Act 2002, and

(b)   'mortgage' includes charge, and 'mortgagor' shall be construed accordingly.'

Trusts of Land and Appointment of Trustees Act 1996 (c. 47)

8   At the end of section 7 of the Trusts of Land and Appointment of Trustees Act 1996 (partition by trustees) there shall be added –

'(6)   Subsection (1) is subject to sections 21 (part-unit: interests) and 22 (part-unit: charging) of the Commonhold and Leasehold Reform Act 2002.'

Commonhold Regulations 2004, SI 2004/1829

Made	14th July 2004
Laid before Parliament	16th July 2004
Coming into force in accordance with regulation 1(1)	

The Lord Chancellor, in exercise of the powers conferred upon him by sections 3, 9(2), 11(3), 13, 17(1), 19(1), 21(2), 24(6), 31(2), 32(1), 37(1), 45(2), 51(3), 57(3), 58(5) and paragraphs 2 and 16 of Schedule 3 to the Commonhold and Leasehold Reform Act 2002, makes the following Regulations:

PART I
GENERAL

1   **Citation, commencement and interpretation**

(1)   These Regulations may be cited as the Commonhold Regulations 2004 and shall come into force on the day on which section 2 of the Act comes into force.

(2)   In these Regulations a section referred to by number alone means the section so numbered in the Act and a Schedule referred to by number alone means the Schedule so numbered in these Regulations.

(3)   In these Regulations–
       (a)   'the Act' means the Commonhold and Leasehold Reform Act 2002; and
       (b)   'the Rules' means the Commonhold (Land Registration) Rules 2004 and a Form referred to by letters alone or by letters and numbers means the Form so designated in Schedule 1 to the Rules.

2   **Joint unit-holders**

(1)   In the application of the following provisions to a commonhold unit with joint unit-holders a reference to a unit-holder is a reference to the joint unit-holders together–

(a)   regulations 10(2), 18(2)(a) and 18(3); and

(b)   paragraphs 4.8.5 to 4.8.9 in Schedule 3.

(2)   In the application of the following provisions to a commonhold unit with joint unit-holders a reference to a unit-holder includes a reference to each joint unit-holder and to the joint unit-holders together–

(a)   regulations 11(1) and 18(2)(b);

(b)   articles 4(d) and 75 in Schedule 2; and

(c)   all provisions in Schedule 3 except paragraphs 4.8.5 to 4.8.9.

(3)   In section 13(2)–

(a)   omit paragraphs (a), (c), (g) and (h);

(b)   in paragraph (b) omit 'and (3)'; and

(c)   in paragraph (f) after 'section 35(1)(b),' insert 'and'.

(4)   In section 13(3)–

(a)   after paragraph (a) insert–

'(aa)   section 14(3),

(ab)   section 15(3),';

(b)   after paragraph (b) insert–

'(ba)   section 19(2) and (3),'; and

(c)   after paragraph (f) insert–

'(fa)   section 38(1),

(fb)   section 39(2),'.

PART II
REGISTRATION

3   **Consents required prior to the creation of a commonhold additional to those required by section 3(1)(a) to (c)**

(1)   An application under section 2 may not be made in respect of a freehold estate in land without the consent of anyone who is–

(a)   the estate owner of any unregistered freehold estate in the whole or part of the land;

(b)   the estate owner of any unregistered leasehold estate in the whole or part of the land granted for a term of more than 21 years;

(c)   the owner of any mortgage, charge or lien for securing money or money's worth over the whole or part of any unregistered land included in the application; or

(d)   subject to paragraph (2), the holder of a lease granted for a term of not more than 21 years which will be extinguished by virtue of section 7(3)(d) or 9(3)(f).

(2)   An application under section 2 may be made without the consent of a person who would otherwise be required to consent by virtue of paragraph (1)(d) if–

(a)   the person is entitled to the grant of a term of years absolute–

(i)   of the same premises as are comprised in the extinguished lease;

(ii)   on the same terms as the extinguished lease, except to the extent necessary to comply with the Act and these Regulations and excluding any terms that are spent;

217

      (iii)   at the same rent as the rent payable under, and including the same provisions for rent review as were included in, the extinguished lease as at the date on which it will be extinguished;

      (iv)   for a term equivalent to the unexpired term of the lease which will be extinguished; and

      (v)   to take effect immediately after the lease is extinguished by virtue of section 7(3)(d) or 9(3)(f); and

(b)   before the application under section 2 is made, the person's entitlement to the grant of a term of years absolute has been protected by a notice in the land register to the freehold title(s) for the land in the application or, in the case of unregistered land, by an entry in the land charges register in the name of the estate owner of the freehold title.

4   Details of consent

(1)   Consent to an application under–

     (a)   section 2 must be given in Form CON 1; and

     (b)   section 8(4) must be given in Form CON 2.

(2)   Subject to paragraphs (3), (4) and (7), consent is binding on a person who gives consent or who is deemed to have given consent.

(3)   Consent may be given subject to conditions.

(4)   Subject to any condition imposing a shorter period, consent will lapse if no application is made within a period of 12 months beginning with the date on which consent was given.

(5)   Consent is deemed to have been given by–

     (a)   the person making the application where that person's consent would otherwise be required in accordance with section 3, but has not been expressly given; and

     (b)   a successor in title to a person who has given consent or who is deemed to have given consent.

(6)   Consent given for the purpose of one application has effect for the purpose of another application ('the new application') only where the new application is submitted–

     (a)   in place of a previous application which has been withdrawn by the applicant, or rejected or cancelled by the Registrar; and

     (b)   within a period of 12 months beginning with the date on which the consent was given.

(7)   Consent may be withdrawn at any time before the date on which any application is submitted to the Registrar.

(8)   In this regulation, 'consent' means consent for the purposes of section 3.

5   Dispensing with a requirement for consent

The court may dispense with the requirement for consent to an application under section 2 if a person whose consent is required–

     (a)   cannot be identified after all reasonable efforts have been made to ascertain his identity;

(b)   has been identified but cannot be traced after all reasonable efforts have been made to trace him; or

(c)   has been sent the request for consent and all reasonable efforts have been made to obtain a response but he has not responded.

6   Statement under section 9(1)(b): Registration with unit-holders

A statement under section 9(1)(b) which accompanies an application under section 2 must, in relation to each commonhold unit, state–

(a)   the full name of the proposed initial unit-holder or if there are proposed joint unit-holders the full name of each of them;

(b)   the address for service of the proposed unit-holder or if there are proposed joint unit-holders the address for service of each of them;

(c)   the unit number of the commonhold unit; and

(d)   the postal address of the commonhold unit (if available).

7   Multiple site commonholds

For the purposes of an application under section 2 made jointly by two or more persons, each of whom is the registered freeholder of part of the land to which the application relates ('a part site') section 11 is modified so that, in addition to complying with the requirements in section 11(3), in defining the extent of a commonhold unit, the commonhold community statement must provide for the extent of each commonhold unit to be situated wholly upon one part site, and not situated partly on one part site and partly on one or more other part sites.

PART III
COMMONHOLD UNIT

8   Requirements of a plan defining the extent of a commonhold unit

A plan referred to in a commonhold community statement for the purposes of defining the extent of a commonhold unit must delineate the boundaries of the commonhold unit with any adjoining property.

9   Definition of a commonhold unit

(1)   In defining the extent of a commonhold unit a commonhold community statement–

(a)   may exclude, from the definition, the structure and exterior of a self-contained building, or of a self-contained part of a building, which only contains one commonhold unit or part of one commonhold unit; and

(b)   must exclude, from the definition, the structure and exterior of a self-contained building, or of a self-contained part of a building, in any other case.

(2)   In this regulation–
'self-contained building' means a building which is structurally detached;
'self-contained part of a building' means a part of a building–

(a)   which constitutes a vertical division of the building;

(b)   the structure of which is such that it could be redeveloped independently of the rest of the building; and

(c)   in relation to which the relevant services provided for occupiers are provided independently of the relevant services provided for the occupiers of the rest of the building, or could be so provided without involving the carrying out of works likely to result in a significant interruption in the provision of any relevant services for occupiers of the rest of the building;

'relevant services' are services provided by the means of pipes, cables or other fixed installations; and

'structure and exterior' includes the relevant services in or to the building but does not include those which are within and exclusively to one commonhold unit.

10   Requirement to notify Registrar

(1)   This regulation applies to an amendment of a commonhold community statement which redefines the extent of a commonhold unit over which there is a registered charge.

(2)   The unit-holder of a commonhold unit over which there is a registered charge must give notice of the amendment to the Registrar in Form COE.

(3)   On receipt of such notification the Registrar must alter the register to reflect the application of section 24(4) or (5).

11   Leasing of a residential commonhold unit

(1)   A term of years absolute in a residential commonhold unit or part only of a residential commonhold unit must not–

(a)   be granted for a premium;

(b)   subject to paragraph (2), be granted for a term longer than 7 years;

(c)   be granted under an option or agreement if–

(i)   the person to take the new term of years absolute has an existing terms of years absolute of the premises to be let;

(ii)   the new term when added to the existing term will be more than 7 years; and

(iii)   the option or agreement was entered into before or at the same time as the existing term of years absolute;

(d)   contain an option or agreement to renew the term of years absolute which confers on the lessee or on the lessor an option or agreement for renewal for a further term which, together with the original term, amounts to more than 7 years;

(e)   contain an option or agreement to extend the term beyond 7 years; or

(f)   contain a provision requiring the lessee to make payments to the commonhold association in discharge of payments which are due, in accordance with the commonhold community statement, to be made by the unit-holder.

(2)   A term of years absolute in a residential commonhold unit or part only of a residential commonhold unit may be granted for a term of not more than 21 years to the holder of a lease which has been extinguished by virtue of section 7(3)(d) or 9(3)(f) if the term of years absolute –

(a)   is granted of the same premises as are comprised in the extinguished lease;

(b)   is granted on the same terms as the extinguished lease, except to the extent necessary to comply with the Act and these Regulations and excluding any terms that are spent;

(c)   is granted at the same rent as the rent payable under, and including the same provisions for rent review as were included in, the extinguished lease as at the date on which it was extinguished;

(d)   is granted for a term equivalent to the unexpired term of the lease immediately before it was extinguished or, if the unexpired term of the lease immediately before it was extinguished is more than 21 years, for a term of 21 years;

(e)   takes effect immediately after the lease was extinguished; and

(f)   does not include any option or agreement which –

      (i)   may create a term or an extension to a term which, together with the term of the term of years absolute, would amount to more than 21 years; or

      (ii)   may result in the grant of a term of years absolute containing an option or agreement to extend the term.

PART IV
COMMONHOLD ASSOCIATION

12   **The name of the commonhold association**

(1)   The name by which a commonhold association is registered under the Companies Act 1985 must end with 'commonhold association limited' or, if the memorandum of association states that the commonhold association's registered office is to be situated in Wales, those words or the Welsh equivalent ('Cymdeithas Cydradd-Ddaliad Cyfyngedig').

(2)   The name by which a company other than a commonhold association is registered may not end with 'commonhold association limited' or the Welsh equivalent 'Cymdeithas Cydradd-Ddaliad Cyfyngedig'.

(3)   In this regulation references to the words 'limited' and 'cyfyngedig' include the abbreviations 'ltd.' and 'cyf.'.

13 Memorandum of association

(1) The memorandum of association of a commonhold association must be in the form in Schedule 1 (memorandum of association) or a form to the same effect.

(2) The memorandum of association of a commonhold association must contain all the provisions contained in the form in Schedule 1 and each provision in that Schedule will have effect for a commonhold association whether or not it is adopted under paragraph 2(2) of Schedule 3 to the Act.

(3) In its memorandum of association, a commonhold association must–

    (a) include the name of the commonhold association on the front page and in paragraph 1;

    (b) omit 'England and Wales' or 'Wales' from paragraph 2; and

    (c) include the name of the commonhold in paragraph 3.

(4) A commonhold association may include additional provisions in its memorandum of association immediately after the provision which appears as paragraph 5 in Schedule 1 where the additional provisions are preceded by a heading which must include 'additional provision specific to this commonhold association' and each new provision must be given a number.

14 Articles of association

(1) The articles of association of a commonhold association must be in the form in Schedule 2 (articles of association) or a form to the same effect.

(2) Subject to the following paragraphs, the articles of association of a commonhold association must contain all the provisions in the form in Schedule 2 and each provision in that Schedule will have effect for a commonhold association whether or not it is adopted under paragraph 2(2) of Schedule 3 to the Act.

(3) In its articles of association a commonhold must include the name of the commonhold association on the front page.

(4) In its articles of association a commonhold association may substitute–

    (a) any time period for the time periods in articles 7, 18 and 48(f) except that the time period may not be reduced below the time periods mentioned in those articles;

    (b) any number of meetings for the number of meetings in article 48(f) except that the number may not be reduced below three;

    (c) any figure for the figures in article 13 except that the figure may not be reduced below the figures mentioned in that article and different provision may be made for different purposes; and

    (d) a time or date for 'at any time' in article 36.

(5) A commonhold association may omit 'Failing that it may be delivered at the meeting to the chairman, secretary or to any director.' from article 36 of its articles of association.

(6) A commonhold association may include additional provisions in its articles of association where each additional provision is immediately preceded by a heading which must include 'additional provision specific to this commonhold association' and is identified with the numeral of the immediately preceding article followed by a capital letter, such letters to be allocated in alphabetical order in respect of each number.

(7) Where the articles of association of a commonhold association contain provisions for the appointment of alternate directors, article 38 is to have effect for a commonhold association with '(other than alternate directors)' inserted after 'the number of directors'.

(8) Where the commonhold community statement gives the developer the right to appoint and remove directors the following provisions have effect for a commonhold association whether or not they are adopted under paragraph 2(2) of Schedule 3 to the Act—

    (a) during the transitional period the developer may appoint up to two directors in addition to any directors appointed by the subscribers, and may remove or replace any director so appointed;

    (b) after the end of the transitional period and for so long as the developer is the unit-holder of more than one quarter of the total number of commonhold units in the commonhold, he may appoint up to one quarter of the directors of the commonhold association, and may remove or replace any director so appointed;

    (c) a director appointed by the developer pursuant to paragraph (a) or (b) is known as a 'developer's director';

    (d) any appointment or removal of a developer's director made pursuant to paragraph (a) or (b) must be by notice in writing signed by or on behalf of the developer and will take effect immediately it is received at the office of the commonhold association or by the secretary, or as and from the date specified in the notice (if later);

    (e) if at any time the commonhold association resolves to specify or reduce the maximum number of directors, and as a consequence the number of developer's directors exceeds the number permitted under paragraph (b), the developer must immediately reduce the number of developer's directors accordingly and where such reduction has not been effected by the start of the next directors' meeting, the longest in office of the developer's directors must cease to hold office immediately so as to achieve the required reduction in numbers;

    (f) if the developer ceases to be the unit-holder of more than one quarter of the total number of units in the commonhold, he may no longer appoint, replace or remove a director and any developer's directors previously appointed by him under this article will cease to hold office immediately;

    (g) a developer's director who is removed from office or who ceases to hold office under this article will not have any claim against the commonhold association in respect of such removal from, or cessation to hold, office;

    (h) at any time at which the developer is entitled to exercise the power to appoint and remove developer's directors, the developer is not entitled to vote upon a resolution fixing the number of directors of the commonhold association, or upon a resolution for the appointment or removal from office of any director not appointed by him, or upon any resolution concerning the remuneration of any director not appointed by him;

    (i) a developer's director may provide information to the developer that he receives by virtue of his being a director; and

    (j) the provisions in articles 40, 41 and 54 do not apply to a developer's director.

(9) Where the provisions in paragraph (8) have effect for a commonhold association–
  (a) articles 45 and 46 are to have effect for a commonhold association but with '(other than a vacancy in respect of a developer's director)' inserted after 'fill a vacancy'; and
  (b) article 61 is to have effect for a commonhold association but with 'At least one of the persons present at the meeting must be a director other than a developer's director.' inserted at the end.

(10) In this regulation an article referred to by number alone means the article so numbered in Schedule 2.

15 Commonhold community statement

(1) The commonhold community statement must be in the form in Schedule 3 (commonhold community statement) or a form to the same effect.

(2) The commonhold community statement must contain all the provisions contained in the form in Schedule 3 and will be treated as including those provisions.

(3) The commonhold community statement must include the name of the commonhold on the front page and signature page and must include the information relevant to the commonhold in the paragraphs in the Annexes.

(4) The commonhold community statement must be signed at the end in the following form–
  (a) on application for registration under section 2–

'Signed [by] [on behalf of] the applicant: . . . .
Name: (please print) . . . .
Title: . . . .'; or

  (b) where an amended commonhold community statement is registered in accordance with section 33–

'Signed [by] [on behalf of] [the commonhold association] [the developer]:
. . . .
Name: (please print) . . . .
Title: . . . .'

(5) The commonhold community statement must include information relevant to the commonhold in–
  (a) paragraph 2 of Annex 3 if the directors of the commonhold association have established funds to finance the repair and maintenance of the common parts or commonhold units; and
  (b) paragraph 5 of Annex 4 if there are other risks insured in addition to fire.

(6) The commonhold community statement is treated as including '0 per cent.' in paragraph 1 of Annex 4 unless different provision is made in its place.

(7) Where, by virtue of regulation 9(1)(b), in defining the extent of a commonhold unit, the commonhold community statement excludes the structure and exterior of a self-contained building, or of a self-contained part of a building, the commonhold community statement is treated as including

provision which imposes a duty on the commonhold association to insure the whole of the self-contained building, or self-contained part of the building.

(8) Subject to paragraphs (9) to (12), the commonhold community statement may include further definitions and may include further numbered provisions relevant to the commonhold at the end of a Part or a Section or in an Annex.

(9) Where further definitions are included in the commonhold community statement each definition must be inserted in alphabetical order into paragraph 1.4.5 in the commonhold community statement.

(10) Where further provisions are included in the commonhold community statement which confer rights on the developer –

    (a) the provisions must be inserted in an Annex headed 'DEVELOP-MENT RIGHTS', such Annex must be numbered and be the last Annex in the commonhold community statement and a reference to its heading must be included in the table of contents in the commonhold community statement;

    (b) a paragraph containing 'Annex [ ] specifies the rights of the developer which are designed to permit him to undertake development business or to facilitate his undertaking of development business.' must be inserted in Section 1.3 in the commonhold community statement with the Annex number inserted in place of the brackets; and

    (c) paragraph 4.8.14 in the commonhold community statement is treated as including

'; or to remove any surrendered development rights' at the end.

(11) Where any other provisions are included in the commonhold community statement in a Part or Section –

    (a) each additional provision must be inserted in numerical order continuing the numbers within the relevant Part or Section;

    (b) each additional provision must be immediately preceded by a heading which must include 'additional provision specific to this commonhold' in the relevant Part or Section; and

    (c) a reference to the heading must be included in the table of contents in the commonhold community statement.

(12) Where any other provisions are included in the commonhold community statement in an Annex –

    (a) a heading which must include 'ADDITIONAL PROVISIONS SPECIFIC TO THIS COMMONHOLD' must be inserted at the end of Part 4 followed by a numbered paragraph which reads 'Additional provisions are set out in Annex' followed by the number given to the Annex by the commonhold association;

    (b) a paragraph must be inserted in Section 1.3 in the commonhold community statement giving the number of the Annex and details of its contents; and

    (c) a reference to its heading must be included in the table of contents in the commonhold community statement.

(13) In this regulation 'commonhold community statement' means the commonhold community statement of a commonhold and a reference to a Part, Section or Annex means a Part, Section or Annex in the commonhold community statement.

16   Forms

The Forms contained in Schedule 4 (forms) or forms to the same effect must be used in accordance with the commonhold community statement of a commonhold.

PART V
OPERATION OF A COMMONHOLD

17   Enforcement

Jurisdiction is conferred on the court to deal with the exercise or enforcement of a right conferred, or duty imposed, by or by virtue of–
   (a)   a commonhold community statement;
   (b)   these Regulations; or
   (c)   Part 1 of the Act.

18   Development Rights

(1)   The rights (if any) conferred on the developer in a commonhold community statement are restricted or regulated in accordance with the following paragraphs.

(2)   The developer must not exercise development rights in such manner as to interfere unreasonably with–
   (a)   the enjoyment by each unit-holder of the freehold estate in his unit; and
   (b)   the exercise by any unit-holder or tenant of his rights under the commonhold community statement.

(3)   The developer may not remove land from the commonhold that has been transferred to a unit-holder unless the unit-holder consents in writing before the land is removed.

(4)   Any damage to the common parts or a commonhold unit caused by the developer in the course of undertaking development business must be put right by the developer as soon as reasonably practicable taking into account the future works required to complete the development and the degree of interference caused by the damage.

(5)   The developer must not exercise development rights if the works for which the development rights were conferred have been completed, save that any rights permitting or facilitating the undertaking of development business of the type referred to in paragraph 3 of Schedule 4 to the Act may be exercised for such further period as the developer continues to undertake that type of development business in relation to the whole or, as the case may be, the relevant part, of the commonhold.

(6)   In this regulation 'developer' includes a person acting on his authority.

PART VI
TERMINATION

19   **Termination**

(1)   The liquidator must, in accordance with section 45(2), apply to the court for an order determining–

    (a)   the terms and conditions on which a termination application may be made; and

    (b)   the terms of the termination statement to accompany a termination application

within the period of 3 months beginning with the date on which the liquidator was appointed.

(2)   An application under section 51(1) must be accompanied by the certificate of incorporation of the successor commonhold association given in accordance with section 13 of the Companies Act 1985 and any altered certificates of incorporation issued under section 28 of that Act.

Schedule 1

Regulation 13

THE COMPANIES ACTS 1985 & 1989

COMPANY LIMITED BY GUARANTEE AND NOT HAVING A SHARE CAPITAL

MEMORANDUM OF ASSOCIATION

OF

[ ]

1.   The name of the company (referred to in this document as 'the commonhold association') is [ ].

2.   The registered office of the commonhold association is to be situated in [England and Wales] [Wales].

3.   The object of the commonhold association is to exercise the functions of a commonhold association in relation to land known as [ ] commonhold in accordance with the commonhold community statement of that commonhold, as amended from time to time, and any provision made by or by virtue of Part 1 of the Commonhold and Leasehold Reform Act 2002 and the doing of all such things as are incidental or conducive to the attainment of that object.

4.   The liability of the members is limited.

5.   Without prejudice to any further liability which he may have under or arising out the commonhold community statement, every member of the commonhold association undertakes to contribute such amount as may be required, not exceeding £1, to the assets of the commonhold association if it should be wound up while he is a member or within one year after he ceases to be a member, for payment of the debts and liabilities of the commonhold association contracted before he ceases to be a member, and of the costs, charges, and expenses of winding up the commonhold association, and for the adjustment of the rights of the contributories among themselves.

We, the subscribers to this memorandum of association, wish to be formed into a company pursuant to this memorandum.

Names and Addresses of subscribers (or subscriber)

Dated
Witness to the above signatures

Schedule 2

THE COMPANIES ACTS 1985 & 1989

COMPANY LIMITED BY GUARANTEE AND NOT HAVING A SHARE CAPITAL

ARTICLES OF ASSOCIATION

OF

[ ]

TABLE OF CONTENTS

INTERPRETATION

1.   In these articles –
'the Act' means the Commonhold and Leasehold Reform Act 2002;

'clear days' in relation to the period of a notice means that period excluding the day when the notice is given or deemed to be given and the day for which it is given or on which it is to take effect;

'the commonhold' means the land in respect of which the commonhold community statement is registered;

'the commonhold association' means the commonhold association named above;

'the commonhold community statement' means the document held by Land Registry which makes provision for the rights and duties of the commonhold association and the unit-holders and defines the extent of each commonhold unit;

'communication' includes a communication comprising sounds or images or both and a communication effecting a payment;

'the Companies Act' means the Companies Act 1985 or any statutory modification or re-enactment of it for the time being in force;

'the developer' means the person who makes an application to register a freehold estate in land as a freehold estate in commonhold land, and his successor in title who is treated as the developer, and who carries on development business on the commonhold land;

'electronic communication' means a communication transmitted (whether from one person to another, from one device to another or from a person to a device or vice versa) –
(a)   by means of a telecommunication system; or
(b)   by other means but while in an electronic form;

'member' means a person whose name is entered as a member in the register of members of the commonhold association but excludes any person who has ceased to be a unit-holder or joint unit-holder or who has resigned as a member;

'pre-commonhold period' means the period beginning with incorporation of a commonhold association and ending when land specified in its memorandum becomes commonhold land;

'secretary' means the secretary of the commonhold association or any other person appointed to perform the duties of the secretary of the commonhold association, including a joint, assistant or deputy secretary;

'subscribers' means the first members of the commonhold association;

'telecommunications system' means a system for the conveyance, through the agency of electric, magnetic, electro-magnetic, electro-chemical or electro-mechanical energy, of–

(a)   speech, music and other sounds;

(b)   visual images;

(c)   signals serving for the impartation (whether as between persons and persons, things and things or persons and things) of any matter otherwise than in the form of sounds or visual images; or

(d)   signals serving for the actuation or control of machinery or apparatus;

'transitional period' means the period between registration of the freehold estate in land as a freehold estate in commonhold land under section 2 of the Act and the event mentioned in section 7(3) of the Act;

'the United Kingdom' means Great Britain and Northern Ireland;

'unit-holder' means a person entitled to be registered as the proprietor of the freehold estate in a commonhold unit (whether or not he is registered).

Unless the context otherwise requires, words and expressions contained in these articles bear the same meaning as in the Act, including any statutory modification or re-enactment of it for the time being in force, or in the Companies Act and words in the singular include the plural and words in the plural include the singular.

MEMBERS

Membership

2.   The persons who are entitled to be entered in the register of members of the commonhold association are–

(a)   in the pre-commonhold period, the subscribers to the memorandum of association of the commonhold association;

(b)   during the transitional period, the subscribers to the memorandum of association of the commonhold association and a person who for the time being is the developer in respect of all or part of the commonhold;

(c)   on transfer of a commonhold unit; or, where a commonhold unit becomes commonhold land by registration with unit-holders under section 9 of the Act; a person who becomes the unit-holder; and

(d)   on transfer of a commonhold unit; or, where a commonhold unit becomes commonhold land by registration with unit-holders under section 9 of the Act; and two or more persons become joint unit-holders of a commonhold unit; and–

(i)   the joint unit-holders nominate, in writing to the commonhold association, one of themselves to be entered in the register of members, the person so nominated;

(ii)   if no nomination is received by the commonhold association in accordance with sub-paragraph (i) within seven days beginning with the date on which the joint unit-holders are entitled to be registered as proprietors of the freehold estate in the commonhold unit, the person whose name appears first in the proprietorship register;

(iii)   the court orders a joint unit-holder to be entered in the register of members in place of a person who is or who would be entitled to be registered under sub-paragraph (ii), the person so ordered by the court; or

(iv)   the joint unit-holders nominate one of themselves to be entered in the register of members in place of the person previously entered by virtue of sub-paragraph (i), (iii) or this sub-paragraph, the person so nominated.

Register of members

3.   The commonhold association must keep a register of members and enter in it–

(a)   the name, address and unit number, where applicable, of each member and an address for correspondence (if different);

(b)   the date on which the person was registered as a member; and

(c)   the date at which the person ceased to be a member.

4.   The commonhold association must enter the particulars of a person in the register of members of a commonhold association where the person is entitled to be entered in the register within fourteen days beginning with–

(a)   in the pre-commonhold period, the date of incorporation of the commonhold association;

(b)   in the transitional period, the date on which the developer notifies the commonhold association of his right to be registered;

(c)   on registration with unit-holders, the date on which Land Registry gives notice that the registration of the land as commonhold land has been completed;

(d)   on the transfer of a commonhold unit, the date on which the commonhold association receives notification, in writing, from the new unit-holder that the transfer has taken place;

(e)   in the event that no nomination is received from joint unit-holders under article 2(d)(i)–

(i)   the date on which the commonhold association becomes aware that the joint unit-holders are registered as the freehold proprietors in the commonhold unit; or

(ii)   if the court orders a joint unit-holder to be entered in the register of members in place of a person who is or who would be entitled to be registered under paragraph (i), the date the commonhold association receives notice of the court order; or

(f)   in the event that joint unit-holders nominate one of themselves to be entitled to be entered in the register of members in place of the person entered by virtue of paragraph (d), (e)(ii) or this paragraph, the date on which the commonhold association receives the nomination.

GENERAL MEETINGS

Annual general meetings

5. Subject to the provisions of the Companies Act, the commonhold association must hold an annual general meeting.

Convening meetings

6. The directors may call general meetings and, on the requisition of members pursuant to the provisions of the Companies Act, must immediately proceed to convene a general meeting for a date not more than twenty-eight days after the date of the notice convening the meeting. If there are insufficient directors in the United Kingdom to call a general meeting, any director or any member of the commonhold association may call a general meeting.

NOTICE OF GENERAL MEETINGS

Period of notice

7. An annual general meeting or any general meeting called for the passing of a special resolution, a unanimous resolution, a termination-statement resolution, a winding-up resolution or a resolution appointing a person as a director must be called by at least twenty-one clear days' notice. All other general meetings must be called by at least fourteen clear days' notice but a general meeting may be called by shorter notice of at least three clear days if it is so agreed –
    (a)   in the case of an annual general meeting, by all the members entitled to attend and vote at that meeting; and
    (b)   in the case of any other meeting, by a majority in number of the members having a right to attend and vote being a majority together holding at least ninety-five per cent. of the total voting rights at that meeting of all the members.

Contents of notice

8. The notice must specify the time and place of the meeting and in the case of an annual general meeting, must specify the meeting as an annual general meeting. The meeting should take place within the commonhold or at a similarly convenient location.

9.   The notice must also include or be accompanied by a statement of the
        agenda of the business to be transacted at the meeting, the text of any reso-
        lution to be proposed (save that the text of ordinary resolutions need not be
        given) and a brief written explanation of them.

Entitlement to receive notice

10.   The notice must be given to the members and the directors of the common-
        hold association; but if any person entitled to receive notice is not sent it or
        does not receive it, this does not invalidate the proceedings at the meeting if
        the failure to notify was accidental.

PROCEEDINGS AT GENERAL MEETINGS

Business to be transacted

11.   Business must not be transacted at any general meeting unless details of it
        were included in the notice convening the meeting in accordance with article
        9. In the event that the text of an ordinary resolution is given in the notice
        convening the meeting in accordance with article 9 a proposal to amend an
        ordinary resolution may, however, be voted upon if the terms of the pro-
        posed amendment were received by the commonhold association at its reg-
        istered office, or at an address specified in the notice convening the meeting
        for the purpose of receiving electronic communications, before the time
        appointed for the meeting. The decision of the chairman as to the admissi-
        bility of any proposed amendment will be final and conclusive and does not
        invalidate any proceedings on the substantive resolution.

Order of business

12.   At any general meeting, so far as practicable and subject to any contrary
        ordinary resolution of the meeting, any business arising from a requisition
        of members will be transacted before any other business and, if there is
        more than one requisition, the business arising from it will be transacted
        in the order in which the requisitions were received by the commonhold
        association.

Quorum

13.   Business must not be transacted at any general meeting unless a quorum is
        present. The quorum for the meeting is one-fifth of the members of the com-
        monhold association or two members of the commonhold association
        (whichever is the greater) present in person or by proxy.
14.   If the relevant quorum is not present within half an hour after the time set
        for the meeting, or if during a meeting such a quorum ceases to be present,

the meeting is adjourned to the same day in the next week, at the same time and place, or to another day, time and place as decided by the directors.

Chairman

15.   The chairman, if any, of the board of directors or in his absence some other director or person nominated by the directors will preside as chairman of the meeting. If neither the chairman nor such other director (if any) is present within fifteen minutes after the time set for the meeting and willing to act, the directors present may elect one of themselves to be chairman or, if there is only one director present and willing to act, he will be chairman.

16.   If no director is willing to act as chairman, or if no director is present within fifteen minutes after the time set for the meeting, the members present and entitled to vote must choose one of themselves to be chairman.

Role of director

17.   A director, despite not being a member, is entitled to attend, speak and propose (but, subject to article 23, not vote upon) a resolution at any general meeting.

Adjournment

18.   The chairman may adjourn the meeting with the consent of any quorate meeting (and must if so required by the meeting), but no business is to be transacted at an adjourned meeting other than business which might properly have been transacted at the meeting had the adjournment not taken place. No notice is required of an adjourned meeting unless the meeting is adjourned for fourteen days or more, in which case at least seven clear days' notice must be given of the time and place of the adjourned meeting and the general nature of the business to be transacted.

Vote on a resolution and demand for a poll

19.   A resolution put to the vote of a meeting will be decided on a show of hands unless, before or on the declaration of the result of the show of hands, a poll is demanded. A poll may be demanded–
       (a)   by the chairman; or
       (b)   by at least two members having the right to vote at the meeting; or
       (c)   by a member or members representing not less than one-tenth of the total voting rights of all the members having the right to vote at the meeting;
       and a demand by a person as proxy for a member is the same as a demand by the member.

20.   Unless a poll is demanded, a declaration by the chairman that a resolution has been carried or lost on a show of hands, whether unanimously or by a

particular majority, and an entry to that effect in the minutes of the meeting is conclusive evidence of the fact, without proof, of the number or proportion of the votes recorded in favour of or against the resolution.

Proceedings on a poll

21.   The demand for a poll may be withdrawn before the poll is taken, but only with the consent of the chairman. The withdrawal of a demand for a poll does not invalidate the result of a show of hands declared before the demand for the poll was made.

22.   A poll will be taken in such manner as the chairman directs, having particular regard to the convenience of members, and he may appoint scrutineers (who need not be members). The result of the poll will be announced at the meeting at which the poll takes place and is deemed to be the resolution of the meeting at which the poll was demanded.

23.   In the case of an equality of votes, whether on a show of hands or on a poll, the chairman is entitled to a casting vote in addition to any other vote he may have.

24.   A poll demanded on the election of a chairman, or on a question of adjournment of a meeting, must be taken immediately. A poll demanded on any other question may be taken at such time as the chairman directs, having regard to the convenience of members, and not being more than thirty days after the poll is demanded. The demand for a poll does not prevent the meeting dealing with any business other than the business being determined by poll. If a poll is demanded before the declaration of the result of a show of hands and the demand is withdrawn, the meeting will continue as if the demand had not been made.

25.   No notice need be given of a poll not taken immediately if the time and place at which it is to be taken are announced at the meeting at which it is demanded. In any other case at least seven clear days' notice must be given of the time and place at which the poll is to be taken.

Written resolutions

26.   A resolution in writing signed by or on behalf of each member who would have been entitled to vote upon it if it had been proposed at a general meeting at which he was present is as effectual as if it had been passed at a general meeting convened and held and may consist of several instruments in similar form each signed by or on behalf of one or more members.

VOTES OF MEMBERS

Allocation of votes on show of hands

27.   On a show of hands, every member who (being an individual) is present in person or (being a corporation) is present by an authorised representative, not being himself a member entitled to vote, has one vote.

Allocation of votes on a poll

28.   On a poll –
- (a)   during the pre-commonhold period or the transitional period, every member has one vote; and
- (b)   at any other time, every member has the number of votes that are allocated in the commonhold community statement to him in respect of the commonhold unit of which he is the member and, where a member is a member in respect of more than one unit, the sum of the votes allocated to him in respect of those units.

Entitlement to vote – mental incapacity

29.   A member in respect of whom an order has been made by any court having jurisdiction (whether in the United Kingdom or elsewhere) in matters concerning mental disorder may vote, whether on a show of hands or on a poll, by his receiver or other person authorised in that behalf appointed by that court, and any such receiver or other person may, on a poll, vote by proxy. Evidence to the satisfaction of the directors of the authority of the person claiming to exercise the right to vote may be deposited at the registered office, or at such other place as is specified in accordance with the articles for the deposit of an appointment of proxy, before the time appointed for the meeting or adjourned meeting at which the right to vote is to be exercised or such evidence may be presented to the directors at the meeting. In default the right to vote is not exercisable.

Entitlement to vote – receiver, administrator, trustee in bankruptcy, commissioner in sequestration or similar person

30.   A receiver appointed by the court or by a mortgagee, an administrator, a trustee in bankruptcy, a commissioner in sequestration or similar person may vote in place of a member, whether on a show of hands or on a poll. Evidence to the satisfaction of the directors of the authority of the person claiming to exercise the right to vote may be deposited at the registered office, or at such other place as is specified in accordance with the articles for the deposit of appointments of proxy, before the time appointed for the meeting or adjourned meeting at which the right to vote is to be exercised or such evidence may be presented to the directors at the meeting. In default the right to vote is not exercisable.

Entitlement to vote – mortgagee in possession

31.   A mortgagee who provides –
- (a)   a certificate confirming that possession has been taken of a commonhold unit; and
- (b)   an official copy of the charges register of the title to the commonhold unit showing it as the registered proprietor of the charge

is entitled to vote in place of a member, whether on a show of hands or on a poll. The person claiming to exercise the right to vote must deposit such evidence at the registered office, or at such other place as is specified in accordance with the articles for the deposit of appointments of proxy, before the time appointed for the meeting or adjourned meeting at which the right to vote is to be exercised or such evidence may be presented to the directors at the meeting. In default the right to vote is not exercisable.

Objections to qualification of voter

32.   Objections to the qualification of any voter may only be raised at the meeting or adjourned meeting at which the vote objected to is tendered, and every vote not disallowed at the meeting is valid. Any objection made in due time must be referred to the chairman whose decision is final and conclusive.

Votes on a poll in person or by proxy

33.   On a poll votes may be given either personally or by proxy. A member may appoint more than one proxy to attend on the same occasion.

Form of appointment of proxy

34.   The appointment of a proxy must be in writing, signed by or on behalf of the appointor and must be in the following form (or a form to the same effect or in any other form which the directors may approve in writing)–

'[Name of commonhold association]
I/We [ ], of [ ], being a member/members of the above-named commonhold association, appoint [ ] of [ ], or failing him, [ ] of [ ], as my/our proxy to vote in my/our name and on my/our behalf at the (annual) general meeting of the commonhold association to be held on [ ], and at any adjournment of it

Signed on [ ]'

35.   Where members are to be given the opportunity to instruct the proxy how he must act, the appointment of a proxy must be in the following form (or a form to the same effect or in any other form which the directors may approve in writing)–

'[Name of commonhold association]
I/We, [ ], of [ ], being a member/members of the above-named commonhold association, appoint [ ] of [ ], or failing him, [ ] of [ ], as my/our proxy to vote in my/our name and on my/our behalf at the (annual) general meeting of the commonhold association, to be held on [ ], and at any adjournment of it.

This form is to be used in respect of the resolutions mentioned below as follows:

Resolution No.1 for* against*
Resolution No.2 for* against*

* Delete as appropriate

Unless instructed otherwise, the proxy may vote as he thinks fit or abstain from voting.

Signed on [ ]'

Notice of proxy

36.　The appointment of a proxy and any authority under which it is signed or a copy of such authority properly certified notarially or approved in another way by the directors may –
　　(a)　　in the case of an appointment contained in an electronic communication, where an address has been specified for the purpose of receiving electronic communications –
　　　　(i)　　in the notice convening the meeting, or
　　　　(ii)　　in any form of appointment of proxy sent out by the commonhold association in relation to the meeting, or
　　　　(iii)　　in any invitation contained in an electronic communication to appoint a proxy issued by the commonhold association in relation to the meeting,
　　　　be received at that address; or
　　(b)　　in any other case, be deposited at the registered office of the commonhold association or at such other place within the United Kingdom as is stated either in the notice convening the meeting or in any form of appointment of proxy sent out by the commonhold association in relation to the meeting;
at any time before the meeting or adjourned meeting, at which the person named in the appointment proposes to vote, is held. Failing that it may be delivered at the meeting to the chairman, secretary or to any director. The appointment of a proxy which is not deposited, received or delivered in accordance with this article is invalid.

Notice of determination of authority

37.　A vote given or poll demanded by a proxy for a member, or by the authorised representative of a corporation remains valid despite the previous determination of the authority of the person voting or demanding a poll unless notice of the determination was received by the commonhold association at –
　　(a)　　the registered office; or
　　(b)　　at such other place at which the appointment of proxy was deposited; or

241

(c)   where the appointment of the proxy was contained in an electronic communication, at the address at which such appointment was received

before the start of the meeting or adjourned meeting at which the vote is given or the poll demanded or (in the case of a poll taken otherwise than on the same day as the meeting or adjourned meeting) the time appointed for taking the poll.

NUMBER OF DIRECTORS

38.   Unless otherwise determined by ordinary resolution, the number of directors is not subject to any maximum but must not be less than two.

APPOINTMENT AND RETIREMENT OF DIRECTORS

Qualification

39.   A director need not be a member of the commonhold association.

Retirement by rotation

40.   At the first annual general meeting after the end of the transitional period, all of the directors must retire from office. At every subsequent annual general meeting, one-third of the directors who are subject to retirement by rotation must retire. If the number of directors is not three or a multiple of three, the number nearest to one-third must retire from office. If there is only one director who is subject to retirement by rotation, he must retire.

41.   Subject to the provisions of the Companies Act, the directors to retire by rotation are those who have been in office longest since their last appointment or reappointment. Where there are directors who were appointed or re-appointed on the same day, those to retire must be determined by lot, unless the directors agree otherwise among themselves.

42.   If the commonhold association, at the meeting at which a director retires by rotation, does not fill the vacancy, the retiring director, if willing to act, is deemed to have been re-appointed unless at the meeting it is resolved not to fill the vacancy or unless a resolution for the reappointment of the director is put to the meeting and lost.

Appointment and re-appointment of directors at general meetings

43.   No person other than a director retiring by rotation may be appointed or re-appointed as a director at any general meeting unless–
(a)   he is recommended by the directors; or
(b)   at least fourteen and not more than thirty-five clear days before the date appointed for the meeting, notice signed by a member quali-

fied to vote at the meeting has been given to the commonhold association of the intention to propose that person for appointment or reappointment and stating the particulars which would be required to be included in the commonhold association's register of directors, if he were appointed or re-appointed, together with notice signed by that person of his willingness to be appointed or re-appointed.

Notice of proposed appointment

44.   At least seven and not more than twenty-eight clear days before the date appointed for holding a general meeting notice must be given to all who are entitled to receive notice of the meeting of any person (other than a director retiring by rotation at the meeting) who is recommended by the directors for appointment or reappointment as a director at the meeting or in respect of whom notice has been given to the commonhold association of the intention to propose him at the meeting for appointment or reappointment as a director. The notice must give the particulars of that person which would, if he were appointed or re-appointed, be required to be included in the commonhold association's register of directors.

Appointment by members

45.   Subject to these articles, the commonhold association may by ordinary resolution appoint a person, who is willing to act, to be a director either to fill a vacancy or as an additional director and may also determine the rotation in which any additional directors are to retire.

Appointment by directors

46.   The directors may appoint a person who is willing to act to be a director, either to fill a vacancy or as an additional director, provided that the appointment does not cause the number of directors to exceed the number fixed by or in accordance with these articles as the maximum number of directors (if any). A director so appointed will hold office only until the next following annual general meeting and is not taken into account in determining the directors who are to retire by rotation at the meeting. If not re-appointed at such annual general meeting, he must vacate office at the end of the meeting.

Re-appointment following retirement at annual general meeting

47.   Subject to these articles, a director who retires at an annual general meeting may, if willing to act, be re-appointed. If he is not re-appointed, he must hold office until the meeting appoints someone in his place, or if it does not do so, until the end of the meeting.

DISQUALIFICATION AND REMOVAL OF DIRECTORS

48.   The office of a director must be vacated if–
   (a)   an ordinary resolution is passed by the members in favour of removing a director (where special notice of the resolution has been given in accordance with the Companies Act);
   (b)   he ceases to be a director by virtue of any provision of the Companies Act or he becomes prohibited by law from being a director; or
   (c)   he becomes bankrupt or makes any arrangement or composition with his creditors generally; or
   (d)   he is, or may be, suffering from mental disorder and either:–
      (i)   he is admitted to hospital in pursuance of an application for admission for treatment under the Mental Health Act 1983 or, in Scotland, an application for admission under the Mental Health (Scotland) Act 1960, or
      (ii)   an order is made by a court having jurisdiction (whether in the United Kingdom or elsewhere) in matters concerning mental disorder for his detention or for the appointment of a receiver or other person to exercise powers with respect to his property or affairs; or
   (e)   he resigns his office by notice to the commonhold association; or
   (f)   he is absent for more than three consecutive months from meetings of the directors held during that period or from three consecutive meetings (whichever is the greater) without permission from the directors and the directors resolve that his office be vacated.

49.   Where there is only one or one remaining director of the commonhold association, an appointment of a new director must take place, before the director disqualified or being removed vacates his office.

POWERS OF DIRECTORS

50.   Subject to the provisions of the Companies Act, the memorandum and the articles, and to any directions given by special resolution, the directors must manage the business of the commonhold association and may exercise all the powers of the commonhold association. No alteration of the memorandum or articles and no such direction invalidates any prior act of the directors which would have been valid if that alteration had not been made or that direction had not been given. The powers given by this article are not limited by any special power given to the directors by the articles and the directors' powers may be exercised at a meeting at which a quorum is present.

51.   The directors may, by power of attorney or otherwise, appoint any person to be the agent of the commonhold association for such purposes and on such conditions as they determine, including authority for the agent to delegate all or any of his powers.

AGENTS

52.   The directors have the power on behalf of the commonhold association to appoint and enter into contracts with managing agents of the commonhold on such terms as they think fit including a term providing for cancellation of the contract and return of records and monies paid. The directors remain bound to supervise the managing agent so appointed.

DELEGATION OF DIRECTORS' POWERS

53.   Where an ordinary resolution is passed in favour, the directors may delegate any of their powers to any committee consisting of one or more directors, members of the commonhold association and others as they think fit, provided that the majority of the persons on any such committee from time to time are members of the commonhold association. They may also delegate to any managing director or any director holding any other executive office or any managing agent such of their powers as they consider desirable to be exercised by him. Any such delegation is subject to any provisions of the commonhold community statement, may be made subject to any conditions the directors may impose, may be made either collaterally with or to the exclusion of their own powers, and may be revoked or altered. Subject to any such conditions, the proceedings of a committee with two or more persons are governed by the articles regulating the proceedings of directors so far as they are capable of applying. A record must be kept giving details of any powers that have been delegated.

REMUNERATION OF DIRECTORS

54.   Directors are entitled to such remuneration as the commonhold association may determine by ordinary resolution, where the directors are not members of the commonhold association, and by special resolution, where the directors are members of the commonhold association. Unless the resolution provides otherwise, the remuneration is deemed to accrue from day to day.

DIRECTORS' EXPENSES

55.   The directors may be paid all travelling, hotel, and other expenses reasonably and properly incurred by them in connection with their attendance at meetings of directors or committees set up by the directors or general meetings or separate meetings of the members of the commonhold association or otherwise in connection with the discharge of their duties.

DIRECTORS' APPOINTMENTS AND INTERESTS

Executive appointments

56.   Subject to the provisions of the Companies Act, the directors may appoint one or more of their number to the office of managing director or to any other executive office under the commonhold association and may enter into an agreement or arrangement with any director for his employment by the commonhold association or for the provision by him of any services outside the scope of the ordinary duties of a director. Any appointment of a director to an executive office must terminate if he ceases to be a director but without prejudice to any claim to damages for breach of the contract of service between the director and the commonhold association.

Directors' interests

57.   Subject to the provisions of the Companies Act, and provided that he has disclosed to the directors the nature and extent of any material interest of his, a director–

    (a)   may be a party to, or otherwise interested in, any transaction or arrangement with the commonhold association or in which the commonhold association is otherwise interested; and

    (b)   may be a director or other officer of, or employed by, or a party to any transaction or arrangement with, or otherwise interested in, any body corporate promoted by the commonhold association or in which the commonhold association is otherwise interested; and

    (c)   is not, by reason of his office, accountable to the commonhold association for any benefit which he derives from any such office or employment or from any such transaction or arrangement or from any interest in any such body corporate and no such transaction or arrangement is liable to be avoided on the ground of any such interest or benefit.

58.   For the purposes of article 57–

    (a)   a general notice given to the directors that a director is to be regarded as having an interest of the nature and extent specified in the notice in any transaction or arrangement in which a specified person or class of persons is interested is deemed to be a disclosure that the director has an interest in any such transaction of the nature and extent so specified; and

    (b)   an interest of which a director has no knowledge and of which it is unreasonable to expect him to have knowledge will not be treated as an interest of his.

59.   A commonhold association must keep a register of directors' interests and whenever it receives information from a director given in fulfilment of an obligation imposed on him by article 57, it is under obligation to enter in the register, against the director's name, the information received and the date of the entry.

PROCEEDINGS OF DIRECTORS

Regulation and notice of meetings

60. Subject to the provisions of these articles, the directors may regulate their proceedings, as they think fit. A director may, and the secretary at the request of a director must, call a meeting of the directors. It is not necessary to give notice of a meeting to a director who is absent from the United Kingdom unless he has given to the commonhold association an address to which notices may be sent using electronic communications. In such case the director is entitled to have notices given to him at that address. In all other cases, a notice calling a meeting of directors need not be in writing. Questions arising at a meeting will be decided by a majority of votes. In the case of an equality of votes, the chairman will have a second or casting vote.

Quorum

61. The quorum for the transaction of the business of the directors may be fixed by the directors and unless so fixed at any other greater number, is half of the number of appointed directors for the time being or two directors (whichever is the greater).

62. The continuing directors or a sole continuing director may act despite any vacancies in their number, but, if the number of directors is less than the number fixed as the quorum, the continuing director or directors may act only for the purpose of filling vacancies or of calling a general meeting.

Chairman

63. The directors may appoint one of their number to be the chairman of the board of directors and may at any time remove him from that office. Unless he is unwilling to do so, the director so appointed must preside at every meeting of directors at which he is present. But if there is no director holding that office, or if the director holding it is unwilling to preside or is not present within fifteen minutes after the time appointed for the meeting, the directors present may appoint one of their number to be chairman of the meeting.

Validity of acts

64. All acts done by a meeting of directors, or of a committee set up by the directors, or by a person acting as a director are valid even if it is discovered later that there was a defect in the appointment of any director or that any of them were disqualified from holding office, or had vacated office, or were not entitled to vote.

Written resolutions

65.   A resolution in writing signed by all the directors entitled to receive notice of a meeting of directors or of a committee set up by the directors is as valid and effectual as if it had been passed at a meeting of directors or (as the case may be) a committee set up by the directors convened and held and may consist of several documents in similar form each signed by one or more directors.

Entitlement to vote – conflict of interest

66.   A director must not vote at a meeting of directors or of a committee set up by the directors on any resolution concerning a matter in which he has, directly or indirectly, an interest or duty which is material and which conflicts or may conflict with the interests of the commonhold association. For the purposes of this article, an interest of a person who is, for any purpose of the Companies Act (excluding any statutory modification of it not in force when this article becomes binding on the commonhold association), connected with a director is treated as an interest of the director.

67.   A director must not be counted in the quorum present at a meeting in relation to a resolution on which he is not entitled to vote.

68.   The commonhold association may by ordinary resolution suspend or relax to any extent, either generally or in respect of any particular matter, any provisions of these articles prohibiting a director from voting at a meeting of directors or of a committee set up by the directors.

69.   If a question arises at a meeting of directors or of a committee set up by the directors as to the right of a director to vote, the question may be referred to the chairman of the meeting before the end of the meeting, and his ruling in relation to any director other than himself must be final and conclusive.

SECRETARY

70.   Subject to the provisions of the Companies Act, the secretary will be appointed by the directors for such terms, at such remuneration and upon such conditions as they may think fit; and any secretary so appointed may be removed by them.

MINUTES

71.   The directors must cause minutes to be made in books kept for the purpose –
        (a)   of all appointments of officers made by the directors or by the developer; and
        (b)   of all proceedings at meetings of the commonhold association and of the directors, and of committees, including the names of the persons present at each such meeting, the date of the meeting and any action agreed at the meeting.

NO DISTRIBUTION OF PROFITS

72.   Save in accordance with a termination statement or in a winding up, the commonhold association must not distribute its profits or assets, whether in cash or otherwise, to its members.

INSPECTION AND COPYING OF BOOKS AND RECORDS

73.   In addition to, and without derogation from, any right conferred by statute, any member has the right, on reasonable notice and at a reasonable time and place, to inspect, and to be provided with a copy of, any book, minute, register, document, or accounting record of the commonhold association, upon payment of any reasonable charge for copying. Such rights are subject to any ordinary resolution of the commonhold association in general meeting, and, in the case of any book, minute, register, document, or accounting record which the directors reasonably consider contains confidential material, the disclosure of which would be contrary to the interests of the commonhold association or to another member, to the exclusion or excision of such confidential material (the fact of such exclusion or excision being disclosed to the member), and to any other reasonable conditions that the directors may impose.

74.   Subject to any statutory requirement, all books, minutes, registers, documents, or accounting records of the commonhold association must be retained for a minimum period of three years.

75.   Up-to-date copies of the commonhold community statement and the memorandum and articles of association must be kept at the registered office of the commonhold association and any unit-holder has the right, on reasonable notice and at a reasonable time and place, to inspect the commonhold community statement or the memorandum and articles of association.

NOTICES

76.   Unless otherwise stated, any notice to be given under these articles must be in writing.

77.   Any notice may be given –
   (a)   personally;
   (b)   by leaving it at an address given to the commonhold association as an address for correspondence;
   (c)   by sending it by first class post in a prepaid envelope properly addressed to the member at an address given to the commonhold association as an address for correspondence; or
   (d)   where an electronic address has been provided as an address for correspondence, by electronic communication to that address in accordance with any terms or conditions as previously specified by the recipient.

78.   Proof that an envelope containing a notice was properly addressed, prepaid and posted by first class post is conclusive evidence that it was given to a

postal address. Electronic confirmation of receipt is conclusive evidence that a notice was given to an address.

79.   A notice is deemed to be given, unless proved otherwise–

    (a)   on the day it was handed to the recipient or left at the address for correspondence;

    (b)   on the second day after it was posted to the recipient; or

    (c)   on the day after it was transmitted by electronic communication.

INDEMNITY

80.   Subject to the provisions of the Companies Act but without affecting any indemnity to which he may otherwise be entitled, every director or other officer of the commonhold association must be indemnified out of the assets of the commonhold association against any liability incurred by him in defending any proceedings, whether civil or criminal, alleging liability for negligence, default, breach of duty or breach of trust in relation to the affairs of the commonhold association, and in which judgment is given in his favour, or in which he is acquitted, or in connection with any application in which relief is granted to him by the Court.

Signed by the subscribers to the memorandum of association of the commonhold association

Dated:

Witness to the above signature(s)

Schedule 3
Commonhold Community Statement

[Not reproduced here but see **www.opsi.gov.uk** and **Appendix B**.]

Schedule 4
Forms

[Not reproduced here but see **www.opsi.gov.uk**.]

Commonhold (Land Registration) Rules 2004, SI 2004/1830

Made 14th July 2004
Laid before Parliament 16th July 2004
Coming into force in accordance with rule 1

The Lord Chancellor, with the advice and assistance of the Rule Committee appointed in pursuance of section 127 of the Land Registration Act 2002, in exercise of the powers conferred upon him by section 65 of the Commonhold and Leasehold Reform Act 2002 hereby makes the following rules:

General

1   Citation and commencement

These rules may be cited as the Commonhold (Land Registration) Rules 2004 and shall come into force on the day that section 2 of the Act comes into force.

2   Interpretation

(1)   In these rules–
'the Act' means Part 1 of the Commonhold and Leasehold Reform Act 2002,
'commonhold entries' means the entries referred to in paragraphs (a) to (c) of rule 28(1) and
'main rules' means the Land Registration Rules 2003.

(2)   In these rules except where otherwise stated, a form referred to by letters or numbers means the form so designated in Schedule 1 to these rules.

3   Land registration rules

(1)   Land registration rules within the meaning of the Land Registration Act 2002 have effect in relation to anything done by virtue of or for the purposes of the Act as they have effect in relation to anything done by virtue of or for the purposes of the Land Registration Act 2002 subject to paragraphs (2) and (3).

(2)   Rules 3(3)(a), 3(4)(a), 126, 127 and 214 of the main rules shall not apply to any application made under the Act.

(3)   In its application to the Act –

    (a)   subject to paragraph (2), rule 3 of the main rules (individual registers and more than one registered estate, division and amalgamation) shall apply as if the words 'and are vested in the same proprietor' in paragraph (1) and the words 'and are vested in the same proprietor' in paragraph (4) were omitted,

    (b)   rule 54 of the main rules (outline applications) shall apply as if paragraph (6) of that rule referred to the forms in Schedule 1 to these rules,

    (c)   rules 136 to 138 of the main rules (exempt information documents) shall apply as if a commonhold community statement and a memorandum and articles of association of a commonhold association were excluded from the definition of a 'relevant document' in rule 136(7),

    (d)   for the purposes of rule 208 of the main rules (Welsh language forms) the forms in Schedule 1 to these rules shall be treated as if they were scheduled forms within the meaning of the main rules,

    (e)   rules 210 and 211 of the main rules (documents in a Schedule 1 form and electronically produced forms) shall apply to the forms in Schedule 1 to these rules as they apply to the forms in Schedule 1 to the main rules, and

    (f)   Parts 3 and 4 of Schedule 6 to the main rules (information to be included in the results of certain official searches) shall apply as if the words 'relevant pending application' included any application made under the Act.

Applications

4   Lodging a copy document

(1)   This rule applies to –

    (a)   the commonhold association's certificate of incorporation,

    (b)   any altered certificate of incorporation,

    (c)   the memorandum and articles of association of the commonhold association,

    (d)   any altered memorandum or articles of association of the commonhold association,

    (e)   a commonhold community statement,

    (f)   any amended commonhold community statement,

    (g)   an order of the court under the Act, and

    (h)   a termination statement.

(2)   Where the Act or these rules requires an application to be accompanied by a document referred to in paragraph (1), a certified copy of that document may be submitted in place of the original.

(3)   Where the original document is lodged a certified copy must accompany it.

5   Application for registration

(1)   An application to register a freehold estate in land as a freehold estate in commonhold land must be made in Form CM1 accompanied, where appropriate, by the statement required by section 9(1)(b) of the Act.

(2)   The statement required by section 9(1)(b) of the Act shall be in Form COV.

(3)   Unless the Registrar otherwise directs, the application must be accompanied by a statutory declaration made by the applicant that complies with rule 6.

6   Statutory declaration

(1)   The statutory declaration referred to in rule 5(3) must comply with paragraphs (2) to (6).

(2)   The declaration must list the consents, or orders of court dispensing with consent, that have been obtained under or by virtue of section 3 of the Act.

(3)   Where there is a restriction entered in any individual register affected by the application, the declaration must confirm that either the restriction does not protect an interest in respect of which the consent of the holder is required or, if it does that the appropriate consent has been obtained.

(4)   The declaration must confirm that–
           (a)   no other consents are required under or by virtue of section 3 of the Act,
           (b)   no consent has lapsed or been withdrawn, and
           (c)   if a consent is subject to conditions, all conditions have been fully satisfied.

(5)   Where the application involves the extinguishment under section 22 of the Act of a charge that is the subject of an entry in the register the declaration must–
           (a)   identify the charge to be extinguished
           (b)   identify the title of the owner of the charge,
           (c)   give the name and address of the owner of the charge, and
           (d)   confirm that the consent of the owner of the charge has been obtained.

(6)   The Registrar must accept the statutory declaration as conclusive evidence that no additional consents are required under or by virtue of section 3 of the Act and must cancel any entry in the register relating to an interest that has been identified in the statutory declaration to be extinguished.

7   Form of consent

The form of consent required under or by virtue of sections 3 and 41 of the Act is Form CON 1.

8   Rejection or cancellation of application

In addition to the Registrar's powers contained in rule 16 of the main rules, the Registrar may reject an application on delivery or he may cancel it at any time thereafter if plans submitted with it (whether as part of the commonhold community statement or otherwise) are insufficiently clear or accurate.

9 Title to interests

(1) Where a consent required under or by virtue of section 3 of the Act has been lodged relating to an interest which is unregistered or is the subject of only a notice, caution or restriction in the register, the applicant must also lodge sufficient evidence to satisfy the Registrar that the person whose consent has been lodged is the person who was entitled to that interest at the time the consent was given.

(2) For the purposes of paragraph (1), the Registrar may accept as sufficient evidence of entitlement a conveyancer's certificate that he is satisfied that the person whose consent has been lodged in relation to that interest is the person who was entitled to it at the time the consent was given and that he holds evidence of this.

10 Service of notice – extinguished leases

(1) Subject to paragraph (3), where, as the result of an application under section 2 of the Act, a lease the title to which is registered is extinguished under section 9(3)(f) of the Act, the Registrar must give notice of the closure of the leasehold title to the following–

    (a) the registered proprietor of the leasehold title,

    (b) the registered proprietor of any charge affecting the leasehold title, and

    (c) the person entitled to the benefit of a notice, a restriction or a caution against dealings entered in the register of the leasehold title.

(2) Subject to paragraph (3), where, as the result of an application under section 2 of the Act, an unregistered lease which is noted in the register of the freehold title is extinguished under section 9(3)(f) of the Act, the Registrar must give notice of the completion of the application to the holder of the leasehold estate that has been extinguished.

(3) The Registrar is not obliged to give notice to a person referred to in paragraph (1) or (2) or in both if–

    (a) that person consented under section 3 of the Act to the application, or

    (b) that person's name and his address for service under rule 198 of the main rules are not set out in the relevant individual register.

11 Service of notice at end of transitional period – extinguished leases

(1) Subject to paragraph (3), where a lease the title to which is registered is extinguished under section 7(3)(d) of the Act and rule 29 (2) applies, the Registrar must give notice of the closure of the leasehold title to the following–

(a)   the registered proprietor of the leasehold title,
(b)   the registered proprietor of any charge affecting the leasehold title, and
(c)   the person entitled to the benefit of a notice, a restriction or a caution against dealings entered in the register of the leasehold title.

(2)   Subject to paragraph (3), where an unregistered lease which is noted in the register of the freehold title is extinguished under section 7(3)(d) and rule 29(2) applies, the Registrar must give notice of the completion of the application to the holder of the leasehold estate that has been extinguished.

(3)   The Registrar is not obliged to give notice to a person referred to in paragraph (1) if–
(a)   that person consented under section 3 of the Act to the application, or
(b)   that person's name and his address for service under rule 198 of the main rules are not set out in the relevant individual register.

12   Court order

An application to give effect in the register to an order of the court under the Act, other than a succession order, must be made in Form AP1 of the main rules.

13   Registration of an amended commonhold community statement

(1)   An application to register an amended commonhold community statement must be made in Form CM3.
(2)   The application must be accompanied by a new version of the commonhold community statement incorporating the amendments.
(3)   On completion of the application, the Registrar must enter a note of the amended commonhold community statement in the register of the title to the common parts in a manner that distinguishes it from previous versions of the commonhold community statement.

14   Cessation of commonhold during the transitional period

(1)   An application for the freehold estate in land to cease to be registered as a freehold estate in commonhold land during the transitional period must be made in Form CM2.
(2)   When satisfied that the application is in order, the Registrar must cancel to the necessary extent the commonhold entries made in the register under rule 28(1)(a) to (c).
(3)   Unless the Registrar otherwise directs, the application must be accompanied by–
(a)   a statutory declaration made by the applicant that complies with rule 6 to the extent necessary, and
(b)   all necessary consents in Form CON2.

15   Transfer of part of a commonhold unit

(1)   An application to register a transfer of the freehold estate in part only of a commonhold unit must be accompanied by an application in Form CM3 to register the commonhold community statement that has been amended in relation to the transfer.

(2)   The Registrar may reject on delivery the application to register the transfer, or he may cancel it at any time thereafter, if it is not accompanied by an application to register the amended commonhold community statement.

16   Transfer of part of the common parts

(1)   An application to register a transfer of the freehold estate in part of the common parts must be accompanied by an application in Form CM3 to register the commonhold community statement that has been amended in relation to the transfer.

(2)   The Registrar may reject on delivery the application to register the transfer, or he may cancel it at any time thereafter, if it is not accompanied by an application to register the amended commonhold community statement.

17   Alteration of the extent of a commonhold unit

(1)   An application to register an amended commonhold community statement in Form CM3 which would have the effect of altering the extent of a commonhold unit (other than by removing the whole of the unit) must be accompanied by an application to register any relevant transfer.

(2)   Where there is a relevant transfer, the Registrar may reject on delivery the application to register the amended commonhold community statement, or he may cancel it at any time thereafter, if paragraph (1) is not complied with.

18   Alteration of the extent of the common parts

(1)   An application to register an amended commonhold community statement in Form CM3 which would have the effect of altering the extent of the common parts (unless section 30(4) of the Act applies) must be accompanied by an application to register any relevant transfer.

(2)   Where there is a relevant transfer, the Registrar may reject on delivery the application to register the amended commonhold community statement, or he may cancel it at any time thereafter, if paragraph (1) is not complied with.

19   Registration of an altered memorandum or articles of association

(1)   An application to register an altered memorandum or articles of association must be made in Form CM3.

257

(2) The application must be accompanied by a new version of the memorandum or articles of association of the commonhold association incorporating the amendments.

(3) On completion of the application, the Registrar must enter a note of the altered memorandum or articles of association in the register of the title to the common parts in a manner that distinguishes them from previous versions of the memorandum or articles of association of the commonhold association.

20 Application to add land

(1) An application to add land within the meaning of section 41 of the Act must be made in Form CM4.

(2) Such an application must be accompanied by an application to register the amended commonhold community statement in Form CM3.

(3) The Registrar may reject on delivery the application to add land, or he may cancel it at any time thereafter, if it is not accompanied by an application to register the amended commonhold community statement.

(4) Unless the Registrar otherwise directs the application must be accompanied by a statutory declaration by the applicant that complies with rule 6 to the extent necessary.

21 Termination application following a voluntary winding up

(1) A termination application must be–
   (a) made in Form CM5, and
   (b) accompanied by the order, appointment by the Secretary of State or resolution under which the liquidator was appointed and such other evidence as the Registrar may require.

(2) Where a termination application is made and the liquidator notifies the Registrar that he is content with the termination statement, or sends to the Registrar a copy of the court's determination of the terms of the termination statement, the Registrar must–
   (a) enter the commonhold association as proprietor of the commonhold units, and
   (b) cancel the commonhold entries on every registered title affected.

22 Application to terminate a commonhold registration following the winding-up of a commonhold association by the court

(1) An application to terminate a commonhold registration where the court has made a winding-up order in respect of a commonhold association and has not made a succession order must be made in Form CM5.

(2) When the Registrar has received notification under section 54(2)(c) to (f) of the Act, and is otherwise satisfied that the application is in order, he may cancel the commonhold entries on the registered titles affected.

23   **Registration of a successor commonhold association**

(1)   Where a succession order is made, an application must be made to the Registrar to register the successor commonhold association in Form CM6.

(2)   Unless the Registrar otherwise directs, the application must be accompanied by –
       (a)   the succession order,
       (b)   the memorandum and articles of association of the successor commonhold association, and
       (c)   the winding up order.

(3)   When satisfied that the application is in order, the Registrar must –
       (a)   cancel the note of the memorandum and articles of association of the insolvent commonhold association in the property register of the registered title to the common parts,
       (b)   enter a note of the memorandum and articles of association of the successor commonhold association in the property register of the registered title to the common parts, and
       (c)   give effect to the terms of the succession order in the individual registers of the registered titles affected.

(4)   Where a succession order includes provisions falling within section 52(4) of the Act, the successor commonhold association must make an application to give effect in the register to those provisions so far as necessary.

24   **Application to register surrender of a development right**

(1)   An application to note the surrender of a right conferred by section 58(2) of the Act in the register must be accompanied by a notice in Form SR1.

(2)   When satisfied as to the application, the Registrar must complete it by entering the notice surrendering the right in the property register of the registered title to the common parts.

25   **Official copies**

An application for official copies of the individual register and title plan of the common parts in relation to a commonhold must be made by inserting the following words in panel 9 of Form OC1 in Schedule 1 of the main rules –

       'official copy(ies) of the register and title plan of the common parts in a commonhold development.'

26   **Searches of the index map**

If a person who applies for a search of the index map requires the title numbers of the units in relation to a commonhold, he must insert the common parts title number followed by the words 'common parts' in panel 2 of Form SIM in Schedule 1 of the main rules or supply a plan of the commonhold land showing sufficient detail to enable the land to be clearly identified on the Ordnance Survey map.

The Register

27   Restrictions

To give effect to the terms of the Act the Registrar must –
(a)   enter a restriction in Form CA in Schedule 2 in the individual register of the common parts title, and
(b)   enter a restriction in Form CB in Schedule 2 in the individual register of each unit title.

28   Completion of application for registration

(1)   When satisfied that an application under section 2 of the Act is in order, the Registrar must complete it by entering in the individual register of the affected registered titles –
(a)   a note that the freehold estate is registered as a freehold estate in commonhold land,
(b)   a note of the memorandum and articles of association of the commonhold association and the commonhold community statement,
(c)   where the application is not accompanied by Form COV, a note that the rights and duties conferred and imposed by the commonhold community statement will not come into force until the end of the transitional period, and
(d)   where the application is not accompanied by Form COV, the applicant as proprietor of the registered title to each of the units and as proprietor of the registered title to the common parts.
(2)   Where an application to register the freehold estate in land as the freehold estate in commonhold land is accompanied by Form COV, the Registrar must –
(a)   cancel notice of any lease extinguished under section 9(3)(f) of the Act, and
(b)   close the title if the lease is registered.

29   End of transitional period

(1)   This rule applies where an application has been made under section 2 of the Act and was not accompanied by Form COV.
(2)   Where the Registrar is aware that the transitional period has come to an end, he must –
(a)   cancel the entries made in the register under rule 28(1)(c),
(b)   cancel notice of any lease extinguished under section 7(3)(d) of the Act, and
(c)   close the title to any such lease where the lease is registered.

30   Leases of commonhold units

When a term of years absolute is created in a commonhold unit and the lease is registered, the Registrar must enter a note in the property register of the leasehold title that it is a lease of a commonhold unit.

31   Changing size: charged unit

On an application to which rule 15 or rule 17 relates and where section 24(1) of the Act applies, on receipt of Form COE, the Registrar must give effect in the register to section 24(4) and (5) of the Act as appropriate.

32   Charges over common parts

Where a charge is extinguished, in whole or in part, under section 28(3) or section 28(4) of the Act, the Registrar must cancel or alter as appropriate any entry of the charge in the register to the extent that it is extinguished.

Schedule 1

[Not reproduced here – prescribed forms – see **www.opsi.gov.uk**.]

Schedule 2

rule 27

COMMONHOLD RESTRICTIONS

Form CA (Restriction in common parts title)

No charge by the proprietor of the registered estate is to be registered other than a legal mortgage which is accompanied by a certificate by a conveyancer or a director or secretary of the commonhold association that the creation of the mortgage was approved by a resolution complying with section 29(2) of the Commonhold and Leasehold Reform Act 2002.

Form CB (Restriction in unit title)

No disposition by the proprietor of the registered estate (other than a transfer or charge of the whole of the land in the title) is to be registered without a certificate by a conveyancer or a director or secretary of the commonhold association that the disposition is authorised by and made in accordance with the provisions of the Commonhold and Leasehold Reform Act 2002.

APPENDIX B

Example commonhold community statement

This is an extract of Appendix 2 from the Department for Constitutional Affairs *Guidance on the drafting of a Commonhold Community Statement including Specimen Local Rules* which was published in February 2005.

* * * * *

APPENDIX 2 – EXAMPLE CCS

This Appendix contains an illustrative example of a completed CCS (excluding the plans). The example is not intended to represent a comprehensive document for a particular commonhold. It simply aims to illustrate how some of the specimen clauses outlined in this guidance would appear when incorporated into the model CCS. Those intending to set up a commonhold are advised to seek professional advice when considering the provisions that need to be included in a particular CCS.

COMMONHOLD AND LEASEHOLD REFORM ACT 2002

COMMONHOLD COMMUNITY STATEMENT OF SUNNYSIDE COMMONHOLD

This document is important.

It creates legally binding rights and duties.

It is recommended that anyone affected by it should take appropriate advice.

TABLE OF CONTENTS Page Number

ANNEX 6: DEVELOPMENT RIGHTS

PART 1: INTRODUCTION

1.1 COMMONHOLD COMMUNITY STATEMENT

1.1.1   This document is a commonhold community statement ('CCS'). It defines the commonhold units and the common parts. It also specifies the rights and duties of the unit-holders and the commonhold association, and the procedure to be followed to enforce them.

1.1.2   This CCS imposes obligations on a tenant of a commonhold unit and specifies the procedure to be followed by a tenant to enforce a duty imposed on the commonhold association, a unit-holder, or another tenant.

1.1.3   These rights and duties are in addition to any rights and duties that may exist under the general law.

1.1.4   The provisions of this CCS are subject to the Act and regulations made under it. In particular, regulations may provide that a CCS is to be treated as including specified provisions or as including provisions of a specified kind, for a specified purpose or about a specified matter.

1.1.5   A provision of this CCS has no effect to the extent that it is–

(a)   inconsistent with any provision made by or by virtue of the Act;

(b)   inconsistent with anything which is treated as included in this CCS by regulations;

(c)   inconsistent with the memorandum or articles of association; or

(d)   prohibited by regulations.

1.2 THE COMMONHOLD AND COMMONHOLD ASSOCIATION

1.2.1   The name of the commonhold is in paragraph 1 of Annex 1.

1.2.2   The name and company number of the commonhold association are in paragraphs 2 and 3 of Annex 1.

1.3 STRUCTURE OF THIS DOCUMENT

1.3.1   This CCS is divided into numbered Parts and Annexes. Each of the Parts is divided into numbered Sections with numbered paragraphs. The Annexes are also divided into numbered paragraphs.

1.3.2   Part 1 contains general provisions. Annex 1 sets out the details of the commonhold and the commonhold association.

1.3.3   Part 2 and Annex 2 define the properties within the commonhold.

1.3.4   Part 3 and Annex 3 define the percentages allocated to each commonhold unit in respect of the commonhold assessment and any levy and the allocation of votes.

1.3.5   Part 4 and Annex 4 specify the rights and duties of the commonhold association and the unit-holders, the obligations imposed on tenants, and the procedures used for enforcement.

1.3.6   Annex 5 contains additional local rules specific to this commonhold.

1.3.7   Annex 6 specifies the rights of the developer which are designed to permit him to undertake development business or to facilitate his undertaking of development business.

1.4 INTERPRETATION OF THIS DOCUMENT

1.4.1   In this CCS, references to a numbered Form are references to the Form so numbered in Schedule 4 to the Commonhold Regulations 2004. A requirement to use a numbered Form is satisfied by the use of a form to the same effect.

1.4.2   Unless otherwise stated, in the application of provisions in this CCS to a commonhold unit with joint unit-holders, a reference to a unit-holder is a reference to each joint unit-holder and to the joint unit-holders together.

1.4.3   Unless otherwise stated, in the application of provisions in this CCS, where two or more persons together hold a tenancy, a reference to a tenant is a reference to each tenant and to the tenants together.

1.4.4   Unless the contrary intention appears, words–
  (a)   referring to one gender include any other gender;
  (b)   in the singular include the plural; and
  (c)   in the plural include the singular.

1.4.5   Unless the contrary intention appears, the following definitions apply:

'the Act' means Part 1 of the Commonhold and Leasehold Reform Act 2002 or any statutory modification or re-enactment of it for the time being in force;

'articles of association' means the articles of association of the commonhold association;

'common parts' means every part of the commonhold which is not for the time being a commonhold unit in accordance with this CCS (section 25(1) of the Act);

'commonhold assessment' means the income required to be raised from unit-holders to meet the expenses of the commonhold association (section 38 of the Act);

'commonhold association' means the commonhold association named in paragraph 2 of Annex 1;

'commonhold land' means the land that is registered at Land Registry as a freehold estate in commonhold land and described in paragraph 2 of Annex 2;

'commonhold unit' means a unit as defined in paragraphs 4 and 5 of Annex 2;

'commonhold unit information certificate' means a certificate stating the debts owed to the commonhold association in respect of the commonhold assessment or levy allocated to a commonhold unit and any interest added in respect of late payment;

'company number' means the number with which the commonhold association is registered under the Companies Act 1985;

'complaint notice' means a notice given in accordance with paragraph 4.11.5 or 4.11.27;

'default notice' means a notice given in accordance with paragraph 4.11.13;

'general meeting' means a meeting of the members of the commonhold association held in accordance with the articles of association of the commonhold association;

'levy' means an amount set by the directors of the commonhold association from time to time to be raised from unit-holders for contribution to a reserve fund (section 39 of the Act);

'limited use areas' means any part of the common parts that may only be used by authorised persons or in a manner consistent with the authorised use specified in paragraph 4 of Annex 4 (section 25(2) of the Act);

'local rules' means provisions, including information contained in the Annexes, inserted by the developer or the commonhold association, that are not prescribed by regulations;

'member' means a person whose name is entered as a member in the register of members of the commonhold association, but excludes any person who has ceased to be a unit-holder or joint unit-holder, or any person who has resigned as a member;

'memorandum' means the memorandum of association of the commonhold association;

'mortgagee' means, in relation to a unit, a person recorded as mortgagee of that unit in the register of charges kept by the commonhold association (additional definition specific to this commonhold);

'ombudsman' means a person whose appointment has been approved in accordance with section 42 of the Act under an approved ombudsman scheme for commonhold;

'ordinary resolution' means a resolution passed by a simple majority of such members as (being entitled to do so) vote in person or, if proxies are allowed, by proxy, at a general meeting of the commonhold association of which notice specifying the intention to propose the resolution as an ordinary resolution has been given in accordance with the articles of association;

'prescribed rate' means the rate of interest specified by the commonhold association in paragraph 1 of Annex 4; 'regulations' means regulations made under the Act from time to time and for the time being in force;

'rent' means such monies as are defined as rent in the relevant tenancy agreement;

'reply notice' means a notice given in accordance with paragraph 4.11.6, 4.11.14 or 4.11.28;

'reserve fund' means a fund set up by the directors of the commonhold association to which unit-holders contribute to finance the repair and maintenance of the common parts or commonhold units (section 39 of the Act);

'reserve study' means an inspection of the common parts to advise the directors whether or not it is appropriate to establish or maintain a reserve fund;

'special resolution' means a resolution passed by a majority of not less than 75 per cent. of such members as (being entitled to do so) vote in person or, if proxies are allowed, by proxy, at a general meeting of the commonhold association of which notice specifying the intention to propose the resolution as a special resolution has been given in accordance with the articles of association;

'tenancy' means a term of years absolute in a commonhold unit or part only of a commonhold unit and includes 'sub-tenancy'; and the term 'tenant' should be interpreted accordingly;

'transfer' means a transfer of the freehold estate in a commonhold unit, whether or not for consideration, whether or not subject to any reservation or other terms, and whether or not by operation of law (section 15 of the Act);

'unanimous resolution' means a resolution passed by every member as (being entitled to do so) votes in person or, if proxies are allowed, by proxy, at a general meeting of the commonhold association of which notice specifying the intention to propose the resolution as a unanimous resolution has been given in accordance with the articles of association;

'unit-holder' means a person entitled to be registered at Land Registry as the proprietor of the freehold estate in a commonhold unit (whether or not he is registered).

PART 2: THE COMMONHOLD

2.1 INTRODUCTION

2.1.1   This Part of this CCS defines the extent and location of the properties within the commonhold and the rights that exist over the commonhold land.

2.2 PLANS

2.2.1   A list of the plans incorporated in this CCS is set out in paragraph 1 of Annex 2.

2.3 COMMONHOLD LAND

2.3.1   The location and extent of the commonhold land are described in paragraph 2 of Annex 2.

2.4 COMMONHOLD UNITS

Number of units in the commonhold

2.4.1   The number of commonhold units in the commonhold is set out in paragraph 3 of Annex 2.

Location and extent of commonhold units

2.4.2   The commonhold units are defined in paragraphs 4 and 5 of Annex 2.

Rights for the benefit of commonhold units

2.4.3   Details of rights existing for the benefit of each commonhold unit over other commonhold units or over the common parts are set out in paragraph 6 of Annex 2.

Rights over commonhold units for the benefit of the common parts

2.4.4   Details of rights existing for the benefit of the common parts over one or more commonhold units are set out in paragraph 7 of Annex 2.

PART 3: COMMONHOLD ALLOCATIONS

3.1 INTRODUCTION

3.1.1   This Part of this CCS defines the commonhold allocations.

3.2 ALLOCATION OF COMMONHOLD ASSESSMENT

3.2.1   The percentage allocated to each commonhold unit in respect of the commonhold assessment is specified in paragraph 1 of Annex 3.

3.3 ALLOCATION OF RESERVE FUND LEVY

3.3.1   The percentage allocated to each commonhold unit in respect of any levy to fund the repair and maintenance of the common parts or the commonhold units is specified in paragraph 2 of Annex 3.

3.4 ALLOCATION OF VOTES

3.4.1   The number of votes allocated to a member in respect of each commonhold unit is specified in paragraph 3 of Annex 3.

PART 4: THE RULES OF THE COMMONHOLD

4.1 INTRODUCTION

4.1.1   This Part of this CCS sets out the rules regulating the affairs of the commonhold community and how they may be enforced.
4.1.2   The rules are for the benefit of, and bind, all unit-holders and the commonhold association. Where stated, rules also bind tenants.

4.2 FINANCIAL MATTERS

Commonhold Assessment – calculation and request for payment

4.2.1   The directors of the commonhold association must make an annual esti-mate of the income required to be raised from unit-holders to meet the expenses of the commonhold association, and may from time to time make estimates of income required to be raised from unit-holders in addition to the annual estimate.

4.2.2   Subject to paragraph 4.2.5, when the directors of the commonhold asso-ciation consider that income is required to be raised from unit-holders they must give a notice containing details of the proposed commonhold assessment to each unit-holder. Form 1 [Notice of proposed commonhold assessment] must be used.

4.2.3   Within 1 month, beginning with the date on which the notice referred to in paragraph 4.2.2 is given, each unit-holder may make written representations to the commonhold association regarding the amount of the proposed com-monhold assessment.

4.2.4   The directors must consider any representations made in accordance with paragraph 4.2.3 and must give a further notice to each unit-holder specify-ing the payments required to be made by that unit-holder and the date on which each payment is due. The notice must not specify a date for payment, which is within 14 days, beginning with the date on which the notice is given. Form 2 [Request for payment of commonhold assessment] must be used.

Emergency commonhold assessment – request for payment

4.2.5   If the commonhold association requires income to meet its expenses in an emergency, then the directors of the commonhold association may give a notice to each unit-holder requiring payment of the commonhold assess-ment without seeking representations from unit-holders. Form 3 [Request for payment of emergency commonhold assessment] must be used.

Reserve Fund – establishment, calculation and request for payment

4.2.6   The directors of the commonhold association must consider whether to commission a reserve study by an appropriately qualified person in the first year in which the commonhold is registered.

4.2.7   The directors of the commonhold association must commission a reserve study by an appropriately qualified person at least once in every 10 years.

4.2.8   The directors of the commonhold association must consider the results of any reserve study to decide whether it is appropriate–
(a)   to establish a reserve fund;
(b)   to maintain any existing reserve fund; and if it is appropriate to establish a reserve fund, or maintain an existing reserve fund, then the directors must do so.

4.2.9   The directors of the commonhold association must at appropriate intervals decide whether it is appropriate to establish one or more reserve funds or maintain any existing reserve fund; and, if they decide that it is appropriate to establish a reserve fund, or maintain an existing reserve fund, then the directors must do so.

4.2.10　The members may, by ordinary resolution, require the directors to establish a reserve fund.

4.2.11　If a reserve fund is established, then the directors of the commonhold association must set a levy from time to time; and in doing so must try to ensure that unnecessary reserves are not accumulated.

4.2.12　When the directors of the commonhold association set a levy they must give a notice containing details of the proposed levy to each unit-holder. Form 4 [Notice of proposed reserve fund levy] must be used.

4.2.13　Within 1 month, beginning with the date on which the notice referred to in paragraph 4.2.12 is given, each unit-holder may make written representations to the commonhold association regarding the amount of the levy.

4.2.14　The directors must consider any representations made in accordance with paragraph 4.2.13 and must give a further notice to each unit-holder specifying the payments required to be made by that unit-holder and the date on which each payment is due. The notice must not specify a date for payment, which is within 14 days, beginning with the date on which the notice is given. Form 5 [Request for payment of reserve fund levy] must be used.

Commonhold assessment and reserve fund – payment

4.2.15　A unit-holder must pay to the commonhold association the amount that is allocated to his commonhold unit in accordance with a notice given under paragraphs 4.2.4, 4.2.5 or 4.2.14.

Commonhold assessment and reserve fund – late payment

4.2.16　If a payment required by paragraph 4.2.15 is not made by the date on which it is due, then the unit-holder must pay interest to the commonhold association at the prescribed rate for the period beginning with the date on which the payment is due and ending on the date on which the payment is made.

Commonhold assessment and reserve fund – unit-holder's failure to pay

4.2.17　In paragraphs 4.2.18 to 4.2.26 – 'tenant' means only an immediate tenant of the unit-holder who has failed to pay; and 'diversion date' means the date on which a period of 14 days ends, beginning with the date on which the notice in paragraph 4.2.18 is given.

Diversion of rent from a tenant

4.2.18　If a unit-holder has not paid all or part of any payment due to the commonhold association under paragraphs 4.2.15 or 4.2.16, then the commonhold association may give a notice requiring a tenant to divert to the commonhold association all or part of the rent payable to the unit-holder from time to time under the tenancy agreement until the commonhold association has recovered from the tenant an equivalent sum to the amount due from the unit-holder. Form 6 [Notice to tenant of diversion of rent] must be used and the commonhold association must also give a copy to the unit-holder.

4.2.19   The commonhold association must specify in the notice the payments that the tenant is required to make. In any single payment, the commonhold association must not require the tenant to pay more rent than is due under the tenancy agreement, to pay rent earlier than is due under the tenancy agreement, or to pay rent earlier than the diversion date.

4.2.20   A tenant who receives a notice under paragraph 4.2.18 must make the payments required by the notice.

4.2.21   Unless the commonhold association specifies a later date in the notice, the tenant must make the first payment on the next date, after the diversion date, that rent is required to be paid under the tenancy agreement.

4.2.22   The commonhold association must, within a period of 14 days, beginning with the date on which all the payments required in the notice have been made, notify the tenant and the unit-holder that the diversion of rent has ended.

Diversion of rent from a tenant – no deduction

4.2.23   A tenant may not rely on any non-statutory right of deduction, set-off or counterclaim that he has against the unit-holder to reduce the amount to be paid to the commonhold association.

Diversion of rent from a tenant – discharge of liability

4.2.24   A payment made in accordance with paragraph 4.2.20 will discharge, to the extent of the payment, the liability of–
(a)   the unit-holder for the amount he has failed to pay to the commonhold association; and
(b)   the tenant for the payment of rent owed to the unit-holder.

4.2.25   A unit-holder is deemed to have received and accepted rent, for the purposes of the tenancy agreement, in an amount equal to the payment made in accordance with paragraph 4.2.20, and may not forfeit the tenancy for the non-payment of rent deemed to have been paid, or bring proceedings for breach of any covenant or condition in the tenancy agreement for the non-payment of the rent deemed to have been paid.

Diversion of rent from a tenant – late payment

4.2.26   If a payment required by paragraph 4.2.20 is not made by the date on which it is due, then the tenant must pay interest to the commonhold association at the prescribed rate for the period beginning with the date on which the payment is due and ending on the date on which the payment is made.

Commonhold assessment and reserve fund – tenant's failure to pay

4.2.27   In paragraphs 4.2.28 to 4.2.37 –
'tenant' means only an immediate tenant of the unit-holder;
'sub-tenant' means only the immediate tenant of the tenant who has failed
to pay; and
'diversion date' means the date on which a period of 14 days ends, beginning
with the date on which the notice in paragraph 4.2.28 is given.

Diversion of rent from a sub-tenant

4.2.28   If a tenant has not paid all or part of any payment due to the commonhold
association under paragraphs 4.2.20 or 4.2.26, then the commonhold association may give a notice requiring a sub-tenant to divert to the commonhold association all or part of the rent payable to the tenant from time to
time under the sub-tenancy agreement until the commonhold association
has recovered from the sub-tenant an equivalent sum to the amount due
from the tenant. Form 7 [Notice to sub-tenant of diversion of rent] must
be used and the commonhold association must also give copies to the
unit-holder and the tenant.

4.2.29   The commonhold association must specify in the notice the payments that
the sub-tenant is required to make and, in any single payment, the commonhold association must not require the sub-tenant to pay more rent than
is due under the sub-tenancy agreement, to pay rent earlier than is due under
the sub-tenancy agreement, or to pay rent earlier than the diversion date.

4.2.30   A sub-tenant who receives a notice under paragraph 4.2.28 must make the
payments required by the notice.

4.2.31   Unless the commonhold association specifies a later date in the notice, the
sub-tenant must make the first payment on the next date, after the diversion
date, that rent is required to be paid under the sub-tenancy agreement.

4.2.32   The commonhold association must, within a period of 14 days, beginning
with the date on which all the payments required in the notice have been
made, notify the sub-tenant, the tenant and the unit-holder that the
diversion of rent has ended.

Diversion of rent from a sub-tenant – no deduction

4.2.33   A sub-tenant may not rely on any non-statutory right of deduction, set off,
or counterclaim that he has against the tenant to reduce the amount to be
paid to the commonhold association.

Diversion of rent from a sub-tenant – discharge of liability

4.2.34   A payment made in accordance with paragraph 4.2.30 will discharge, to the
extent of the payment, the liability of –
(a)   the unit-holder for the amount he has failed to pay to the
commonhold association;

(b)   the tenant for the payment owed to the commonhold association in accordance with paragraph 4.2.20;

(c)   the tenant for the payment of rent owed to the unit-holder; and

(d)   the sub-tenant for the payment of rent owed to the tenant.

4.2.35   A unit-holder is deemed to have received and accepted rent, for the purposes of the tenancy agreement, in an amount equal to the payment made in accordance with paragraph 4.2.30, and may not forfeit the tenancy for the non-payment of rent deemed to have been paid, or bring proceedings for breach of any covenant or condition in the tenancy agreement for the non-payment of the rent deemed to have been paid.

4.2.36   A tenant is deemed to have received and accepted rent, for the purposes of the sub-tenancy agreement, in an amount equal to the payment made in accordance with paragraph 4.2.30, and may not forfeit the sub-tenancy for the non-payment of rent deemed to have been paid, or bring proceedings for breach of any covenant or condition in the sub-tenancy agreement for the non-payment of the rent deemed to have been paid.

Diversion of rent from a sub-tenant – late payment

4.2.37   If a payment required by paragraph 4.2.30 is not made by the date on which it is due, then the sub-tenant must pay interest to the commonhold association at the prescribed rate for the period beginning with the date on which the payment is due and ending on the date on which the payment is made.

Commonhold assessment and reserve fund – sub-tenant's failure to pay

4.2.38   If the sub-tenant fails to pay in accordance with paragraph 4.2.30, then paragraphs 4.2.28 to 4.2.37 may be applied with necessary modifications as against the immediate tenant of that sub-tenant and so on. The terms 'tenant' and 'sub-tenant' must be interpreted accordingly.

Reimbursement of tenant

4.2.39   If a tenant has suffered any loss as a result of a payment being made to the commonhold association in accordance with paragraph 4.2.20 or 4.2.30, then he may give a notice requiring the unit-holder to reimburse him for that loss.

4.2.40   Within 14 days, beginning with the date on which the notice referred to in paragraph 4.2.39 is given, the unit-holder must reimburse the tenant for the loss suffered.

Commonhold association's right to request details of tenancy

4.2.41   If a commonhold unit is let under a tenancy agreement, then the commonhold association may give a notice to one or all of the parties to the tenancy agreement requesting details of the length of the tenancy and the rent payable. Part A of Form 8 [Notice requesting further details about a tenancy] must be used.

4.2.42   Within 14 days, beginning with the date on which the notice referred to in paragraph 4.2.41 is given, the recipient must give a notice to the commonhold association providing the details requested. Part B of Form 8 [Notice requesting further details about a tenancy] must be used.

Notice to mortgagee – additional provision specific to this commonhold

4.2.43   Whenever the commonhold association gives notice under paragraph 4.2.18 requiring a tenant of a unit-holder to divert to it all or part of the rent payable by a unit-holder, the commonhold association must at the same time give a copy of the notice to any mortgagee of the unit.

4.3 USE

4.3.1   A unit-holder or tenant must not use a commonhold unit other than in accordance with its permitted use as specified in paragraph 2 of Annex 4.

4.3.2   A unit-holder or tenant must not use the common parts other than in accordance with their permitted use as specified in paragraphs 3 or 4 of Annex 4, or other than in accordance with the rights specified in paragraph 6 of Annex 2.

Further restrictions on use of a commonhold unit – additional provision specific to this commonhold

4.3.3   A unit-holder or tenant must not use a commonhold unit, or allow anyone else to use a commonhold unit, for any of the following.

    (a)   anything which causes, or might become, a nuisance or annoyance to a unit-holder or tenant of any other commonhold unit;

    (b)   anything which is dangerous or noxious;

    (c)   storage of any flammable or explosive substance (except in the fuel tank of a vehicle);

    (d)   installing or storing anything which overloads the floors or the structure of the building;

    (e)   anything which contravenes a term of the policy insuring the property or causes an increase in the premium;

    (f)   a public meeting or anything which attracts casual callers; or

    (g)   playing music or amplifying or reproducing any sound so that it can be heard outside the unit between the hours of 11.00pm and 7.00am.

Further restriction on use of the common parts – additional provision specific to this commonhold

4.3.4   A unit-holder or tenant must not obstruct the common parts or leave any goods there.

4.4 INSURANCE

4.4.1   The commonhold association must insure the common parts to their full rebuilding and reinstatement costs against loss or damage by fire and such other risks as are specified in paragraph 5 of Annex 4.

4.4.2   The commonhold association must use the proceeds of any insurance taken out in accordance with paragraph 4.4.1 for the purpose of rebuilding or reinstating the common parts.

4.4.3   The commonhold association must keep details of common parts insurance and evidence of payment of the most recent premium at its registered office or such other place as the directors think fit.

4.4.4   A unit-holder may, on reasonable notice and at a reasonable time and place, inspect the common parts insurance policy taken out by the commonhold association and may also, upon payment of the commonhold association's reasonable charges, require the commonhold association to provide a copy of the insurance policy.

4.4.5   If a request is made by a unit-holder to provide a copy of the common parts insurance policy, the commonhold association must provide the copy to the unit-holder as soon as reasonably practicable upon payment of the charge.

4.4.6   The duties imposed by this CCS in respect of the insurance of the commonhold units are specified in paragraph 6 of Annex 4.

Directors' liability – additional provision specific to this commonhold

4.4.7   The commonhold association may take out insurance against losses incurred as a result of negligence, misbehaviour or dishonesty of directors.

Fire precautions – additional provision specific to this commonhold

4.4.8   A unit-holder or tenant must provide and maintain fire prevention, fire detection, fire fighting and escape instructions and equipment as directed or recommended by the property insurers or the local fire prevention officer.

4.5 REPAIR AND MAINTENANCE

4.5.1   The commonhold association must repair and maintain the common parts. This includes decorating them and putting them into sound condition.

4.5.2   The duties imposed by this CCS in respect of the repair and maintenance of the commonhold units are specified in paragraph 7 of Annex 4.

4.6 ALTERATION OF THE COMMON PARTS

4.6.1 The commonhold association must not make any alterations to the common parts or cause or permit the common parts to be altered unless the proposed alteration is approved by ordinary resolution.

Alteration of a commonhold unit – additional provision specific to this commonhold

4.6.2 A unit-holder or tenant must obtain the written consent of the commonhold association before–
  (a) making any alteration to a commonhold unit which affects the common parts;
  (b) altering or adapting the electrical or water supply to a commonhold unit or wiring or plumbing within the unit.

4.7 DEALINGS WITH THE LAND

Transfer of a commonhold unit – commonhold unit information certificate

4.7.1 A unit-holder may give a notice requiring the commonhold association to provide a commonhold unit information certificate in respect of his commonhold unit.
4.7.2 Within 14 days, beginning with the date on which the notice referred to in paragraph 4.7.1 is given, the commonhold association must provide a commonhold unit information certificate to the unit-holder and for the purposes of Section 4.9, a commonhold unit information certificate is a notice. Form 9 [Commonhold unit information certificate] must be used.

Transfer of a commonhold unit – new unit-holder's liability

4.7.3 Subject to paragraph 4.7.4, following a transfer of a commonhold unit, the commonhold association may give a notice requiring the new unit-holder to pay to the commonhold association the debts owed under paragraphs 4.2.15 and 4.2.16 by any former unit-holder in respect of that commonhold unit.
4.7.4 When the commonhold association has provided a commonhold unit information certificate the new unit-holder cannot be required to pay more than the amount specified in that certificate for the period up to and including the date of the certificate.
4.7.5 Within 14 days, beginning with the date on which the notice referred to in paragraph 4.7.3 is given, the new unit-holder must pay to the commonhold association the sum required by the notice.
4.7.6 If a payment required by paragraph 4.7.5 is not made by the date on which it is due, then the new unit-holder must pay interest to the commonhold association at the prescribed rate for the period beginning with the date on which the payment is due and ending on the date on which the payment is made.

4.7.7   When payment is made in accordance with paragraph 4.7.5 the common-hold association's right to enforce the payment of the sum paid against the former unit-holder is deemed to have been assigned to the new unit-holder.

Transfer of a commonhold unit – notification

4.7.8   Subject to paragraph 4.7.9, when a person becomes entitled to be registered as the proprietor of a freehold estate in a commonhold unit, he must notify the commonhold association within 14 days, beginning with the date on which he is entitled to be registered. Form 10 [Notice of transfer of a com-monhold unit] or 11 [Notice of transfer of part of a commonhold unit] must be used.

4.7.9   When a person becomes entitled to be registered as the proprietor of a free-hold estate in a commonhold unit by operation of law, he must notify the commonhold association within 14 days, beginning with the date on which he becomes aware of his entitlement. Form 12 [Notice of vesting of a commonhold unit by operation of law] must be used.

Application to add land

4.7.10   The commonhold association may not apply to Land Registry to add land to a commonhold unless the application is approved by a unanimous resolution.

Leasing – grant of a tenancy

4.7.11   A unit-holder or tenant may not grant a tenancy in a residential common-hold unit–
         (a)   for a premium;
         (b)   for a term of more than 7 years, unless regulation 11(2) of the Commonhold Regulations 2004 applies;
         (c)   under an option or agreement if–
                 (i)   the person to take the new tenancy has an existing tenancy of the premises to be let;
                 (ii)   the new term added to the existing term will be more than 7 years; and
                 (iii)   the option or agreement was entered into before or at the same time as the existing tenancy;
         (d)   containing an option or agreement to renew which confers on either party to the tenancy an opt agreement for renewal for a further term which, together with the original term, amounts to more than 7 years;
         (e)   containing an option or agreement to extend the term beyond 7 years; or
         (f)   containing a provision requiring a tenant to make payments to the commonhold association in discharge of payments which are due, in accordance with this CCS, to be made by the unit-holder.

4.7.12 Before granting a tenancy in a commonhold unit, a prospective landlord must give the prospective tenant—

    (a)   a copy of this CCS, including such of the plans or parts of plans as are relevant to that commonhold unit; and

    (b)   a notice informing him that he will be required to comply with the paragraphs in the CCS that impose duties on him if he takes the tenancy. Form 13 [Notice to a prospective tenant] must be used.

4.7.13 If a landlord has not complied with paragraph 4.7.12 and a tenant has suffered loss as a result of an obligation in this CCS being enforced against him, then the tenant may give a notice requiring the landlord to reimburse him for that loss, unless the obligation is reproduced in the tenancy agreement.

4.7.14 Within 14 days, beginning with the date on which the notice referred to in paragraph 4.7.13 is given, the landlord must reimburse the tenant for the loss suffered.

Leasing – notification of the grant of a tenancy

4.7.15 Within 14 days, beginning with the date on which a tenancy is granted, the unit-holder or tenant who grants the tenancy must notify the commonhold association that the tenancy has been granted and must give a copy of any written tenancy agreement, or details of the terms of any oral tenancy, to the commonhold association. Form 14 [Notice of grant of a tenancy in a commonhold unit] must be used.

Leasing – assignment of a tenancy

4.7.16 Before assigning a tenancy in a commonhold unit a tenant must give the prospective assignee—

    (a)   a copy of this CCS, including such of the plans or parts of plans as are relevant to that commonhold unit; and

    (b)   a notice informing him that he will be required to comply with those paragraphs in the CCS that impose duties on him if he takes the assignment of the tenancy. Form 15 [Notice to a prospective assignee] must be used.

4.7.17 If a tenant has not complied with paragraph 4.7.16 and an assignee has suffered loss as a result of any obligation in this CCS being enforced against him, then the assignee may give a notice requiring the tenant to reimburse him for that loss, unless the obligation is reproduced in the tenancy agreement.

4.7.18 Within 14 days, beginning with the date on which the notice referred to in paragraph 4.7.17 is given, the tenant must reimburse the assignee for the loss suffered.

Leasing – notification of the assignment of a tenancy

4.7.19 Within 14 days, beginning with the date on which the tenancy is assigned, the new tenant must notify the commonhold association that the assignment has been completed. Form 16 [Notice of assignment of a tenancy in a commonhold unit] must be used.

Leasing – tenant's failure to comply with a duty

4.7.20   If the commonhold association has suffered loss because a tenant of a commonhold unit has not complied with a duty in this CCS, and the duty is one which must be complied with by both a unit-holder and a tenant, the commonhold association may give a notice requiring the unit-holder to reimburse it for that loss.

4.7.21   Within 14 days, beginning with the date on which the notice referred to in paragraph 4.7.20 is given, the unit-holder must reimburse the commonhold association for the loss.

4.8 AMENDMENT OF THE COMMONHOLD COMMUNITY STATEMENT

4.8.1   In the application of the provisions in paragraphs 4.8.5 to 4.8.9 to a commonhold unit with joint unit-holders, a reference to a unit-holder is a reference to the joint unit-holders together.

4.8.2   A paragraph in Parts 1 to 4 of this CCS cannot be amended unless it is a local rule.

4.8.3   Except where this CCS provides otherwise and subject to the Companies Act 1985, local rules cannot be amended unless the proposed amendment is approved by ordinary resolution.

4.8.4   The format for paragraphs 1 to 3 of Annex 1, paragraphs 1 to 7 of Annex 2, paragraphs 1 to 3 of Annex 3 and paragraphs 1 to 7 of Annex 4 to this CCS cannot be amended.

4.8.5   An amendment to the rights for, or over, a commonhold unit specified in paragraphs 6 or 7 of Annex 2 cannot be made unless the unit-holder and the registered proprietor of any charge over that commonhold unit have consented in writing to the proposed amendment before it is made.

4.8.6   An amendment to remove a reference to a unit-holder in the column headed 'Authorised users' in paragraph 4 of Annex 4 cannot be made unless the unit-holder and the registered proprietor of any charge over his commonhold unit have consented in writing to the proposed amendment before it is made.

4.8.7   An amendment to the permitted use of a commonhold unit specified in paragraph 2 of Annex 4 cannot be made unless the proposed amendment is approved by special resolution and the unit-holder has consented in writing to the proposed amendment before it is made.

4.8.8   An amendment to this CCS, which redefines the extent of a commonhold unit, cannot be made unless the unit-holder and the registered proprietor of any charge over that commonhold unit have consented in writing to the proposed amendment before it is made.

4.8.9   An amendment to this CCS which specifies that land which forms part of the commonhold unit is to be added to the common parts cannot be made unless the unit-holder and the registered proprietor of any charge over that land have consented in writing to the proposed amendment before it is made.

4.8.10   This CCS cannot be amended to record a change in the boundaries of the commonhold, a commonhold unit or the common parts following a transfer unless any consent required under paragraphs 4.8.8 and 4.8.9 has been given and the approval of the members by special resolution has been given.

4.8.11   An amendment to the following provisions cannot be made unless the proposed amendment is approved by special resolution –

(a)   the percentage of the commonhold assessment or levy allocated to a commonhold unit in paragraphs 1 and 2 of Annex 3; and

(b)   the number of votes allocated to a member in paragraph 3 of Annex 3.

4.8.12   A unit-holder has the right not to have the percentage of the commonhold assessment or levy allocated to his/her, or any other, commonhold unit altered if the effect of the alteration, taking into account all the circumstances of the case, would be to allocate a significantly disproportionate percentage of the commonhold assessment or levy to his/her commonhold unit.

4.8.13   A unit-holder who is a member has the right not to have the number of votes allocated to him, or any other member, in respect of a commonhold unit altered if the effect of the alteration, taking into account all the circumstances of the case, would be to allocate a significantly disproportionate number of votes to him.

4.8.14   The directors of the commonhold association may amend this CCS without any resolution of the members to include specified provisions, or provisions of a specified kind, for a specified purpose or about a specified matter required by the Act and regulations or to delete any provisions that are of no effect for the reasons set out in paragraph 1.1.5; or to remove any surrendered development rights.

4.8.15   If this CCS has been amended, then the directors must apply, as soon as practicable, to Land Registry for the registration of the amended CCS.

4.8.16   Amendments to this CCS only take effect when the amended version is registered at Land Registry.

Termination statement – additional provision specific to this commonhold

4.8.17   An amendment to the requirements of a termination statement specified in paragraph 5.1 of Annex 5 cannot be made unless the proposed amendment is approved by special resolution.

4.9 NOTICES

4.9.1   Any notice given by the commonhold association under this CCS must contain the name of the commonhold association, its company number, and an address for correspondence. If a notice does not specify an address for correspondence, it will be deemed to be the same address as the address of the registered office.

4.9.2   Any Form used in accordance with this CCS must be completed in full.

4.9.3   Within 14 days, beginning with the date on which a person becomes a unit-holder or tenant, he must give a notice to the commonhold association specifying a full postal address in the United Kingdom including postcode as his/her address for correspondence, unless notice of that address has already been given to the commonhold association under paragraphs 4.7.8, 4.7.9, 4.7.15 or 4.7.19.

4.9.4 A unit-holder or tenant may give a notice to the commonhold association specifying up to two more addresses for correspondence, which may be postal or electronic.

4.9.5 A unit-holder or tenant may give a notice to the commonhold association requesting that an address for correspondence held by the commonhold association is amended or removed, or requesting that an additional address for correspondence is to be held by the commonhold association, provided that the notice does not request the commonhold association to hold more than three addresses for the unit-holder or tenant at any time and that at least one of those addresses is at all times, a full postal address in the United Kingdom including postcode.

4.9.6 When giving notice to a unit-holder or tenant, the commonhold association must give notice to each of the addresses for correspondence for that unit-holder or tenant held by the commonhold association in the register referred to in paragraph 4.10.1 or 4.10.2.

4.9.7 If a commonhold unit has joint unit-holders, then any notice to be given in accordance with this CCS must be addressed to all the joint unit-holders together.

4.9.8 Any notice to be given in accordance with this CCS must be in writing and given–
   (a)   personally;
   (b)   by leaving it at an address given as an address for correspondence;
   (c)   by sending it by first class post in a prepaid envelope properly addressed to an address given as an address for correspondence; or
   (d)   if an electronic address has been provided as an address for correspondence, by electronic communication to that address in accordance with any terms or conditions previously specified by the intended recipient.

4.9.9 Proof that an envelope containing a notice was properly addressed, prepaid and posted by first class post is conclusive evidence that it was given to a postal address. Electronic confirmation of receipt is conclusive evidence that a notice was given to an e-mail address.

4.9.10 A notice is deemed to have been given, unless proved otherwise–
   (a)   on the day it was handed to the recipient or left at the address for correspondence;
   (b)   on the second day after it was posted to the recipient; or
   (c)   on the day after it was transmitted by electronic communication.

Notices received – additional provision specific to this commonhold

4.9.11 A unit-holder or tenant must promptly give the commonhold association a copy of any notice received concerning.
   (a)   an application for permission to develop any part of the commonhold or any neighbouring land;
   (b)   a proposal to enforce planning control;
   (c)   an intention to acquire any part of the commonhold compulsorily;
   (d)   a party wall or a proposal to do work affecting a party structure;
   (e)   an application for an order authorising access to any part of the commonhold; or

(f)   action to prohibit or limit any activity undertaken on any part of the commonhold or a use to which any part is put.

Notice of creation of a charge – additional provision specific to this commonhold

4.9.12   Within 14 days, beginning with the date on which a charge over a commonhold unit is created, the unit-holder must give a notice to the commonhold association specifying name and address for the correspondence of the mortgagee and the account number (if any).

Notice of discharge of a charge – additional provisions specific to this commonhold

4.9.13   Within 14 days, beginning with the date on which a charge over a commonhold unit is discharged, the unit-holder must give a notice to the commonhold association specifying that the charge over the commonhold unit has been discharged

4.10 COMMONHOLD REGISTERS AND DOCUMENTS

4.10.1   The commonhold association must maintain a register of unit-holders and their commonhold units and, within 14 days of receiving notice from a unitholder under–
    (a)   paragraph 4.7.8, 4.7.9, 4.9.3 or 4.9.4, enter in the register the name and address for correspondence of the unit-holder; or
    (b)   paragraph 4.9.5, amend the register in accordance with the notice if, as a result of the amendment proposed, the commonhold association will hold in the register in respect of the unit-holder at least one full postal address in the United Kingdom including postcode and no more than three addresses in total.

4.10.2   The commonhold association must maintain a register of tenants and, within 14 days of receiving notice under–
    (a)   paragraph 4.7.15, 4.7.19, 4.9.3 or 4.9.4, enter in the register–
        (i)   a description of the premises let;
        (ii)   the name and address of the tenant; and
        (iii)   the length of the tenancy; or
    (b)   paragraph 4.9.5, amend the register in accordance with the notice, if as a result of the amendment proposed, the commonhold association will hold in the register in respect of the tenant at least one full postal address in the United Kingdom including postcode and no more than three addresses in total.

4.10.3   The commonhold association must keep up-to-date copies of the CCS and the memorandum and articles of association at the registered office of the commonhold association.

4.10.4   A unit-holder or tenant may, on reasonable notice and at a reasonable time and place, inspect the CCS or the memorandum and articles of association, and may also, on payment of the commonhold association's reasonable charges, require the commonhold association to provide a copy of such documents.

Register of charges – additional provision specific to this commonhold

4.10.5   The commonhold association must maintain a register of charges over commonhold units and, within 14 days of receiving notice under–
   (a)   Paragraph 4.9.12, enter in the register the name and address for correspondence of the mortgagee and the account number (if any);
   (b)   Paragraph 4.9.13, delete the entry in the register relating to any charge which is discharged.

4.11 DISPUTE RESOLUTION

4.11.1   The dispute resolution procedure contained in the following paragraphs applies only to the enforcement of rights and duties that arise from this CCS or from a provision made by or by virtue of the Act. References to enforcing a right include enforcing the terms and conditions to which a right is subject.

Procedure for enforcement by unit-holder or tenant against the commonhold association

4.11.2   Subject to paragraph 4.11.3, a unit-holder or tenant must use the dispute resolution procedure contained in paragraphs 4.11.4 to 4.11.9 when seeking to enforce against the commonhold association a right or duty contained in this CCS or a provision made by or by virtue of the Act.

4.11.3   A unit-holder or tenant, when seeking to enforce against the commonhold association a duty to pay money or a right or duty in an emergency may–
   (a)   use the dispute resolution procedure contained in paragraphs 4.11.4 to 4.11.9;
   (b)   if the commonhold association is a member of an approved ombudsman scheme, refer a dispute directly to the ombudsman; or
   (c)   bring legal proceedings.

4.11.4   When seeking to enforce a right or duty a unit-holder or tenant (the 'complainant') must first consider resolving the matter by–
   (a)   negotiating directly with the commonhold association; or
   (b)   using arbitration, mediation, conciliation, or any other form of dispute resolution procedure involving a third party, other than legal proceedings.

4.11.5   If the matter is not resolved in accordance with paragraph 4.11.4, then the complainant must, if he wishes to take further action to enforce the right or duty, give a complaint notice to the commonhold association. Form 17 [Complaint notice against commonhold association] must be used.

4.11.6   The commonhold association may respond to the complaint notice by giving a reply notice to the complainant. Form 18 [Reply to complaint notice against commonhold association] must be used.

4.11.7   Upon receipt of the reply notice or when 21 days have passed, beginning with the date on which the complaint notice is given, (whichever is earlier) the complainant must, if he wishes to take further action to enforce the right or duty, first reconsider whether the matter could be resolved–
   (a)   by negotiating directly with the commonhold association; or

(b)   by using arbitration, mediation, conciliation, or any other form of dispute resolution procedure involving a third party, other than legal proceedings.

4.11.8   If the matter is not resolved in accordance with paragraph 4.11.7 and the complainant wishes to take further action to enforce the right or duty, then he must, if the commonhold association is a member of an approved ombudsman scheme, refer the matter to the ombudsman.

4.11.9   If the commonhold association is a member of an approved ombudsman scheme, then legal proceedings may only be brought once the ombudsman has investigated and determined the matter and he has notified the parties of his/her decision. If the commonhold association is not a member of an approved ombudsman scheme, then legal proceedings may be brought upon completion of the dispute resolution procedure contained in paragraphs 4.11.4 to 4.11.7.

Procedure for enforcement by commonhold association against a unit-holder or tenant

4.11.10   Subject to paragraph 4.11.11, the commonhold association must use the dispute resolution procedure contained in paragraphs 4.11.12 to 4.11.16 when seeking to enforce against a unit-holder or tenant a right or duty contained in this CCS or a provision made by or by virtue of the Act.

4.11.11   The commonhold association, when seeking to enforce against a unit-holder or tenant a duty to pay money or a right or duty in an emergency, may–

(a)   use the dispute resolution procedure contained in paragraphs 4.11.12 to 4.11.16;

(b)   if the commonhold association is a member of an approved ombudsman scheme, refer a dispute directly to the ombudsman; or

(c)   bring legal proceedings.

4.11.12   When seeking to enforce a right or duty the commonhold association must first consider–

(a)   resolving the matter by–

(i)   negotiating directly with the unit-holder or tenant (the 'alleged defaulter'); or

(ii)   using arbitration, mediation, conciliation, or any other form of dispute resolution procedure involving a third party, other than legal proceedings; or

(b)   taking no action if it reasonably thinks that inaction is in the best interests of establishing or maintaining harmonious relationships between all the unit-holders, and that it will not cause any unit-holder (other than the alleged defaulter) significant loss or significant disadvantage.

4.11.13   If the matter is not resolved in accordance with paragraph 4.11.12, then the commonhold association must, if it wishes to take further action to enforce the right or duty, give a default notice to the alleged defaulter. Form 19 [Default notice] must be used.

4.11.14   The alleged defaulter may respond to the default notice by giving a reply notice to the commonhold association. Form 20 [Reply to default notice] must be used.

4.11.15   Upon receipt of the reply notice or when 21 days have passed, beginning with the date on which the default notice is given, (whichever is earlier) the commonhold association must, if it wishes to take further action to enforce the right or duty, first reconsider whether the matter could be resolved –

(a)   by negotiating directly with the alleged defaulter; or

(b)   by using arbitration, mediation, conciliation, or any other form of dispute resolution procedure involving a third party, other than legal proceedings.

4.11.16   If the matter is not resolved in accordance with paragraph 4.11.15, then the commonhold association may either, if it is a member of an approved ombudsman scheme, refer the matter to the ombudsman, or, if it is satisfied that the interests of the commonhold require it, bring legal proceedings.

Procedure for enforcement by unit-holder or tenant against another unit-holder or tenant

4.11.17   Subject to paragraph 4.11.18, a unit-holder or tenant must use the dispute resolution procedure contained in paragraphs 4.11.19 to 4.11.30 when seeking to enforce against another unit-holder or tenant a right or duty contained in this CCS or a provision made by or by virtue of the Act.

4.11.18   A unit-holder or tenant, when seeking to enforce against another unit-holder or tenant a duty to pay money or a right or duty in an emergency may –

(a)   use the dispute resolution procedure contained in paragraphs 4.11.19 to 4.11.30; or

(b)   bring legal proceedings.

4.11.19   When seeking to enforce a right or duty a unit-holder or tenant (the 'complainant') must first consider resolving the matter by –

(a)   negotiating directly with the other unit-holder or tenant (the 'alleged defaulter'); or

(b)   using arbitration, mediation, conciliation, or any other form of dispute resolution procedure involving a third party, other than legal proceedings.

4.11.20   If the matter is not resolved in accordance with paragraph 4.11.19, then the complainant must, if he wishes to take further action to enforce the right or duty, give a notice to the commonhold association requesting that the commonhold association take action to enforce the right or duty against the alleged defaulter. Form 21 [Request for action] must be used.

4.11.21   The commonhold association must consider the notice referred to in paragraph 4.11.20 and decide whether to –

(a)   take action to enforce the right or duty against the alleged defaulter; and if it so decides, then to take action as soon as reasonably practicable using the dispute resolution procedure contained in paragraphs 4.11.12 to 4.11.16; or

(b)   take no action in accordance with paragraph 4.11.22; and if it so decides, then to decide whether, in accordance with paragraph 4.11.23, to allow the complainant to enforce the right or duty against the alleged defaulter directly.

4.11.22   The commonhold association may decide to take no action in respect of the matters specified in the notice referred to in paragraph 4.11.20 if it reasonably thinks that inaction is in the best interests of establishing or maintaining harmonious relationships between all the unit-holders or tenants, and that it will not cause any unit-holder or tenant (other than the alleged defaulter) significant disadvantage.

4.11.23   The commonhold association may refuse the complainant the right to take further action in relation to the matter specified in the notice referred to in paragraph 4.11.20, if the commonhold association reasonably thinks that the complaint—

(a)   does not amount to a breach of a right enjoyed by, or a duty owed to, the complainant; or

(b)   is vexatious, frivolous or trivial.

4.11.24 The commonhold association must, as soon as practicable after making a decision in accordance with paragraph 4.11.21, inform the complainant of outcome of its decision. Form 22 [Reply to request for action] must be used.

4.11.25 If the complainant wishes to challenge the decision made by the commonhold association under paragraph 4.11.21 he may use the dispute resolution procedure contained in paragraphs 4.11.4 to 4.11.9, save that for these purposes the time period mentioned in paragraph 4.11.7 is to be 7 days.

4.11.26 If the commonhold association fails to comply with paragraph 4.11.24 within 21 days, beginning with the date on which the notice referred to in paragraph 4.11.20 is given, the complainant may enforce the right or duty against the alleged defaulter directly, and if he does so, he must use the dispute resolution procedure in paragraphs 4.11.27 to 4.11.30.

4.11.27 If, by virtue of the notice referred to in paragraph 4.11.24, the complainant has the right to enforce the right or duty against the alleged defaulter directly then the complainant must, if he wishes to take further action to enforce the right or duty, give a complaint notice to the alleged defaulter. Form 23 [Complaint notice against unit-holder or tenant] must be used.

4.11.28 The alleged defaulter may respond to the complaint notice by giving a reply notice to the complainant. Form 24 [Reply to complaint notice against unit-holder or tenant] must be used.

4.11.29 Upon receipt of the reply notice or when 21 days have passed, beginning with the date on which the complaint notice is given, (whichever is earlier) the complainant must, if he wishes to take further action to enforce the right or duty, reconsider whether the matter could be resolved—

(a)   by negotiating directly with the alleged defaulter; or

(b)   by using arbitration, mediation, conciliation, or any other form of dispute resolution procedure involving a third party, other than legal proceedings.

4.11.30 If the matter is not resolved in accordance with paragraph 4.11.29 the complainant may bring legal proceedings against the alleged defaulter in respect of the complaint specified in the notice given under paragraph 4.11.20.

4.12 ADDITIONAL PROVISIONS SPECIFIC TO THIS COMMONHOLD

4.12.1   Additional provisions are set out in Annex 5.

ANNEX 1: IDENTITY OF THE COMMONHOLD AND THE COMMONHOLD ASSOCIATION

1. Name of the commonhold

Sunnyside Commonhold

2. Name of the commonhold association

Sunnyside Commonhold Association Limited

3. Company number of the commonhold association

1234567

ANNEX 2: DEFINITION OF THE PROPERTIES WITHIN THE COMMONHOLD

1. List of plans

Plan Number	Plan reference number (if different)	Date of plan (if any)
1	SC1/001/001	27.09.04
2	SC1/002/001	27.09.04
3	SC1/002/002	27.09.04

2. Description of the location and extent of commonhold land

Land adjoining Sunny Street, Sundale, extending to an area of 5000 square metres shown edged red on Plan 1.

3. Total number of commonhold units in the commonhold

4

4. Description of the location and extent of commonhold units

Commonhold unit number	Plan number	Details of how the commonhold unit is shown on the plan	Property description
1	2	Edged red and numbered 1	Ground floor flat with garden known as Flat 1, Sunnyside Court, extending to an area of 900 square metres.
2	2	Edged red and numbered 2	Ground floor flat with garden known as Flat 2, Sunnyside Court, extending to an area of 800 square metres.
3	3	Edged red and numbered 3	First floor flat known as Flat 3, Sunnyside Court, extending to an area of 600 square metres.
4	3	Edged red and numbered 4	First floor flat known as Flat 4, Sunnyside Court, extending to an area of 600 square metres.

5. Further description of commonhold units

5.1   A commonhold unit does not include–
        (a)   the structure and exterior of the building of which it is part;
        (b)   the beams and joists supporting the floor and ceiling of the unit;
        (c)   the pipes, cables or other fixed service installations in the unit, other than those exclusively serving the unit.

5.2   Units 1 and 2 include the fences marked on Plan 2 with an inwards 'T'

6. Rights for commonhold units

6.1   The unit-holder of each commonhold unit is at all times entitled to–
        (a)   use the hallways, stairs, corridors, lifts, paths and drives in the common parts, for obtaining access to that unit;
        (b)   use the pipes, cables and other fixed installations in the common parts, for receiving and using services in and to that unit;
        (c)   have rights of air and light over the common parts and support from the common parts and other commonhold units, for the enjoyment of that unit.

7. Rights over commonhold units

7.1   In relation to each commonhold unit, the commonhold association and the unit-holders of the other commonhold units are entitled to rights of air and light over that unit and support from that unit, for the enjoyment of other parts of the commonhold.

7.2   A unit-holder or tenant must allow a person authorised by the commonhold association to enter the commonhold unit at any reasonable time, when it is necessary for any of the following purposes–
        (a)   to repair, maintain, improve, or to prevent damage to the common parts;
        (b)   to inspect the state of repair and maintenance of the commonhold unit or of the common parts;
        (c)   to ascertain how the commonhold unit is being used; or
        (d)   to make a valuation for insurance purposes.

7.3   A unit-holder or tenant must allow a person authorised by another unit-holder to enter the commonhold unit at any reasonable time, where such entry is necessary to repair, maintain, or to prevent damage to that other unit-holder's commonhold unit.

7.4   Any authority given under paragraph 7.2 or paragraph 7.3 is subject to the following conditions–
        (a)   reasonable notice is given to the unit-holder or tenant, unless there is an emergency;
        (b)   there is as little interference as possible with the occupation and enjoyment of the commonhold unit; and

(c)   **ANY DAMAGE TO THE COMMONHOLD UNIT CAUSED BY THE PERSON AUTHORISED IS PROMPTLY MADE GOOD.**

ANNEX 3: COMMONHOLD ALLOCATIONS

1. Allocation of commonhold assessment

Commonhold unit number	Percentage allocation (total 100%)
1	25%
2	25%
3	25%
4	25%

2. Allocation of reserve fund levy

Name of reserve fund	Commonhold unit number	Percentage allocation (total 100%)
Car park maintenance	1	25%
	2	25%
	3	25%
	4	25%
Lift maintenance	1	0%
	2	0%
	3	50%
	4	50%

3. Allocation of votes

Commonhold unit number	Number of votes allocated to member
1	1
2	1
3	1
4	1

ANNEX 4: LOCAL RULES

1. Prescribed rate of interest
5% above the Bank of England's base rate for the time being in force

2. Permitted use of commonhold units

Commonhold unit number	Permitted use
1	Residential
2	Residential
3	Residential
4	Residential

3. Permitted use of common parts

3.1   The common parts (other than limited use areas: see paragraph 4 of this Annex) may be used as follows–

    (a)   the pipes, cables and other fixed service installations for providing the appropriate services to the commonhold;

    (b)   the garden, coloured green on Plan 1, for recreation;

    (c)   the driveway, coloured blue on Plan 3, for access by motor vehicles;

    (d)   the parking areas, coloured violet on Plan 3, for parking motor vehicles; and

    (e)   other areas, both outside and inside the buildings, for pedestrian access to commonhold units.

4. Limited use areas

Description of area	Plan number	Authorised users	Authorised use
Lift motor room	1	Officers of, and agents and contractors appointed by, the commonhold association	Servicing and maintenance of lift machinery
Boiler Room	1	Officers of, and agents and contractors appointed by, the commonhold association	Servicing and maintenance of the boiler
Oil Storage area	1	Officers of, and agents and contractors appointed by, the commonhold association	Delivery and storage of fuel oil and maintenance of tanks
Dustbin area	3	All unit-holders and tenants	Deposit of rubbish in the receptacles provided
Garage forecourt	3	Unit-holders and tenants of those units which include a garage	Driving and parking private motor vehicles, but not so as to obstruct any garage entrance
Tennis court	3	All unit-holders, tenants and those they invite	Playing tennis, observing regulations about reservations and conduct made by the commonhold association

5. Insurance of common parts – insured risks

So far as cover is generally available for that type of property in that location, loss or damage by lightning, aircraft, explosion, earthquake, storm, flood, escape of water or oil, riot, malicious damage, theft or attempted theft, falling trees and branches and aerials, subsidence, heave, landslip, collision, accidental damage to underground services, professional fees, demolition and site clearance costs, public liability to anyone else, and such other risks as the members of the commonhold association approve from time to time by ordinary resolution.

6. Insurance of commonhold units – duties

6.1   The commonhold association must insure all the commonhold units to their full rebuilding and reinstatement costs, together with cover for the cost of alternative accommodation for 2 years.

6.1   That insurance must, so far as cover is generally available for that type of property in that location, be against loss or damage by lightning, aircraft, explosion, earthquake, storm, flood, escape of water or oil, riot, malicious damage, theft or attempted theft, falling trees and branches and aerials, subsidence, heave, landslip, collision, accidental damage to underground services, professional fees, demolition and site clearance costs, public liability to anyone else, and such other risks as the members of the commonhold association approve from time to time by ordinary resolution.

6.2   The commonhold association must, whenever required, provide a unit-holder with written evidence of the terms of the insurance and of the payment of most recent premium.

6.3   In the event of any loss or damage covered by the insurance, the commonhold association must promptly make a claim under the policy and make good the loss or damage.

7. Repair and maintenance of commonhold units – duties

7.1   The unit-holder must repair and maintain the unit. This includes decorating it and putting it into sound condition.

ANNEX 5: SUPPLEMENTARY LOCAL RULES

1. Services

1.1   The commonhold association must, unless prevented by circumstances beyond its control, provide the following services to each commonhold unit–
    (a)   heating from 1 October to 15 April;
    (b)   hot water; and
    (c)   television reception from a communal aerial.

1.2   The commonhold association must, unless prevented by circumstances beyond its control, provide the following services in relation to the common parts–
    (a)   cleaning and lighting;
    (b)   keeping the garden appropriately planted, tended and tidy;
    (c)   maintaining signs and equipment to regulate the access and parking of vehicles; and
    (d)   supply and maintenance of the equipment and marking needed for using the tennis court.

2. Security

2.1   The commonhold association must install and maintain in the common-hold appropriate security arrangements, designed to prohibit the entry of unauthorised persons.

2.2   A unit-holder or tenant must co-operate in the use of the security arrange-ments controlling entry to the commonhold and must require all visitors to comply.

3. Notices

3.1   The commonhold association must erect and maintain an appropriate notice at the entrance to the commonhold displaying the names of the unit-holders and directions to the units.

3.2   The commonhold association must erect and maintain signs and directions to regulate traffic and parking in the grounds of the commonhold.

3.3   A unit-holder or tenant must comply with signs and directions which are displayed regulating traffic and parking in the grounds of the commonhold and must require all visitors to comply.

4. Advertisements

4.1   A unit-holder or tenant must not allow any advertisement to be displayed on the commonhold unit in such a way that it is visible from outside the unit, other than a notice stating that the unit is for sale or to let.

5. Termination statement

5.1   Any termination statement must state that the commonhold association's surplus assets are to be divided between the members in the same propor-tion as the allocation of votes, as specified in paragraph 3 of Annex 3.

ANNEX 6: DEVELOPMENT RIGHTS

1. Construction

1.1   The developer, his agents and workmen, are entitled to access to the common parts as necessary to complete constructing the commonhold.

1.2   In the course of completing construction work, the developer is entitled to interfere temporarily with access and the provision of services to a com-monhold unit, so long as the unit is not rendered unusable for its permitted use.

1.3   Until construction work is completed, the developer is entitled to use the grounds of the commonhold for storing building materials, equipment and machinery.

2. Adding land to the commonhold

2.1   An application to Land Registry by the developer to add land to the commonhold does not require approval by resolution of the commonhold association.

3. Unit-holder's application for planning permission

3.1   A unit-holder must obtain the developer's written consent before applying for planning permission to carry out any development on the commonhold.

4. Advertisements and sales

4.1   The developer is entitled to erect and maintain an advertisement hoarding on the common parts announcing that commonhold units are for sale.

4.2   The developer is entitled to use one commonhold unit as a 'show unit' for display to prospective buyers and for negotiating sales.

4.3   A prospective buyer of a commonhold unit, authorised by the developer, is entitled to have access to the common parts, including the right to park a car while on the property, for the purpose of viewing units for sale and the common parts.

5. Appointment and removal of directors

5.1   The developer has the right to appoint and remove directors of the commonhold association in accordance with the articles of association.

SIGNATURE

This is the commonhold community statement of Sunnyside Commonhold signed in the form required by the Commonhold Regulations 2004

Signed on behalf of the applicant: *A Commonhold*

Name: (please print): A COMMONHOLD

Title: Mr

Date: 27 September 2004

Solicitors' Practice (Conveyancing) Amendment Rules 2005

[NB. Underlined text has been inserted. Text in square brackets has been removed.]

Rules dated 9 February 2005 made by the Council of the Law Society with the concurrence of the Master of the Rolls under section 31 of the Solicitors Act 1974 and section 9 of the Administration of Justice Act 1985.

1. Rules 6 and 6A of the Solicitors' Practice Rules 1990 shall be amended in accordance with Schedule 1.
2. Rule 3 of The Law Society's Code of Conduct [2005] shall be amended in accordance with Schedule 2. [The Code of Conduct will eventually supersede the Practice Rules but is not yet in force.]

SCHEDULE 1

SOLICITORS' PRACTICE RULES 1990

*****

Rule 6 (Avoiding conflicts of interest in conveyancing, property selling and mortgage related services)

*****

(3) (Solicitor acting for lender and borrower)

*****

(c) A solicitor acting for both lender and borrower in a standard mortgage may only accept or act upon instructions from the lender which are limited to the following matters:
*****

(ix) in the case of a leasehold property, confirming that the lease contains the terms stipulated by the lender and does not include any terms specified by the lender as unacceptable; obtaining a suitable deed of variation or indemnity insurance if the terms of the lease are unsatisfactory; enquiring of the seller or the borrower (if the property is already owned by the borrower) as to any known breaches of covenant by the landlord or any superior landlord and reporting any such breaches to the lender; reporting if the solicitor becomes aware of the landlord's absence or insolvency; making a company search and checking the last three years' published accounts of any management company with responsibilities under the lease; if the borrower is required to be a shareholder in the management company, obtaining the share certificate, a blank stock transfer form signed by the borrower and a copy of the memorandum and articles of association; obtaining any necessary consent to or prior approval of the assignment and mortgage; obtaining a clear receipt for the last payment of rent and service charge; and serving notice of the assignment and mortgage on the landlord;

(ixA)   in the case of a commonhold unit, confirming receipt of satisfactory evidence that common parts insurance is in place for at least the sum required by the lender and covers the risks specified by the lender; confirming that the commonhold community statement contains the terms specified by the lender and does not include any restrictions on occupation or use specified by the lender as unacceptable; enquiring of the seller (or the borrower if the property is already owned by the borrower) and the commonhold association as to any known breaches of the commonhold community statement by the commonhold association or any unit-holder, and reporting any such breaches to the lender; making a company search to verify that the commonhold association is in existence and remains registered, and that there is no registered indication that it is to be wound up; obtaining the last three years' published accounts of the commonhold association and reporting any apparent problems with the association to the lender; obtaining a commonhold unit information certificate; and serving notice of the transfer and mortgage of the commonhold unit on the commonhold association;

*****

(d)   In addition, a solicitor acting for both lender and borrower in a standard mortgage of property to be used as the borrower's private residence only:

(i)   must use the certificate of title set out in the Appendix, or as substituted from time to time by the Council with the concurrence of the Master of the Rolls, ('the approved certificate'); and

(ii)   unless the lender has certified that its mortgage instructions are subject to the limitations contained in paragraphs (3)(c) and (3)(e), must notify the lender on receipt of instructions that the approved certificate will be used, and that the solicitor's duties to the lender are limited to the matters contained in the approved certificate.

*****

APPENDIX

CERTIFICATE OF TITLE

*****

WE THE CONVEYANCERS NAMED ABOVE CERTIFY as follows:

*****

(2)   Except as otherwise disclosed to you in writing:

*****

(iv)   if the Property is leasehold the terms of the lease accord with your instructions, including any requirements you have for covenants by the Landlord and/or a management company and/or by a deed of mutual covenant for the insurance, repair and maintenance of the structure, exterior and common parts of any building of which the Property forms part, and we have or will obtain on or before completion a clear receipt for the last payment of rent and service charge;

(ivA)   if the property is a commonhold unit, the commonhold community statement contains the terms specified by you and does not include any restrictions on occupation or use specified by you as unacceptable, and we have or will obtain on or before completion a commonhold unit information certificate;

(v)   we have received satisfactory evidence that the buildings insurance is in place, or will be on completion, for the sum and in the terms required by you;

*****

WE:

*****

(c)   will within the period of protection afforded by the searches referred to in paragraph (b) above:

(i)   complete the mortgage;

(ii)   arrange for the issue of a stamp duty land tax certificate [stamping of the transfer] if appropriate;

(iii)   deliver to the Land Registry the documents necessary to register the mortgage in your favour and any relevant prior dealings;

(iv)   effect any other registrations necessary to protect your interests as mortgagee;

(d)   will despatch to you such deeds and documents relating to the Property as you require with a list of them in the form pre-scribed by you within ten working days of receipt by us of the <u>title information document</u> [Charge Certificate] from the Land Registry;

*****

Rule 6A (Seller's solicitor dealing with more than one prospective buyer)

(1)   This rule applies to the conveyancing of freehold (including commonhold) and leasehold property. The rule is to be interpreted in the light of the notes.

Notes

(i)   *Rule 6A applies to all conveyancing of land, whether the transaction is of a 'commercial' or 'domestic' nature.*

(ii)   *Rule 6A does not set terms for a contract race. It lays down require-ments which must be met when a solicitor is instructed to deal with more than one prospective buyer.*

*****

SCHEDULE 2

THE LAW SOCIETY'S CODE OF CONDUCT [2005]

[The Code of Conduct will eventually supersede the Practice Rules but is not yet in force.]

*****

Rule 3 – Conflict of interests

*****

3.16 Acting for lender and borrower in conveyancing transactions

(1)   3.16 to 3.22 cover the grant of a mortgage of land and are intended to avoid conflicts of interests. 'Mortgage' includes a remortgage. Both commercial and residential conveyancing transactions are covered.

*****

3.19 Types of instruction which may be accepted

If acting for both lender and borrower in a standard mortgage, your firm and the individual solicitor or REL conducting or supervising the transaction may only accept or act upon instructions from the lender which are limited to the following matters:

*****

(i)   in the case of a leasehold property:

      (i)   confirming that the lease contains the terms stipulated by the lender and does not include any terms specified by the lender as unacceptable;

      (ii)   obtaining a suitable deed of variation or indemnity insurance if the terms of the lease are unsatisfactory;

      (iii)   enquiring of the seller or the borrower (if the property is already owned by the borrower) as to any known breaches of covenant by the landlord or any superior landlord and reporting any such breaches to the lender;

      (iv)   reporting if you become aware of the landlord's absence or insolvency;

      (v)   making a company search and checking the last three years' published accounts of any management company with responsibilities under the lease;

      (vi)   if the borrower is required to be a shareholder in the management company, obtaining the share certificate, a blank stock transfer form signed by the borrower and a copy of the memorandum and articles of association;

      (vii)   obtaining any necessary consent to or prior approval of the assignment and mortgage;

      (viii)   obtaining a clear receipt for the last payment of rent and service charge; and

      (ix)   serving notice of the assignment and mortgage on the landlord;

(iA)   in the case of a commonhold unit:

      (i)   confirming receipt of satisfactory evidence that common parts insurance is in place for at least the sum required by the lender and covers the risks specified by the lender;

      (ii)   confirming that the commonhold community statement contains the terms specified by the lender and does not include any restrictions on occupation or use specified by the lender as unacceptable;

      (iii)   enquiring of the seller (or the borrower if the property is already owned by the borrower) and the commonhold association as to any known breaches of the commonhold community statement by the commonhold association or any unit-holder, and reporting any such breaches to the lender;

      (iv)   making a company search to verify that the commonhold association is in existence and remains registered, and that there is no registered indication that it is to be wound up;

      (v)   obtaining the last three years' published accounts of the commonhold association and reporting any apparent problems with the association to the lender;

      (vi)   obtaining a commonhold unit information certificate; and

(vii)   serving notice of the transfer and mortgage of the commonhold
           unit on the commonhold association;

*****

3.20 Using the approved certificate of title

In addition, if acting for both lender and borrower in a standard mortgage of property to be used as the borrower's private residence only:

(a)   you must use the certificate of title set out in the annex to rule 3
           (below), or as substituted from time to time by the Council of the
           Law Society with the concurrence of the Master of the Rolls ('the
           approved certificate'); and

(b)   unless the lender has certified that its mortgage instructions are
           subject to the limitations contained in 3.19 and 3.21, you must
           notify the lender on receipt of instructions that the approved cer-
           tificate will be used, and that your duties to the lender are limited
           to the matters contained in the approved certificate.

*****

ANNEX

CERTIFICATE OF TITLE

*****

WE THE CONVEYANCERS NAMED ABOVE CERTIFY as follows:

*****

(2)   Except as otherwise disclosed to you in writing:

*****

(iv)   if the Property is leasehold the terms of the lease accord with your instruc-
           tions, including any requirements you have for covenants by the Landlord
           and/or a management company and/or by a deed of mutual covenant for the
           insurance, repair and maintenance of the structure, exterior and common
           parts of any building of which the Property forms part, and we have or will
           obtain on or before completion a clear receipt for the last payment of rent
           and service charge;

(ivA)   if the property is a commonhold unit, the commonhold community state-
           ment contains the terms specified by you and does not include any restric-
           tions on occupation or use specified by you as unacceptable, and we have or
           will obtain on or before completion a commonhold unit information certifi-
           cate;

(v)   we have received satisfactory evidence that the buildings insurance is in
           place, or will be on completion, for the sum and in the terms required by
           you;

*****

WE:

*****

(c)   will within the period of protection afforded by the searches referred to in paragraph (b) above:

     (i)   complete the mortgage;

     (ii)   arrange for the <u>issue of a stamp duty land tax certificate</u> [stamping of the transfer] if appropriate;

     (iii)   deliver to the Land Registry the documents necessary to register the mortgage in your favour and any relevant prior dealings;

     (iv)   effect any other registrations necessary to protect your interests as mortgagee;

(d)   will despatch to you such deeds and documents relating to the Property as you require with a list of them in the form prescribed by you within ten working days of receipt by us of the <u>title information document</u> [Charge Certificate] from the Land Registry;

Seller's commonhold information form

SELLER'S COMMONHOLD INFORMATION FORM (1st edition)

Address of the Property:

If the property being sold is a commonhold property, please answer the following questions. The instructions set out at the front of the Seller's Property Information Form apply to this form as well. Please read them again before giving your answers to these questions.

If you are unsure how to answer any of the questions, ask your solicitor.

Part I – to be completed by the seller

1   Commonhold association

Please mark the appropriate box

1.1   Please supply copies of the commonhold association's accounts for the last three years, if you have them.

ENCLOSED	TO FOLLOW	LOST

1.2   Please supply the names and addresses of:

(a) the directors of the association

(b) the secretary of the association

(c) any managing agents appointed by the association

1.3   Do you know of any proposal to amend the terms of the commonhold community statement?

YES	NO

If "YES", please give details:

1.4   Do you know of any proposal to enlarge the commonhold?

YES	NO

If "YES", please give details:

_____
_____
_____

1.5   Is the commonhold association a member of an approved ombudsman scheme?

YES	NO

If "YES", please give the ombudsman's name and address:

_____
_____
_____

2   Commonhold assessments and reserve fund levies

2.1   Please give details of the commonhold assessments which the association has made in respect of your unit during the last three years.

_____
_____
_____

2.2   Has the association established any reserve funds (to pay for major expenditure on such items as outside painting, roof repairs, lift replacement)?

_____
_____
_____

2.3   For which of those funds has the association made levies (demanded contributions) in respect of your unit during the last three years, and how much was payable?

_____
_____
_____

2.4   Do you know of any expense, which is not usually incurred every year and is not covered by a reserve fund (e.g. redecoration, repairing drives), which the commonhold association is likely to incur within the next three years?

YES	NO

If "YES", please give details:

_____
_____

2.5   Have you challenged, or do you know of any other unit-holder who has challenged, the amount of any commonhold assessment or reserve fund levy during the last three years?

YES	NO

If "YES", please give details:

2.6   Do you know of any problems in the last three years between unit-holders and the commonhold association about the payment of commonhold assessments or reserve fund levies?

YES	NO

If "YES", please give details:

2.7   Please obtain a commonhold unit information certificate from the commonhold association and supply a copy.

ENCLOSED	TO FOLLOW

3   Notices

A notice may be in a printed form or in the form of a letter. It may come from the commonhold association, another unit-holder, a neighbouring owner or an official body. Your buyer will wish to know if anything of this sort has been received.

3.1   Have you had any notice about your unit or any other part of the commonhold, its use, its condition, or its repair and maintenance?

NO	YES	ENCLOSED	TO FOLLOW

4   Common parts

4.1   Do you know of any dispute about the use of the common parts during the last three years?

YES	NO

If "YES", please give details:

4.2   Do you know of any proposal to lease or dispose of any of the common parts?

YES	NO

If "YES", please give details:

4.3   Do you know of any proposal to mortgage all or any part of the common parts?

YES	NO

If "YES", please give details:

5   Insurance

5.1   Please supply a copy of the insurance policy covering your unit (whether or not the policy also covers other property) and evidence of payment of the latest premium. (If the commonhold association arranges the insurance, please obtain particulars from the association.)

ENCLOSED	TO FOLLOW

5.2   If the common parts are separately insured, please obtain from the commonhold association, and supply a copy of, the insurance policy covering the common parts and evidence of payment of the latest premium.

ENCLOSED	TO FOLLOW

6   Consents

6.1   Do you know if the commonhold association has given its consent to the transfer of part only of any of the units?

YES	NO

If "YES", please give details:

6.2   Do you know if the commonhold association has refused to give its consent to the transfer of part only of any of the units?

YES	NO

If "YES", please give details:

7   Complaints

7.1   Have you received any complaint from the commonhold association, another unit-holder or the occupier of any unit about anything you have or have not done?

YES	NO

If "YES", please give details:

7.2   Have you complained to the commonhold association, another unit-holder or the occupier of any unit about anything they have or have not done?

YES	NO

If "YES", please give details:

_____

7.3   Please supply a copy of any decision made by the ombudsman affecting the property or the common parts.

ENCLOSED	TO FOLLOW	NONE KNOWN

8   Rights for the developer

Please respond to these questions if the commonhold community statement gives "development rights" to a developer. (They may be rights to complete the building work, rights in connection with marketing units or the right to appoint directors of the commonhold association.)

8.1   Has the developer ceased to be entitled to exercise any of the rights?

YES	NO

If "YES", please give details:

_____

8.2   Please give the name and address of the developer who is now entitled to exercise the rights:

_____

Reminder
Copies of any relevant documents should be supplied with this form, e.g. commonhold association memorandum and articles of association, commonhold community statement, commonhold unit information certificate, commonhold association accounts for the last three years, any notices about your commonhold unit, the insurance policy covering your unit, the insurance policy covering common parts, and any decision made by an ombudsman affecting the property or the common parts.

Signature(s):..

....

Date:...

311

Part II – to be completed by the seller's solicitor

The seller's solicitor should check the seller's replies to Part I against the information in the solicitor's possession. When replying to A-F below the solicitor should have checked the documents carefully, read the file and any other relevant file the firm may have by checking filing records, and following this, make any other reasonable and prudent investigation (see guidance from the Law Society's Conveyancing and Land Law Committee [2003] *Gazette*, 16 October, 43).

Please mark the appropriate box

A. Is the information provided by the seller in this form consistent with the information in your possession?

YES	NO

If "NO", please give details:

B. Do you have any information in your possession to supplement the information provided by the seller?

YES	NO

If "YES", please give details:

C. Please provide the name and address of the recipient of the notice of transfer and charge.

D. Do the insurers make a practice of recording the interest of the unit-holder and the unit-holder's mortgagee on the policy?

YES	NO	NOT KNOWN

E. Please supply a copy of the fire certificate.

ENCLOSED	TO FOLLOW	NOT APPLICABLE

F. Is the property part of a converted building?

YES	NO

If "YES", please supply a copy of the planning permission or an established use certificate, or evidence of permitted use.

ENCLOSED	TO FOLLOW

Seller's solicitor: ....

Date:..

The Law Society

APPENDIX E

Extract from the CML Lenders' Handbook for England and Wales[1]

Commonhold

5.5.5   If any part of the property comprises of commonhold, check **part 2** to see if we will accept it as security.

5.5.6   If we are prepared to accept a title falling within 5.5.5, you must:

5.5.6.1 ensure that the commonhold association has obtained insurance for the common parts which complies with our requirements (see 6.13);

5.5.6.2 obtain a commonhold unit information certificate and ensure that all of the commonhold assessment in respect of the property has been paid up to the date of completion;

5.5.6.3 ensure that the commonhold community statement does not include any material restrictions on occupation or use (see 5.4 and 5.6);

5.5.6.4 ensure that the commonhold community statement provides that in the event of a voluntary termination of the commonhold the termination statement provides that the unit holders will ensure that any mortgage secured on their unit is repaid on termination;

5.5.6.5 make a company search to verify that the commonhold association is in existence and remains registered, and that there is no registered indication that it is to be wound up; and

5.5.6.6 within 14 days of completion, send the notice of transfer of a commonhold unit and notice of the mortgage to the commonhold association.

---

[1] © Council of Mortgage Lenders. The CML Lenders' Handbook is published and updated by the CML online at **www.cml.org.uk**. Paragraph 5.5.5 was introduced on 6 May 2005.

APPENDIX F

Further reading

Office of Public Sector Information (OPSI)

Previously Her Majesty's Stationery Office, the OPSI website (**www.opsi.gov.uk**) includes all the relevant legislation:

- Commonhold and Leasehold Reform Act 2002, Part 1
- Commonhold Regulations 2004 (SI 2004/1829)
- Commonhold (Land Registration) Rules 2004 (SI 2004/1830)
- The Land Registration Fee (Amendment) Order 2004 (SI 2004/1833)

Department of Constitutional Affairs (DCA)

The DCA website has a page of links to essential documents on commonhold (**www.dca.gov.uk**), including:

- Commonhold – Proposals for Commonhold Regulations (consultation October 2002)
- Analysis of the responses to an LCD consultation paper Proposals for Commonhold Regulations (August 2003)
- Memorandum of Association (Schedule 1 to the Commonhold Regulations 2004)
- Articles of Association (Schedule 2 to the Commonhold Regulations 2004)
- Commonhold Community Statement (Schedule 3 to the Commonhold Regulations 2004)
- Forms (Schedule 4 to the Commonhold Regulations 2004)
- Non-Statutory Guidance on the Commonhold Regulations 2004 (September 2004)
- Guidance on the drafting of a Commonhold Community Statement (February 2005)

Land Registry

The Land Registry website has pages dedicated to commonhold (**www.landregistry.gov.uk/legislation/commonhold**), including:

- A Guide to Commonhold (E-learning module)
- Practice Guide 60 Commonhold (June 2004)

314

Council of Mortgage Lenders

Paragraph 5.5.5 on commonhold was added to Part 1 of the CML Lenders' Handbook for England and Wales on 6 May 2005. Part 1 and Part 2 of the Handbook are published and updated at **www.cml.org.uk**.

Law Society of England and Wales

The Law Society website www.lawsociety.org.uk includes the Solicitors Practice Rules and forthcoming Code of Conduct.

The Property Section's website may also contain useful news and information on commonhold – **www.propertysection.org.uk**.

LEASE The Leasehold Advisory Service

The LEASE website contains pages on commonhold at **www.lease-advice.org**.

Index

Conveyancing Handbook

12th Edition

General Editor:
Frances Silverman

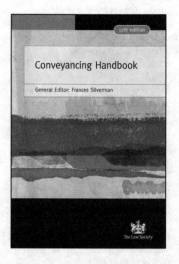

The most reliable, accurate, and up-to-date source of information and guidance on all aspects of conveyancing practice, this book has been specifically designed to give busy practitioners the answers to their everyday questions.

The Handbook collects all the relevant guidance from a multitude of sources so practitioners never have to search far for an answer or authority.

Specific elements new to the 12th edition include:

- a new chapter on Licensing
- the Stamp Duty Land Tax guidance and rates
- the Solicitors' Practice (Conveyancing) Amendment Rules 2005
- revisions to Part 1 of the CML Lenders' Handbook
- an outline of the Land Registry's plans for e-conveyancing
- an introduction to Home Information Packs.

Available from Marston Book Services:
Tel. 01235 465 656.

1 85328 928 0
1344 pages
£79.95
October 2005

The Law Society

Environmental Law Handbook

6th Editon

Trevor Hellawell

This established and trusted
Handbook for non-environmental law
specialists provides a succinct
account of how environmental law
affects property, financial and
business transactions.

Substantially revised and updated, this edition includes:

- discussion of the implications of *Van de Walle et al*
- commentary on *Circular Facilities* v. *Sevenoaks DC* - the first
  case under Part IIA of the Contaminated Land regime
- new precedents for lease clauses
- sample environmental reports
- an enhanced section on planning considerations and planning
  searches
- new regulations on environmental information
- standard enquiries in property transactions
- a new chapter on environmental liability insurance.

The book helps you to identify risk and to mitigate liabilities,
reinforcing understanding with useful precedents and checklists.

Available from Marston Book Services:
Tel. 01235 465 656.

1 85328 978 7
Approx: 288 pages
£44.95
Due November 2005

The Law Society

Licensing for Conveyancers

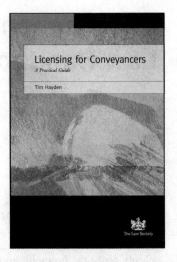

A Practical Guide

Tim Hayden and Jane Hanney

The Licensing Act 2003 is a radical departure from the previous regime under the 1964 Act.

Conveyancing transactions frequently involve licensed premises of different types. This handy book provides conveyancers with a basic understanding of new licensing law and procedures in order to be able to advise clients effectively.

Concise and practical, *Licensing for Conveyancers* includes:

- precedents
- guidance on preliminary enquiries
- extracts from the Secretary of State's Guidance
- extracts from the Licensing Act 2003.

Available from Marston Book Services:
Tel. 01235 465 656.

1 85328 966 3
336 pages
£44.95
August 2005

The Law Society

Planning and Compulsory Purchase Act 2004

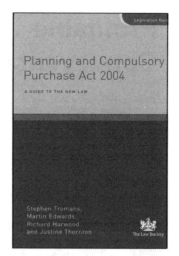

A Guide to the New Law

Stephen Tromans, Martin Edwards, Richard Harwood and Justine Thornton

Sets the Act and its supporting regulations in context in order to ensure a thorough understanding of its implications. Major proposals contained in the Act include:

- changes to development control
- the introduction of regional spatial strategies and local development documents prepared by LPAs
- changes to the basis on which a local authority may acquire land compulsorily
- regional planning bodies and LPAs will have a statutory duty to contribute to the achievement of sustainable development
- the Crown will no longer be immune from planning control.

Contains a copy of the Act in full, together with extracts from the new regulations and guidance implementing it.

Available from Marston Book Services:
Tel. 01235 465 656.

1 85328 925 6
328 pages
£39.95
April 2005

The Law Society

Profitable Conveyancing

A Practical Guide for Residential Conveyancers

Stephanie Dale

This practical book for conveyancers shows how to minimise costs, source more clients and retain existing ones, convert telephone callers into new business and make more efficient use of available technology.

Using examples from practice, and written in plain English, the book helps you to:

- assess your firm or conveyancing department and plan ahead to face the new challenges
- devise business and marketing plans
- learn how to minimise costs and utilise low cost marketing solutions
- understand how to maximise the use of technology and appreciate the role of e-conveyancing.

The author is a Law Society authorised trainer, and practising solicitors contribute chapters on costs, IT and e-conveyancing.

Available from Marston Book Services:
Tel. 01235 465 656.

1 85328 862 4
304 pages
£34.95
March 2005

The Law Society